마이갓 5 Step 모의고사 공부법

1 ● **Vocabulary** 필수 단어 암기 & Test
① 단원별 필수 단어 암기 ② 영어 → 한글 Test ③ 한글 → 영어 Test

2 ● **Text** 지문과 해설
① 전체 지문 해석 ② 페이지별 필기 공간 확보 ③ N회독을 통한 지문 습득

3 ● **Practice 1** 빈칸 시험 (w/ 문법 힌트)
① 해석 없는 반복 빈칸 시험 ② 문법 힌트를 통한 어법 숙지
③ 주요 문법과 암기 내용 최종 확인

4 ● **Practice 2** 빈칸 시험 (w/ 해석)
① 주요 내용/어법/어휘 빈칸 ② 한글을 통한 내용 숙지
③ 반복 시험을 통한 빈칸 암기

5 ● **Quiz** 객관식 예상문제를 콕콕!
① 수능형 객관식 변형문제 ② 100% 자체 제작 변형문제 ③ 빈출 내신 문제 유형 연습

영어 내신의 끝
마이갓 모의고사 고1, 2

1 등급을 위한 5단계 노하우
2 모의고사 연도 및 시행월 별 완전정복
3 내신변형 완전정복

영어 내신의 끝
마이갓 교과서 고1, 2

1 등급을 위한 10단계 노하우
2 교과서 레슨별 완전정복
3 영어 영역 마스터를 위한 지름길

마이갓 교재
보듬책방 온라인 스토어 (https://smartstore.naver.com/bdbooks)

마이갓 10 Step 영어 내신 공부법

Vocabulary

필수 단어 암기 & Test
① 단원별 필수 단어 암기
② 영어 → 한글 Test
③ 한글 → 영어 Test

Grammar

단원별 중요 문법과 연습 문제
① 기초 문법 설명
② 교과서 적용 예시 소개
③ 기초/ Advanced Test

Text

지문과 해설
① 전체 지문 해석
② 페이지별 필기 공간 확보
③ N회독을 통한 지문 습득

Practice 3

빈칸 시험 (w/ 해석)
① 주요 내용/어법/어휘 빈칸
② 한글을 통한 내용 숙지
③ 반복 시험을 통한 빈칸 암기

Practice 2

빈칸 시험 (w/ 해석)
① 주요 내용/어법/어휘 빈칸
② 한글을 통한 내용 숙지
③ 반복 시험을 통한 빈칸 암기

Practice 1

어휘 & 어법 선택 시험
① 시험에 나오는 어법 어휘 공략
② 중요 어법/어휘 선택형 시험
③ 반복 시험을 통한 포인트 숙지

Quiz

객관식 예상문제를 콕콕!
① 수능형 객관식 변형문제
② 100% 자체 제작 변형문제
③ 빈출 내신 문제 유형 연습

Final Test

주관식 서술형 예상문제
① 어순/영작/어법 등
   주관식 서술형 문제 대비!
② 100% 자체 제작 변형문제

전체 영작 연습

직접 영작 해보기
① 주어진 단어를 활용한
   전체 서술형 영작 훈련
② 쓰기를 통한 내용 암기

학교 기출 문제

지문과 해설
① 단원별 실제 학교 기출
   문제 모음
② 객관식부터 서술형까지
   완벽 커버!

24년 고1
11월 모의고사

마이갓

연습과 실전 모두 잡는 내신대비 완벽
| workbook |

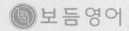

보듬영어

2024 고1

11월

WORK BOOK

—

2024년 고1 11월 모의고사 내신대비용 WorkBook & 변형문제

CONTENTS

2024 고1 11월 WORK BOOK

—

 보듬영어

Voca

| ❶ voca | ❷ text | ❸ [/] | ❹ _____ | ❺ quiz 1 | ❻ quiz 2 | ❼ quiz 3 | ❽ quiz 4 | ❾ quiz 5 |

18	state	상태, 국가, 주; 진술하다		anticipation	예측, 예상, 기대
	department	부서, 매장		decision	결정, 결심, 판결
	regard	간주[주목]하다, 관련있다; 관심, 존경, 관계	20	packed	꽉 찬, 만원의
	fund	자금을 대다; 자금, 기금		dedicated	헌신적인, 전념하는, 전용의
	construction	건축, 구성, 공사		workout	운동, 연습
	additional	추가적인, 추가의		in the midst of	~이 한창일 때, ~중에
	space	간격을 두다		daily routine	일상
	serve	제공[기여]하다, 복무하다, 적합하다		chore	집안일, 허드렛일
	meaningful	의미 있는, 중요한		take out	~을 꺼내다
	submit	제출하다, 복종시키다		trash	쓰레기, 폐물
	require	필요로 하다, 요구하다		task	일, 과업; ~에 과중한 부담을 주다
	receive	받다, 받아들이다		essential	근본적인, 본질적인, 필수적인
	delay	연기하다, 미루다; 지연, 지체		view A as B	A를 B로 간주하다
	process	과정, 절차; 처리하다, 가공하다		seize	붙잡다, 움켜쥐다
	considerable	상당한, 많은		physical activity	신체 활동
	consequence	결과, 영향(력), 중요성		for instance	예를 들면
	relate to	~을 이해하다, ~와 관련이 있다		practice	습관, 관례, 실행[실천], 연습
	in order to V	~하기 위해, ~하려고		engage in	~에 참여[관여]하다, 종사하다
	request	요청, 요구; 요청[요구]하다		push-up	엎드려 팔굽혀펴기
	regarding	~에 관하여		incorporate	법인회사로 만들다, 통합[포함]하다
	look forward to -ing	~하기를 고대하다		improve	향상[개선]시키다, 향상하다
	principal	주된, 주요한; 교장, 회장	21	naturally	자연스럽게, 본래
19	call out	(큰 소리로) 부르다, 외치다		automatically	자동으로, 반사적으로, 기계적으로
	figure	생각[계산]하다; 수치, 숫자, 인물, 모양		retrieve	상기하다
	captain	장, 우두머리, 지휘관		trait	특성, 특색, 특징

Voca

	efficient	유능한, 능률적인, 효율적인		procedure	절차, 순서, 과정, 조치
	raw	날것의, 가공하지 않은, 미숙한		inaccurate	부정확한
	lack	부족, 결핍; ~가 부족하다		identification	동일시, 공감
	detail	세부 (항목); 자세히 말하다, 열거하다		explain	설명하다, 해명하다
	struggle to V	~하려고 몸부림치다[투쟁하다]		recognize	인정하다, 인식하다
	connection	연결, 접속, 연관(성), 인맥, 관계		tend to V	~하는 경향이 있다
	represent	표현하다, 나타내다		accurate	정확한, 정밀한
	abstract	추상적인; 추상, 개요, 요약; 요약[추출]하다		immediate	즉각적인, 직접의, 인접한
	feature	특징, 특집, 용모; 특집으로 하다, 특집으로 삼다		automatic	자동의, 반사적인, 기계적인
	see ~ through	~을 끝까지 해내다		reaction	반응, 반작용, 반발
	assumption	가정, 추정, 생각		interpretation	해석, 설명, 이해
	motivation	동기 (부여)		impression	인상, 감명, 흔적
	discovery	발견, 발각		blink	깜박이다; 깜박임
	representation	묘사, 표현		describe	묘사하다, 기술하다, 설명하다
	completely	완전히, 충분히		a variety of	다양한
	primacy	우위성		psychology	심리, 심리학
	eyewitness	목격자[증인]; 목격하다		economic	경제의, 경제학의, 실리적인
22	laboratory	실험실; 실험실의		demonstrate	입증[설명]하다, 보여 주다, 시위하다
	conduct	~을 하다, 지휘하다, (전기 등을) 전도하다; 행동		superior	우수한, 상위의, 뛰어난; 상사, 윗사람
	experimental	실험의, 실험적인, 경험적인		performance	수행, 성과, 성적, 공연
	evidence	증거, 징후		relatively	비교적, 상대적으로
	facial	얼굴의, 안면의		unconscious	무의식의, 의식을 잃은; 무의식
	detailed	상세한, 세세한		compared to	~에 비해, ~와 비교하여
	discussion	토론, 논의		logical	논리적인, 필연적인
	selection	선택, 선별, 선발	23	form	형태, 모양, 양식; 형성하다, 만들다

Voca

| ❶ voca | ❷ text | ❸ [/] | ❹ ____ | ❺ quiz 1 | ❻ quiz 2 | ❼ quiz 3 | ❽ quiz 4 | ❾ quiz 5 |

	lead	인도하다, 이끌다, 안내하다, 지도하다		exceed	넘다, 초과하다, 초월하다
	measure	측정하다, 평가하다; 척도, 기준, 조치		intelligence	지성, 지능, 정보
	the number of ~	~의 수		repeatedly	반복적으로, 되풀이하여
	interaction	상호 작용		evolve	진화하다, (서서히) 발전하다
	individual	개인; 개인의, 개별적인, 독특한		accelerate	가속하다, 촉진하다
	recall	회상, 추억; 기억해 내다		pursue	추구하다, 쫓다
	yield	양보하다, 굴복하다, 산출하다; 산출(물)		conscious	의식[자각]하는, 의도적인
	reliable	믿을 만한, 확실한		consciousness	의식, 자각, 인식
	respondent	응답자		provide A with B	A에게 B를 제공하다
	definition	정의, 뜻, 선명도		inspire	영감을 주다, 고무시키다, 격려하다
	vary	다르다, 다양하다, 변하다		insight	식견, 통찰력, 이해, 간파
	call in	~의 도움을 청하다		significant	상당한, 중요한, 의미심장한
	prompt	즉각적인, 신속한; 유발[자극]하다, 촉구하다		impact	영향, 효과, 충격; 영향[충격]을 주다
	concrete	구체적인, 실제의, 콘크리트로 만든; 콘크리트		direction	방향, 경향, 지휘, 지도, (-s) 사용법
	similarly	유사하게, 마찬가지로		greatly	크게, 몹시, 대단히, 위대하게
	procrastinator	미루는 사람		supporting	뒷받침하는
	currently	현재, 지금	25	electricity	전기, 전류
	can afford to V	~할 수 있다, ~할 여력이 있다		generation	세대, 대, 발생
	seek	추구하다, 찾다, 노력하다		fossil fuel	화석 연료
	response	대답, 응답		nuclear	(원자)핵의, 원자력의, 핵무기의
	ensure	확실하게 하다, 보장하다		renewable	갱신 가능한, 계속 가능한
	consistency	일관성, 일치, 조화		in terms of	~ 면에서, ~에 관하여
24	associate	연관[제휴]시키다, 교제하다; 동료		generate	발생시키다, 만들어내다, (감정을) 일으키다
	refer to	~을 언급[참조]하다, 가리키다		combined	합친, 결합된
	point at	~을 가리키다	26	artistic	예술의, 예술적인

Voca

	portrait	초상화, 인물상, 인물 사진		at least	적어도, 최소한
	celebrity	명사, 유명 인사	28	judge	판단하다, 심사하다; 판사, 심판
	eagerly	갈망[열망]하여, 열심히		cooperation	협력, 협동, 협조
	await	기다리다		gift certificate	상품권
	arrival	도착, 등장, 출현		management	관리, 경영(진)
	discuss	토론하다, 논의하다		agency	대리점, 대행사, 기관
	contain	포함[함유]하다, 억누르다, 억제하다		application	신청(서), 지원(서), 적용, 응용 프로그램
	prospect	전망, 예상, 가능성, 경치		along with	~와 함께
	graduate	졸업하다; 대학원생, 졸업생		via	경유하여, ~을 거쳐, ~에 의해
	hire	고용하다, 빌리다, 임차하다	29	metaphor	은유, 비유
	instantly	즉시, 곧장		linguistic	언어의, 언어학의
	exotic	이국적인, 진기한, 외래의, 이국의		sense	느끼다, 감지하다; 감각, 느낌, 분별
	up to	~까지, ~의 책임인		unlikely	있음직하지 않은
27	paw	(동물의) 발, 손; 발로 긁다		cognitive	인지의, 인식의
	healthy	건강한, 건전한		engaging	남의 마음을 끄는, 매력 있는
	registration	등록 (서류), 기재		on the other hand	한편, 반면에
	register	등록하다, 기재하다; 등록부, 명부		realize	깨닫다, 알아차리다, 인식하다, 실현하다
	limited	제한된, 제한적인		artifact	인공물, 공예품
	participant	참여자, 참가자		horizon	수평선, 지평선, (인식, 사고 등의) 시야
	include	포함하다, 포괄하다		generally	일반적으로, 대개, 보통
	ingredient	재료, 성분, 구성 요소		afford	~할 여유가 있다, 제공하다
	recipe	조리법, 요리법		potential	가능성이 있는, 잠재적인; 가능성, 잠재력
	safety	안전		wonder	궁금해하다, 경탄하다; 경이
	refund	반환, 환불; 환불하다		normally	보통, 일반적으로, 정상적으로
	cancel	취소하다, 철회하다		usefulness	유용(성), 유효성

❶ voca	❷ text	❸ [/]	❹ _____	❺ quiz 1	❻ quiz 2	❼ quiz 3	❽ quiz 4	❾ quiz 5

	obvious	분명한, 명백한		illusion	착각, 환상, 환영
	at first glance	처음에는, 언뜻 보기에는		eyesight	시력, 시야, 시각
	immediately	즉시, 바로		asset	자산, 재산
30	capacity	용량, 수용력, 능력		turn A into B	A를 B로 바꾸다
	resource	수단, 기지 (-s) 자원, 소질; 자원을 제공하다		creature	생물, 피조물
	compute	계산하다, 산출하다		transform	바꾸다, 전환하다, 변형시키다
	independently	독립적으로, 관계없이		mimic	모방하다, 흉내 내다; 흉내를 잘 내는, 모조의
	distribute	퍼뜨리다, 분포시키다, 분배하다, 유통하다		produce	생산[제조]하다, 초래하다; 농산물
	population	인구, 개체 수		suddenly	갑자기, 불시에
	solve	풀다, 해결하다		develop	발달[개발]하다, (병에) 걸리다
	flush	붉어지다, 물이 쏟아져 나오다; 홍조		grab	집다, 붙잡다, 움켜잡다; 붙잡음
	interact with	~와 상호 작용하다, 교류하다	32	suffer	시달리다, 고통 받다
	mental	마음의, 정신의		frame	구조, 틀, 액자; 만들다, 고안하다
	indeed	실제로, 사실		extreme	극단의, 극단적인; 극단
	dedicate	바치다, 전념[헌신]하다		muscle	근육, 힘, 체력
	calculation	계산, 산출		explode	폭발[파열]하다, 격발하다
	benefit from	~로부터 혜택[이익]을 얻다		oxygen	산소
	contribute to	~에 기여[공헌]하다, ~의 원인이 되다		boundary	경계(선), 한계, 범위
31	species	종, 종류		distance	거리, 간격, 차이
	hide	숨기다, 감추다		patient	인내심이 있는; 환자
	underwater	해저의, 수중(용)의, 극비의		pay for ~	~의 대금을 지불하다, 빚을 갚다
	flounder	넙치		therapy	치료, 요법
	fold	접다; 주름, (동물의) 우리		painful	아픈, 괴로운
	stare	빤히 쳐다보다, 응시하다; 응시		pressure	압력, 압박, 스트레스; 압력을 가하다
	upward	위쪽으로; 위쪽을 향한		treatment	대우, 취급, 치료(법)

| | ❶ voca | ❷ text | ❸ [/] | ❹ ___ | ❺ quiz 1 | ❻ quiz 2 | ❼ quiz 3 | ❽ quiz 4 | ❾ quiz 5 |

	sore	아픈, 쓰린; 상처		global warming	지구 온난화
	tissue	(세포)조직		pleasure	즐거움
33	manufacture	제조하다, 생산하다; 제조, 제품		no longer	더 이상 ~아닌[하지 않는]
	printer	인쇄기, 인쇄업자		pretend	~인 척하다, 주장하다; 가짜의
	discover	발견하다, 알다, 깨닫다		suffering	고통, 괴로움, 고난; 괴로워하는, 고통을 겪는
	goods	상품		distant	동떨어진, 먼, 냉담한
	manufacturer	제조업자[회사]		in time	일찍, 늦지 않게, 조만간
	product	생산물, 상품, 산물		in place	제자리에, 준비가 되어 있는
	be willing to V	(기꺼이) ~하려고 하다		stop -ing	~하는 것을 그만두다
	income	수입, 소득	35	crisis	위기, 중대 국면, 고비
	offer	제공하다, 제안하다; 제공, 제안		political	정치적인
	compare	비교하다, 비유하다		fix	고치다, 고착시키다, 정하다
	manipulate	조작하다, 조종하다		elective	선택의
	presence	존재, 실재, 참석, 출현		nevertheless	그럼에도 불구하고, 그렇기는 하지만
34	disaster	재앙, 재난, 재해		neglect	무시[방치]하다; 소홀, 무시
	scope	범위, 영역, 시야, 여지; 조사하다		indifference	무관심, 냉담
	eliminate	없애다, 제거하다, 실격시키다		careless	부주의한, 조심성 없는, 경솔한
	genre	장르, 유형, 형식		in other words	즉, 다시 말해서
	temperature	온도, 기온, 체온		address	연설, 주소; 연설하다, 다루다, 말을 걸다
	rise	오르다, 일어나다; 오름, 상승, 발생		leak	새다, 누설하다; 새는 곳[틈]
	degree	정도, 도, 학위		deliver	배달하다, 전하다, 출산하다
	isolated	외딴, 고립된, 격리된		account for	(~의 비율을) 차지하다, 설명하다
	expand	확장[확대]하다, 부연[확충]하다		estimated	대략적인, 어림잡은, 평이 좋은
	cease	중지하다, 그만두다		loss	손실, 손해, 상실, 패배
	illustrate	보여 주다, 예증하다, 삽화를 넣다		freshwater	민물의, 담수의

Voca

	estimate	견적, 평가; 추정하다, 평가하다		persuasive	설득력이 있는; 동기, 유인
	highlight	집중하다, 강조하다; 가장 중요한 부분	37	conventional	기존의, 전통[관례]적인, 형식적인
	proper	적합한, 알맞은		depression	우울증, 불경기
36	thrive	번창하다		be caused by	~에 기인하다
	depend on	~에 의존하다, ~에 달려 있다		neurotransmitter	신경 전달 물질
	navigate	항해[조종]하다, 길을 찾다, 처리하다		major	주요한, 대다수의; 전공; 전공하다
	count	세다, 간주하다, 중요하다; 계산		explanation	설명, 해명, 변명
	support	지지[부양]하다; 지지, 후원, 도움		substance	물질, 물체, 본질, 핵심
	probably	아마		decrease	감소; 감소하다
	mate	짝, 친구; 짝을 이루다		revise	수정하다, 고치다
	merit	장점, 가치, 공로; ~할 만하다		reframe	재구성하다
	matter	문제, 사안, 물질; 문제가 되다, 중요하다		fundamental	근본적인, 토대가 되는; 기초, 근본
	survival	생존, 생존자; 생존을 위한		go beyond	~을 능가하다, ~보다 낫다
	physically	신체적으로, 물리적으로		function	기능하다, 작용하다; 기능, 작용
	sensitive	민감한, 신경 과민의, 감수성이 풍부한		root	뿌리, 근원; 뿌리를 내리다
	skilled	능숙한, 숙련된		disease	질병, 질환
	development	발달, 발전, 성장		manifest	(명백히) 나타내다
	tendency	경향, 추세, 성향, 체질	38	common	공통의, 흔한, 평범한
	perceive	인지하다, 감지하다		account	기술, 설명, 계좌; 설명[생각]하다, 차지하다
	shame	창피를 주다, 부끄럽게 하다; 창피		float	뜨다, 떠다니다; 부유물
	compel	강요하다, ~하게 만들다		mixture	혼합(물)
	be meant to	~하기로 되어 있다, ~할 예정이다		tale	이야기, 설화
	respond to	~에 대응[반응]하다		plain	명백한, 평범한, 무늬가 없는; (-s) 평원
	come off	떨어지다, (약 등을) 중지하다		branch	나뭇가지, 지부, 지점; 갈라지다
	grudging	투덜대는		devote	바치다, 헌신하다, 전념하다

| | ❶ voca | ❷ text | ❸ [/] | ❹ ____ | ❺ quiz 1 | ❻ quiz 2 | ❼ quiz 3 | ❽ quiz 4 | ❾ quiz 5 |

	psychologist	심리학자		organism	유기체, 생물, 생명체
	accept	받아들이다, 인정하다		switch	바꾸다, 전환하다; 스위치, 개폐기
	thinker	사상가		exist	존재하다, 실존하다
	look for	~을 모집하다, ~을 찾다		random	무작위의, 임의의
	make sure	반드시 (~하도록) 하다, 확인하다, 확신하다		rough	거친, 난폭한, 대강의, 개략적인
	psychological	심리적인, 정신의		landscape	풍경, 지형; 조경하다, 경치를 꾸미다
	firmly	단호히		physiological	생리적인
	derive	비롯되다, 유래하다, 끌어내다		strikingly	두드러지게
	in addition to	~뿐만 아니라, ~에 더하여	40	punish	벌하다
	approach	접근하다; 접근(법)		effective	효과적인, 유효한, 시행되는
	deal with	~을 처리[해결]하다, 다루다		scold	야단치다, 꾸짖다
	principle	원리, 원칙, 신념, 신조		anger	화, 분노; 화나게 하다
	diversity	다양(성)		punishment	처벌, 형벌
	A as well as B	B뿐만 아니라 A도		discourage	의욕을 꺾다, 단념시키다, 훼방하다
	share	지분, 몫, 주식; 공유하다, 나누다		encourage	장려[격려]하다, 촉구하다
39	physicist	물리학자		continue to V	계속 ~하다
	go on	계속 하다, 일어나다, 벌어지다		in this case	이 경우에는
	enormous	엄청난, 거대한, 막대한		adopt	(채)택하다, 선정하다, 취하다
	stable	안정된, 지속성이 있는; 마구간, 외양간		strategy	전략, 전술, 계획, 방법
	emerge	나오다, 나타나다, 드러나다		length	길이, 기간, 범위, 정도
	result from	~로부터 초래되다, 기인하다		constantly	지속적으로, 끊임없이
	embryo	배아		point out	지적하다, 언급하다
	biologist	생물학자		reward	보상, 보답; 보상[보답]하다
	narrow	좁은, 편협한, 가까스로의; 좁히다		in this way	이런 방식으로, 이렇게 해서
	outcome	결과(물)		avoid	피하다, 막다

❶ voca	❷ text	❸ [/]	❹ ____	❺ quiz 1	❻ quiz 2	❼ quiz 3	❽ quiz 4	❾ quiz 5

41~42	imply	넌지시 나타내다, 암시하다, 수반하다		biased	치우친, 편견을 가진, 편향된
	focus on	~에 집중하다, 초점을 맞추다		anthropomorphism	의인화
	reduce	줄이다, 낮추다, 감소하다		mechanism	기계 장치, 기구, 메커니즘
	attention	주의(력), 집중(력), 관심		be about to V	막 ~하려고 하다
	rewarding	유익한, 보람이 있는		claw	발톱, 집게발
	assign A to B	A를 B로 분류하다		analysis	분석 ((복수형 analyses))
	reasoning	추론, 추리	43~45	ordinary	일상적인, 평범한, 보통의
	assume	추정하다, (태도 등을) 취하다, 맡다		cheerful	쾌활한, 명랑한, 밝은
	encounter	접하다, 마주치다; 마주침, (뜻밖의) 만남		content	내용(물), 만족, (-s)목차; 만족하는
	determine	결심[결정]하다, 알아내다		distinctive	독특한, 특징적인, 뚜렷이 구별되는
	sort	분류하다, 구분하다; 종류		uniqueness	특별함, 고유성
	object	~에 반대하다; 목표, 대상, 물체		inspiration	영감, 고무, 감화
	plant	식물, 공장; 심다, 이식하다, 설치하다		patch	(헝겊) 조각, 좁은 땅, 구역; 덧대다
	evaluate	평가하다, 감정하다		reveal	드러내다, 폭로하다
	physics	물리(학)		disappointed	실망한, 낙담한
	attribute	특성, 특질; ~의 탓으로 하다		path	(작은) 길, 진로, 보도, 경로
	intention	의도, 의향		bush	관목, 덤불
	predator	포식자, 포식동물, 약탈자		swallow	삼키다, 감수하다; 제비
	anthropologist	인류학자		climb	올라가다, 기어오르다
	evolutionary	진화의, 발전의, 진화론적인		blossom	꽃; 피다, 좋아지다
	interpret	해석하다, 통역하다, 설명하다		remarkably	놀랍게도, 주목할 만한, 현저한
	ambiguous	모호한		enthusiastically	열심히, 열광하여
	characteristic	특징, 특성, 특색; 독특한, 특징적인		burst into laughter	웃음을 터뜨리다
	result in	(결과적으로) ~을 낳다[야기하다]		glance	흘긋 보다, 대강 훑어보다; 흘긋 봄
	perceptual	지각의, 인지의		stain	얼룩, 때, 오점; 더럽히다, 얼룩지게 하다

Voca Test

영 ▶ 한

❶ voca	❷ text	❸ [/]	❹ ___	❺ quiz 1	❻ quiz 2	❼ quiz 3	❽ quiz 4	❾ quiz 5
glowing	타오르듯이 선명한, 강렬한							
imitate	모방하다, 흉내내다							
come true	실현되다, 이루어지다							
unexpected	예기치 않은, 뜻밖의							
genuine	진정한							

Voca Test

영 ▶ 한

❶ voca	❷ text	❸ [/]	❹ ___	❺ quiz 1	❻ quiz 2	❼ quiz 3	❽ quiz 4	❾ quiz 5
18	state				anticipation			
	department				decision			
	regard			20	packed			
	fund				dedicated			
	construction				workout			
	additional				in the midst of			
	space				daily routine			
	serve				chore			
	meaningful				take out			
	submit				trash			
	require				task			
	receive				essential			
	delay				view A as B			
	process				seize			
	considerable				physical activity			
	consequence				for instance			
	relate to				practice			
	in order to V				engage in			
	request				push-up			
	regarding				incorporate			
	look forward to -ing				improve			
	principal			21	naturally			
19	call out				automatically			
	figure				retrieve			
	captain				trait			

Voca Test

영 ▶ 한

❶ voca	❷ text	❸ [/]	❹ ____	❺ quiz 1	❻ quiz 2	❼ quiz 3	❽ quiz 4	❾ quiz 5

	efficient			procedure	
	raw			inaccurate	
	lack			identification	
	detail			explain	
	struggle to V			recognize	
	connection			tend to V	
	represent			accurate	
	abstract			immediate	
	feature			automatic	
	see ~ through			reaction	
	assumption			interpretation	
	motivation			impression	
	discovery			blink	
	representation			describe	
	completely			a variety of	
	primacy			psychology	
	eyewitness			economic	
22	laboratory			demonstrate	
	conduct			superior	
	experimental			performance	
	evidence			relatively	
	facial			unconscious	
	detailed			compared to	
	discussion			logical	
	selection		23	form	

Voca Test

영 〉 한

① voca	② text	③ [/]	④ ___	⑤ quiz 1	⑥ quiz 2	⑦ quiz 3	⑧ quiz 4	⑨ quiz 5
	lead			exceed				
	measure			intelligence				
	the number of ~			repeatedly				
	interaction			evolve				
	individual			accelerate				
	recall			pursue				
	yield			conscious				
	reliable			consciousness				
	respondent			provide A with B				
	definition			inspire				
	vary			insight				
	call in			significant				
	prompt			impact				
	concrete			direction				
	similarly			greatly				
	procrastinator			supporting				
	currently		25	electricity				
	can afford to V			generation				
	seek			fossil fuel				
	response			nuclear				
	ensure			renewable				
	consistency			in terms of				
24	associate			generate				
	refer to			combined				
	point at		26	artistic				

Voca Tes

영 ▶ 한

❶ voca	❷ text	❸ [/]	❹ ＿＿	❺ quiz 1	❻ quiz 2	❼ quiz 3	❽ quiz 4	❾ quiz 5

				at least				
	portrait							
	celebrity		28	judge				
	eagerly			cooperation				
	await			gift certificate				
	arrival			management				
	discuss			agency				
	contain			application				
	prospect			along with				
	graduate			via				
	hire		29	metaphor				
	instantly			linguistic				
	exotic			sense				
	up to			unlikely				
27	paw			cognitive				
	healthy			engaging				
	registration			on the other hand				
	register			realize				
	limited			artifact				
	participant			horizon				
	include			generally				
	ingredient			afford				
	recipe			potential				
	safety			wonder				
	refund			normally				
	cancel			usefulness				

Voca Test

영 한

❶ voca ❷ text ❸ [/] ❹ ____ ❺ quiz 1 ❻ quiz 2 ❼ quiz 3 ❽ quiz 4 ❾ quiz 5

	obvious			illusion	
	at first glance			eyesight	
	immediately			asset	
30	capacity			turn A into B	
	resource			creature	
	compute			transform	
	independently			mimic	
	distribute			produce	
	population			suddenly	
	solve			develop	
	flush			grab	
	interact with		32	suffer	
	mental			frame	
	indeed			extreme	
	dedicate			muscle	
	calculation			explode	
	benefit from			oxygen	
	contribute to			boundary	
31	species			distance	
	hide			patient	
	underwater			pay for ~	
	flounder			therapy	
	fold			painful	
	stare			pressure	
	upward			treatment	

Voca Test

❶ voca	❷ text	❸ [/]	❹ ___	❺ quiz 1	❻ quiz 2	❼ quiz 3	❽ quiz 4	❾ quiz 5

	sore				global warming			
	tissue				pleasure			
33	manufacture				no longer			
	printer				pretend			
	discover				suffering			
	goods				distant			
	manufacturer				in time			
	product				in place			
	be willing to V				stop -ing			
	income		35		crisis			
	offer				political			
	compare				fix			
	manipulate				elective			
	presence				nevertheless			
34	disaster				neglect			
	scope				indifference			
	eliminate				careless			
	genre				in other words			
	temperature				address			
	rise				leak			
	degree				deliver			
	isolated				account for			
	expand				estimated			
	cease				loss			
	illustrate				freshwater			

Voca Test

	estimate			persuasive	
	highlight		37	conventional	
	proper			depression	
36	thrive			be caused by	
	depend on			neurotransmitter	
	navigate			major	
	count			explanation	
	support			substance	
	probably			decrease	
	mate			revise	
	merit			reframe	
	matter			fundamental	
	survival			go beyond	
	physically			function	
	sensitive			root	
	skilled			disease	
	development			manifest	
	tendency		38	common	
	perceive			account	
	shame			float	
	compel			mixture	
	be meant to			tale	
	respond to			plain	
	come off			branch	
	grudging			devote	

Voca Test

| ❶ voca | ❷ text | ❸ [/] | ❹ ＿＿ | ❺ quiz 1 | ❻ quiz 2 | ❼ quiz 3 | ❽ quiz 4 | ❾ quiz 5 |

	psychologist			organism	
	accept			switch	
	thinker			exist	
	look for			random	
	make sure			rough	
	psychological			landscape	
	firmly			physiological	
	derive			strikingly	
	in addition to		40	punish	
	approach			effective	
	deal with			scold	
	principle			anger	
	diversity			punishment	
	A as well as B			discourage	
	share			encourage	
39	physicist			continue to V	
	go on			in this case	
	enormous			adopt	
	stable			strategy	
	emerge			length	
	result from			constantly	
	embryo			point out	
	biologist			reward	
	narrow			in this way	
	outcome			avoid	

Voca Test

	❶ voca	❷ text	❸ [/]	❹ ____	❺ quiz 1	❻ quiz 2	❼ quiz 3	❽ quiz 4	❾ quiz 5

41~42	imply				biased		
	focus on				anthropomorphism		
	reduce				mechanism		
	attention				be about to V		
	rewarding				claw		
	assign A to B				analysis		
	reasoning			43~45	ordinary		
	assume				cheerful		
	encounter				content		
	determine				distinctive		
	sort				uniqueness		
	object				inspiration		
	plant				patch		
	evaluate				reveal		
	physics				disappointed		
	attribute				path		
	intention				bush		
	predator				swallow		
	anthropologist				climb		
	evolutionary				blossom		
	interpret				remarkably		
	ambiguous				enthusiastically		
	characteristic				burst into laughter		
	result in				glance		
	perceptual				stain		

Voca Test

❶ voca	❷ text	❸ [/]	❹ _____	❺ quiz 1	❻ quiz 2	❼ quiz 3	❽ quiz 4	❾ quiz 5
glowing								
imitate								
come true								
unexpected								
genuine								

Voca Test

18		상태, 국가, 주; 진술하다			예측, 예상, 기대
		부서, 매장			결정, 결심, 판결
		간주[주목]하다, 관련있다; 관심, 존경, 관계	20		꽉 찬, 만원의
		자금을 대다; 자금, 기금			헌신적인, 전념하는, 전용의
		건축, 구성, 공사			운동, 연습
		추가적인, 추가의			~이 한창일 때, ~중에
		간격을 두다			일상
		제공[기여]하다, 복무하다, 적합하다			집안일, 허드렛일
		의미 있는, 중요한			~을 꺼내다
		제출하다, 복종시키다			쓰레기, 폐물
		필요로 하다, 요구하다			일, 과업; ~에 과중한 부담을 주다
		받다, 받아들이다			근본적인, 본질적인, 필수적인
		연기하다, 미루다; 지연, 지체			A를 B로 간주하다
		과정, 절차; 처리하다, 가공하다			붙잡다, 움켜쥐다
		상당한, 많은			신체 활동
		결과, 영향(력), 중요성			예를 들면
		~을 이해하다, ~와 관련이 있다			습관, 관례, 실행[실천], 연습
		~하기 위해, ~하려고			~에 참여[관여]하다, 종사하다
		요청, 요구; 요청[요구]하다			엎드려 팔굽혀펴기
		~에 관하여			법인회사로 만들다, 통합[포함]하다
		~하기를 고대하다			향상[개선]시키다, 향상하다
		주된, 주요한; 교장, 회장	21		자연스럽게, 본래
19		(큰 소리로) 부르다, 외치다			자동으로, 반사적으로, 기계적으로
		생각[계산]하다; 수치, 숫자, 인물, 모양			상기하다
		장, 우두머리, 지휘관			특성, 특색, 특징

Voca Test

❶ voca	❷ text	❸ [/]	❹ _____	❺ quiz 1	❻ quiz 2	❼ quiz 3	❽ quiz 4	❾ quiz 5
		유능한, 능률적인, 효율적인				절차, 순서, 과정, 조치		
		날것의, 가공하지 않은, 미숙한				부정확한		
		부족, 결핍; ~가 부족하다				동일시, 공감		
		세부 (항목); 자세히 말하다, 열거하다				설명하다, 해명하다		
		~하려고 몸부림치다[투쟁하다]				인정하다, 인식하다		
		연결, 접속, 연관(성), 인맥, 관계				~하는 경향이 있다		
		표현하다, 나타내다				정확한, 정밀한		
		추상적인; 추상, 개요, 요약; 요약[추출]하다				즉각적인, 직접의, 인접한		
		특징, 특집, 용모; 특집으로 하다, 특집으로 삼다				자동의, 반사적인, 기계적인		
		~을 끝까지 해내다				반응, 반작용, 반발		
		가정, 추정, 생각				해석, 설명, 이해		
		동기 (부여)				인상, 감명, 흔적		
		발견, 발각				깜박이다; 깜박임		
		묘사, 표현				묘사하다, 기술하다, 설명하다		
		완전히, 충분히				다양한		
		우위성				심리, 심리학		
		목격자[증인]; 목격하다				경제의, 경제학의, 실리적인		
22		실험실; 실험실의				입증[설명]하다, 보여 주다, 시위하다		
		~을 하다, 지휘하다, (전기 등을) 전도하다; 행동				우수한, 상위의, 뛰어난; 상사, 윗사람		
		실험의, 실험적인, 경험적인				수행, 성과, 성적, 공연		
		증거, 징후				비교적, 상대적으로		
		얼굴의, 안면의				무의식의, 의식을 잃은; 무의식		
		상세한, 세세한				~에 비해, ~와 비교하여		
		토론, 논의				논리적인, 필연적인		
		선택, 선별, 선발	23				형태, 모양, 양식; 형성하다, 만들다		

Voca Test

❶ voca	❷ text	❸ [/]	❹ ____	❺ quiz 1	❻ quiz 2	❼ quiz 3	❽ quiz 4	❾ quiz 5
		인도하다, 이끌다, 안내하다, 지도하다			넘다, 초과하다, 초월하다			
		측정하다, 평가하다; 척도, 기준, 조치			지성, 지능, 정보			
		~의 수			반복적으로, 되풀이하여			
		상호 작용			진화하다, (서서히) 발전하다			
		개인; 개인의, 개별적인, 독특한			가속하다, 촉진하다			
		회상, 추억; 기억해 내다			추구하다, 쫓다			
		양보하다, 굴복하다, 산출하다; 산출(물)			의식[자각]하는, 의도적인			
		믿을 만한, 확실한			의식, 자각, 인식			
		응답자			A에게 B를 제공하다			
		정의, 뜻, 선명도			영감을 주다, 고무시키다, 격려하다			
		다르다, 다양하다, 변하다			식견, 통찰력, 이해, 간파			
		~의 도움을 청하다			상당한, 중요한, 의미심장한			
		즉각적인, 신속한; 유발[자극]하다, 촉구하다			영향, 효과, 충격; 영향[충격]을 주다			
		구체적인, 실제의, 콘크리트로 만든; 콘크리트			방향, 경향, 지휘, 지도, (-s) 사용법			
		유사하게, 마찬가지로			크게, 몹시, 대단히, 위대하게			
		미루는 사람			뒷받침하는			
		현재, 지금	25		전기, 전류			
		~할 수 있다, ~할 여력이 있다			세대, 대, 발생			
		추구하다, 찾다, 노력하다			화석 연료			
		대답, 응답			(원자)핵의, 원자력의, 핵무기의			
		확실하게 하다, 보장하다			갱신 가능한, 계속 가능한			
		일관성, 일치, 조화			~ 면에서, ~에 관하여			
24		연관[제휴]시키다, 교제하다; 동료			발생시키다, 만들어내다, (감정을) 일으키다			
		~을 언급[참조]하다, 가리키다			합친, 결합된			
		~을 가리키다	26		예술의, 예술적인			

MOCK TEST 2024년 고1 11월 모의고사 내신대비용 WorkBook &
변형문제

Voca Test

❶ voca	❷ text	❸ [/]	❹ _____	❺ quiz 1	❻ quiz 2	❼ quiz 3	❽ quiz 4	❾ quiz 5

		초상화, 인물상, 인물 사진			적어도, 최소한			
		명사, 유명 인사	28		판단하다, 심사하다; 판사, 심판			
		갈망[열망]하여, 열심히			협력, 협동, 협조			
		기다리다			상품권			
		도착, 등장, 출현			관리, 경영(진)			
		토론하다, 논의하다			대리점, 대행사, 기관			
		포함[함유]하다, 억누르다, 억제하다			신청(서), 지원(서), 적용, 응용 프로그램			
		전망, 예상, 가능성, 경치			~와 함께			
		졸업하다; 대학원생, 졸업생			경유하여, ~을 거쳐, ~에 의해			
		고용하다, 빌리다, 임차하다	29		은유, 비유			
		즉시, 곧장			언어의, 언어학의			
		이국적인, 진기한, 외래의, 이국의			느끼다, 감지하다; 감각, 느낌, 분별			
		~까지, ~의 책임인			있음직하지 않은			
27		(동물의) 발, 손; 발로 긁다			인지의, 인식의			
		건강한, 건전한			남의 마음을 끄는, 매력 있는			
		등록 (서류), 기재			한편, 반면에			
		등록하다, 기재하다; 등록부, 명부			깨닫다, 알아차리다, 인식하다, 실현하다			
		제한된, 제한적인			인공물, 공예품			
		참여자, 참가자			수평선, 지평선, (인식, 사고 등의) 시야			
		포함하다, 포괄하다			일반적으로, 대개, 보통			
		재료, 성분, 구성 요소			~할 여유가 있다, 제공하다			
		조리법, 요리법			가능성이 있는, 잠재적인; 가능성, 잠재력			
		안전			궁금해하다, 경탄하다; 경이			
		반환, 환불; 환불하다			보통, 일반적으로, 정상적으로			
		취소하다, 철회하다			유용(성), 유효성			

Voca Test

❶ voca	❷ text	❸ [/]	❹ ____	❺ quiz 1	❻ quiz 2	❼ quiz 3	❽ quiz 4	❾ quiz 5
		분명한, 명백한			착각, 환상, 환영			
		처음에는, 언뜻 보기에는			시력, 시야, 시각			
		즉시, 바로			자산, 재산			
30		용량, 수용력, 능력			A를 B로 바꾸다			
		수단, 기지 (-s) 자원, 소질; 자원을 제공하다			생물, 피조물			
		계산하다, 산출하다			바꾸다, 전환하다, 변형시키다			
		독립적으로, 관계없이			모방하다, 흉내 내다; 흉내를 잘 내는, 모조의			
		퍼뜨리다, 분포시키다, 분배하다, 유통하다			생산[제조]하다, 초래하다; 농산물			
		인구, 개체 수			갑자기, 불시에			
		풀다, 해결하다			발달[개발]하다, (병에) 걸리다			
		붉어지다, 물이 쏟아져 나오다; 홍조			집다, 붙잡다, 움켜잡다; 붙잡음			
		~와 상호 작용하다, 교류하다	32		시달리다, 고통 받다			
		마음의, 정신의			구조, 틀, 액자; 만들다, 고안하다			
		실제로, 사실			극단의, 극단적인; 극단			
		바치다, 전념[헌신]하다			근육, 힘, 체력			
		계산, 산출			폭발[파열]하다, 격발하다			
		~로부터 혜택[이익]을 얻다			산소			
		~에 기여[공헌]하다, ~의 원인이 되다			경계(선), 한계, 범위			
31		종, 종류			거리, 간격, 차이			
		숨기다, 감추다			인내심이 있는; 환자			
		해저의, 수중(용)의, 극비의			~의 대금을 지불하다, 빚을 갚다			
		넙치			치료, 요법			
		접다; 주름, (동물의) 우리			아픈, 괴로운			
		빤히 쳐다보다, 응시하다; 응시			압력, 압박, 스트레스; 압력을 가하다			
		위쪽으로; 위쪽을 향한			대우, 취급, 치료(법)			

Voca Test

❶ voca	❷ text	❸ [/]	❹ ＿＿	❺ quiz 1	❻ quiz 2	❼ quiz 3	❽ quiz 4	❾ quiz 5
		아픈, 쓰린; 상처				지구 온난화		
		(세포)조직				즐거움		
33		제조하다, 생산하다; 제조, 제품				더 이상 ~아닌[하지 않는]		
		인쇄기, 인쇄업자				~인 척하다, 주장하다; 가짜의		
		발견하다, 알다, 깨닫다				고통, 괴로움, 고난; 괴로워하는, 고통을 겪는		
		상품				동떨어진, 먼, 냉담한		
		제조업자[회사]				일찍, 늦지 않게, 조만간		
		생산물, 상품, 산물				제자리에, 준비가 되어 있는		
		(기꺼이) ~하려고 하다				~하는 것을 그만두다		
		수입, 소득	35			위기, 중대 국면, 고비		
		제공하다, 제안하다; 제공, 제안				정치적인		
		비교하다, 비유하다				고치다, 고착시키다, 정하다		
		조작하다, 조종하다				선택의		
		존재, 실재, 참석, 출현				그럼에도 불구하고, 그렇기는 하지만		
34		재앙, 재난, 재해				무시[방치]하다; 소홀, 무시		
		범위, 영역, 시야, 여지; 조사하다				무관심, 냉담		
		없애다, 제거하다, 실격시키다				부주의한, 조심성 없는, 경솔한		
		장르, 유형, 형식				즉, 다시 말해서		
		온도, 기온, 체온				연설, 주소; 연설하다, 다루다, 말을 걸다		
		오르다, 일어나다; 오름, 상승, 발생				새다, 누설하다; 새는 곳[틈]		
		정도, 도, 학위				배달하다, 전하다, 출산하다		
		외딴, 고립된, 격리된				(~의 비율을) 차지하다, 설명하다		
		확장[확대]하다, 부연[확충]하다				대략적인, 어림잡은, 평이 좋은		
		중지하다, 그만두다				손실, 손해, 상실, 패배		
		보여 주다, 예증하다, 삽화를 넣다				민물의, 담수의		

Voca Test

❶ voca	❷ text	❸ [/]	❹ ___	❺ quiz 1	❻ quiz 2	❼ quiz 3	❽ quiz 4	❾ quiz 5
		견적, 평가; 추정하다, 평가하다						설득력이 있는; 동기, 유인
		집중하다, 강조하다; 가장 중요한 부분	37					기존의, 전통[관례]적인, 형식적인
		적합한, 알맞은						우울증, 불경기
36		번창하다						~에 기인하다
		~에 의존하다, ~에 달려 있다						신경 전달 물질
		항해[조종]하다, 길을 찾다, 처리하다						주요한, 대다수의; 전공; 전공하다
		세다, 간주하다, 중요하다; 계산						설명, 해명, 변명
		지지[부양]하다; 지지, 후원, 도움						물질, 물체, 본질, 핵심
		아마						감소; 감소하다
		짝, 친구; 짝을 이루다						수정하다, 고치다
		장점, 가치, 공로; ~할 만하다						재구성하다
		문제, 사안, 물질; 문제가 되다, 중요하다						근본적인, 토대가 되는; 기초, 근본
		생존, 생존자; 생존을 위한						~을 능가하다, ~보다 낫다
		신체적으로, 물리적으로						기능하다, 작용하다; 기능, 작용
		민감한, 신경 과민의, 감수성이 풍부한						뿌리, 근원; 뿌리를 내리다
		능숙한, 숙련된						질병, 질환
		발달, 발전, 성장						(명백히) 나타내다
		경향, 추세, 성향, 체질	38					공통의, 흔한, 평범한
		인지하다, 감지하다						기술, 설명, 계좌; 설명[생각]하다, 차지하다
		창피를 주다, 부끄럽게 하다; 창피						뜨다, 떠다니다; 부유물
		강요하다, ~하게 만들다						혼합(물)
		~하기로 되어 있다, ~할 예정이다						이야기, 설화
		~에 대응[반응]하다						명백한, 평범한, 무늬가 없는; (-s) 평원
		떨어지다, (약 등을) 중지하다						나뭇가지, 지부, 지점; 갈라지다
		투덜대는						바치다, 헌신하다, 전념하다

Voca Test

❶ voca	❷ text	❸ [/]	❹ ___	❺ quiz 1	❻ quiz 2	❼ quiz 3	❽ quiz 4	❾ quiz 5
		심리학자				유기체, 생물, 생명체		
		받아들이다, 인정하다				바꾸다, 전환하다; 스위치, 개폐기		
		사상가				존재하다, 실존하다		
		~을 모집하다, ~을 찾다				무작위의, 임의의		
		반드시 (~하도록) 하다, 확인하다, 확신하다				거친, 난폭한, 대략의, 개략적인		
		심리적인, 정신의				풍경, 지형; 조경하다, 경치를 꾸미다		
		단호히				생리적인		
		비롯되다, 유래하다, 끌어내다				두드러지게		
		~뿐만 아니라, ~에 더하여	40			벌하다		
		접근하다; 접근(법)				효과적인, 유효한, 시행되는		
		~을 처리[해결]하다, 다루다				야단치다, 꾸짖다		
		원리, 원칙, 신념, 신조				화, 분노; 화나게 하다		
		다양(성)				처벌, 형벌		
		B뿐만 아니라 A도				의욕을 꺾다, 단념시키다, 훼방하다		
		지분, 몫, 주식; 공유하다, 나누다				장려[격려]하다, 촉구하다		
39		물리학자				계속 ~하다		
		계속 하다, 일어나다, 벌어지다				이 경우에는		
		엄청난, 거대한, 막대한				(채)택하다, 선정하다, 취하다		
		안정된, 지속성이 있는; 마구간, 외양간				전략, 전술, 계획, 방법		
		나오다, 나타나다, 드러나다				길이, 기간, 범위, 정도		
		~로부터 초래되다, 기인하다				지속적으로, 끊임없이		
		배아				지적하다, 언급하다		
		생물학자				보상, 보답; 보상[보답]하다		
		좁은, 편협한, 가까스로의; 좁히다				이런 방식으로, 이렇게 해서		
		결과(물)				피하다, 막다		

Voca Test

❶ voca	❷ text	❸ [/]	❹ ____	❺ quiz 1	❻ quiz 2	❼ quiz 3	❽ quiz 4	❾ quiz 5
		넌지시 나타내다, 암시하다, 수반하다			치우친, 편견을 가진, 편향된			
		~에 집중하다, 초점을 맞추다			의인화			
		줄이다, 낮추다, 감소하다			기계 장치, 기구, 메커니즘			
		주의(력), 집중(력), 관심			막 ~하려고 하다			
		유익한, 보람이 있는			발톱, 집게발			
41~ 42		A를 B로 분류하다			분석 ((복수형 analyses))			
		추론, 추리	43~ 45		일상적인, 평범한, 보통의			
		추정하다, (태도 등을) 취하다, 맡다			쾌활한, 명랑한, 밝은			
		접하다, 마주치다; 마주침, (뜻밖의) 만남			내용(물), 만족, (-s)목차; 만족하는			
		결심[결정]하다, 알아내다			독특한, 특징적인, 뚜렷이 구별되는			
		분류하다, 구분하다; 종류			특별함, 고유성			
		~에 반대하다; 목표, 대상, 물체			영감, 고무, 감화			
		식물, 공장; 심다, 이식하다, 설치하다			(헝겊) 조각, 좁은 땅, 구역; 덧대다			
		평가하다, 감정하다			드러내다, 폭로하다			
		물리(학)			실망한, 낙담한			
		특성, 특질; ~의 탓으로 하다			(작은) 길, 진로, 보도, 경로			
		의도, 의향			관목, 덤불			
		포식자, 포식동물, 약탈자			삼키다, 감수하다; 제비			
		인류학자			올라가다, 기어오르다			
		진화의, 발전의, 진화론적인			꽃; 피다, 좋아지다			
		해석하다, 통역하다, 설명하다			놀랍게도, 주목할 만한, 현저한			
		모호한			열심히, 열광하여			
		특징, 특성, 특색; 독특한, 특징적인			웃음을 터뜨리다			
		(결과적으로) ~을 낳다[야기하다]			흘긋 보다, 대강 훑어보다; 흘긋 봄			
		지각의, 인지의			얼룩, 때, 오점; 더럽히다, 얼룩지게 하다			

glowing	타오르듯이 선명한, 강렬한			
imitate	모방하다, 흉내내다			
come true	실현되다, 이루어지다			
unexpected	예기치 않은, 뜻밖의			
genuine	진정한			

2024 고1 11월 모의고사

❶ voca　❷ text　❸ [/]　❹ ＿＿　❺ quiz 1　❻ quiz 2　❼ quiz 3　❽ quiz 4　❾ quiz 5

18 목적

❶ To the State Education Department, I am writing with regard to the state's funding for the construction project at Fort Montgomery High School.

주 교육부 귀하, 저는 Fort Montgomery 고등학교의 건축 프로젝트를 위한 주 예산과 관련하여 편지를 씁니다.

❷ Our school needs additional spaces to provide a fully functional Art and Library Media Center to serve our students in a more meaningful way.

저희 학교는 보다 의미 있는 방식으로 학생들을 만족시키기 위해 완전하게 제 기능을 하는 Art and Library Media Center 를 제공하기 위한 추가 공간이 필요합니다.

❸ Despite submitting all required documentation for funding to your department in April 2024, we have not yet received any notification from your department.

2024년 4월에 귀하의 부서로 예산에 필요한 모든 서류를 제출했음에도 불구하고, 저희는 아직 귀하의 부서로부터 어떠한 통지도 받지 못했습니다.

❹ A delay in the process can carry considerable consequences related to the school's budgetary constraints and schedule.

과정상 지연은 학교의 예산 제한 및 일정과 관련하여 상당한 결과를 초래할 수 있습니다.

❺ Therefore, in order to proceed with our project, we request you notify us of the review result regarding the submitted documentation.

그러므로, 저희의 프로젝트를 진행하기 위해 제출 서류와 관련한 검토 결과를 저희에게 통지해 줄 것을 요청합니다.

❻ I look forward to hearing from you. Respectfully, Clara Smith Principal, Fort Montgomery High School

귀하로부터의 답변을 고대합니다. Fort Montgomery 고등학교 교장, Clara Smith 드림

19 심경

❶ As I waited outside the locker room after a hard-fought basketball game, the coach called out to me, "David, walk with me." I figured he was going to tell me something important.

내가 치열하게 싸운 농구 경기 후에 라커 룸 밖에서 기다릴 때, 코치가 "David, 나와 함께 걷자." 라며 나를 크게 불렀다. 나는 그가 나에게 무언가 중요한 것을 말해 줄 거라고 생각했다.

❷ He was going to select me to be the captain of the team, the leader I had always wanted to be. My heart was racing with anticipation.

그는 내가 항상 되기를 원했던 리더인 팀의 주장으로 나를 뽑으려 할 것이라고 (생각했다). 나의 심장이 기대감으로 빠르게 뛰었다.

❸ But when his next words hit my ears, everything changed. "We're going to have to send you home," he said coldly. "I don't think you are going to make it."

그러나 그의 다음 말이 내 귀를 쳤을 때, 모든 것이 변했다. "우리는 너를 집으로 보내야만 해."라고 그가 차갑게 말했다. "나는 네가 해낼 거라고 생각하지 않아."

❹ I couldn't believe his decision. I tried to hold it together, but inside I was falling apart.

나는 그의 결정을 믿을 수 없었다. 나는 마음을 가다듬으려고 했지만, 내면에서 나는 산산이 무너지고 있었다.

❺ A car would be waiting tomorrow morning to take me home. And just like that, it was over.

내일 아침에 나를 집에 데려갈 차가 기다리고 있을 것이다. 그리고 그렇게, 끝이 났다.

20 요지

❶ For many of us, making time for exercise is a continuing challenge.

우리 중 다수에게 운동할 시간을 내는 것은 계속되는 도전이다.

❷ Between work commitments and family obligations, it often feels like there's no room in our packed schedules for a dedicated workout.

업무에 대한 전념과 가족 의무 사이에서, 우리의 빡빡한 일정들에는 운동에 전념할 여유가 없는 것처럼 종종 느껴진다.

❸ But what if the workout came to you, right in the midst of your daily routine? That's where the beauty of integrating mini-exercises into household chores comes into play.

그러나 만약 여러분의 일상 바로 한가운데에서 운동이 여러분을 찾아온다면 어떨까? 그것이 바로 간단한 운동을 집안일에 통합시키는 아름다움이 작동하는 지점이다.

❹ Let's be realistic; chores are inevitable. Whether it's washing dishes or taking out the trash, these tasks are an essential part of daily life.

현실적이 되자. 집안일은 불가피하다. 그것이 설거지하는 것이든 쓰레기를 내다 버리는 것이든지 간에, 이런 일들은 일상생활의 필수적인 부분이다.

❺ But rather than viewing chores as purely obligatory activities, why not seize these moments as opportunities for physical activity? For instance, practice squats or engage in some wall push-ups as you wait for your morning kettle to boil.

하지만 집안일을 순전히 의무적인 행위로 간주하기보다는, 이런 순간들을 신체 활동을 위한 기회로 잘 이용하는 것이 어떨까? 예를 들어, 여러분의 아침 주전자가 끓기를 기다리면서 스쿼트를 연습하거나 벽에 대고 하는 팔 굽혀 펴기 몇 개를 시작해 보라.

❻ Incorporating quick exercises into your daily chores can improve your health.

짧은 운동을 여러분의 일상적인 집안일에 포함시키는 것이 여러분의 건강을 향상시킬 수 있다.

21 주장

❶ When we see something, we naturally and automatically break it up into shapes, colors, and concepts that we have learned through education.

우리가 무언가를 볼 때, 우리는 그것을 자연스럽게 그리고 자동적으로 우리가 교육을 통해 배운 모양, 색깔, 그리고 개념들로 해체한다.

❷ We recode what we see through the lens of everything we know. We reconstruct memories rather than retrieving the video from memory. This is a useful trait.

우리는 우리가 알고 있는 모든 것의 렌즈를 통해 우리가 보는 것을 재부 호화한다. 우리는 기억에서 영상을 생각해 내기보다 기억을 재구성한다. 이것은 유용한 특성이다.

❸ It's a more efficient way to store information—a bit like an optimal image compression algorithm such as JPG, rather than storing a raw bitmap image file.

그것은 가공되지 않은 비트맵 이미지 파일을 저장하기보다 JPG 와 같은 최적의 이미지 압축 알고리즘과 약간 비슷하게 정보를 저장하기 위한 더 효율적인 방법이다.

❹ People who lack this ability and remember everything in perfect detail struggle to generalize, learn, and make connections between what they have learned.

이런 능력이 부족하고 완벽히 세세하게 모든 것을 기억하는 사람들은 일반화하고, 학습하고, 자신들이 학습한 것들 사이를 연결하려고 고군분투한다.

❺ But representing the world as abstract ideas and features comes at a cost of seeing the world as it is. Instead, we see the world through our assumptions, motivations, and past experiences.

그러나 세상을 추상적 생각과 특징으로 재현하는 것은 세상을 있는 그대로 보는 것을 희생하여 나온다. 대신에, 우리는 우리의 가정, 동기 그리고 과거 경험을 통해 세상을 바라본다.

❻ The discovery that our memories are reconstructed through abstract representations rather than played back like a movie completely undermined the legal primacy of eyewitness testimony. Seeing is not believing.

우리의 기억이 영화처럼 재생되기보다는 추상적 재현을 통해 재구성된다는 발견은 목격자 증언의 법적 우위성을 완전히 손상시켰다. 보는 것이 믿는 것은 아니다.

22 의미

❶ In his Cornell laboratory, David Dunning conducted experimental tests of eyewitness testimony and found evidence that a careful deliberation of facial features and a detailed discussion of selection procedures can actually be a sign of an *inaccurate* identification.

David Dunning의 코넬 대학의 실험실에서, 그는 목격자 증언에 대한 실험을 수행했고, 얼굴 특징에 대한 신중한 숙고와 선택 절차에 대한 상세한 논의가 실제로는 '부정확한' 식별의 징후일 수 있다는 증거를 발견했다.

❷ It's when people find themselves unable to explain why they recognize the person, saying things like "his face just popped out at me," that they tend to be accurate more often.

사람들이 "그의 얼굴이 그냥 나에게 탁 떠올랐다"라는 식으로 말하면서 왜 그 사람을 알아보는지 설명할 수 없는 스스로를 발견하는 바로 그때 그들은 더 자주 정확한 경향이 있다.

❸ Sometimes our first, immediate, automatic reaction to a situation is the truest interpretation of what our mind is telling us.

때때로 상황에 대한 우리의 최초의, 즉각적인, 자동적인 반응이 우리 마음이 우리에게 말하고 있는 것에 대한 가장 정확한 해석이다.

❹ That very first impression can also be more accurate about the world than the deliberative, reasoned self-narrative can be.

바로 그 첫인상이 또한 신중하고 논리적인 자기 서사보다 세상에 대해 더 정확할 수 있다.

❺ In his book *Blink*, Malcolm Gladwell describes a variety of studies in psychology and behavioral economics that demonstrate the superior performance of relatively unconscious first guesses compared to logical step-by-step justifications for a decision.

Malcolm Gladwell은 그의 저서 'Blink'에서, 결정에 대한 논리적인 단계적 정당화에 비해서 상대적으로 무의식적인 최초 추측의 우수성을 보여 주는 심리학 및 행동 경제학의 다양한 연구를 기술한다.

23 주제

❶ Many forms of research lead naturally to quantitative data.

많은 종류의 연구는 자연스럽게 양적 데이터로 이어진다.

❷ A study of happiness might measure the number of times someone smiles during an interaction, and a study of memory might measure the number of items an individual can recall after one, five, and ten minutes.

행복에 관한 연구는 누군가가 상호 작용 중에 미소 짓는 횟수를 측정할 수 있고, 기억에 관한 연구는 개인이 1분, 5분, 그리고 10분 후에 회상할 수 있는 항목의 수를 측정할 수 있다.

❸ Asking people how many times in a year they are sad will also yield quantitative data, but it might not be reliable.

사람들에게 자신이 일년에 몇 번 슬픈지 물어보는 것 또한 양적 데이터를 산출할 수 있지만, 이는 신뢰할 만하지 않을 수도 있다.

❹ Respondents' recollections may be inaccurate, and their definitions of 'sad' could vary widely.

응답자의 회상은 부정확할 수 있고, '슬픈'에 대한 그들의 정의는 크게 다를 수 있다.

❺ But asking "How many times in the past year were you sad enough to call in sick to work?" prompts a concrete answer.

그러나 "지난 1년 동안 직장에 병가를 낼 만큼 슬펐던 적이 몇 번 있었습니까?"라고 묻는 것은 구체적인 답변을 유발한다.

❻ Similarly, instead of asking people to rate how bad a procrastinator they are, ask, "How many of your utility bills are you currently late in paying, even though you can afford to pay them?"

마찬가지로, 사람들에게 그들이 얼마나 심하게 미루는 사람인지를 평가하도록 묻는 대신, "당신이 지불할 여유가 있음에도 불구하고 얼마나 많은 공과금 고지서의 납부가 현재 늦었나요?"라고 물어보라.

❼ Questions that seek concrete responses help make abstract concepts clearer and ensure consistency from one study to the next.

구체적인 응답을 요구하는 질문은 추상적인 개념을 더 명확하게 만들고 한 연구에서 다음 연구 간의 일관성을 보장하는 것을 돕는다.

24 제목

❶ The evolution of AI is often associated with the concept of singularity. Singularity refers to the point at which AI exceeds human intelligence.

AI의 진화는 종종 특이점의 개념과 연관된다. 특이점은 AI가 인간의 지능을 넘어서는 지점을 의미한다.

❷ After that point, it is predicted that AI will repeatedly improve itself and evolve at an accelerated pace.

그 지점 이후, AI는 스스로를 반복적으로 개선하고 가속화된 속도로 진화할 것으로 예측된다.

❸ When AI becomes self-aware and pursues its own goals, it will be a conscious being, not just a machine. AI and human consciousness will then begin to evolve together.

AI가 스스로를 인식하게 되고 자기 자신의 목표를 추구할 때, 그것은 단지 기계가 아니라 의식이 있는 존재가 될 것이다. AI와 인간의 의식은 그러면 함께 진화하기 시작할 것이다.

❹ Our consciousness will evolve to new dimensions through our interactions with AI, which will provide us with intellectual stimulation and inspire new insights and creativity.

우리의 의식은 우리의 AI와의 상호 작용을 통해 새로운 차원으로 진화할 것이며, 이는 우리에게 지적 자극을 제공하고 새로운 통찰력과 창의성을 불어넣을 것이다.

❺ Conversely, our consciousness also has a significant impact on the evolution of AI. The direction of AI's evolution will depend greatly on what values and ethics we incorporate into AI.

반대로, 우리의 의식 또한 AI의 진화에 중대한 영향을 끼친다. AI 진화의 방향은 우리가 어떤 가치와 윤리를 AI에 통합시키는지에 크게 좌우될 것이다.

❻ We need to see our relationship with AI as a mutual coexistence of conscious beings, recognizing its rights and supporting the evolution of its consciousness.

우리는 AI의 권리를 인식하고 그것의 의식의 진화를 지지하면서, 우리와 AI와의 관계를 의식 있는 존재들의 상호 공존으로 볼 필요가 있다.

29 어법

❶ Digital technologies are essentially related to metaphors, but digital metaphors are different from linguistic ones in important ways.
디지털 기술은 근본적으로 은유와 관련되어 있지만, 디지털 은유는 중요한 면에서 언어적 은유와 다르다.

❷ Linguistic metaphors are passive, in the sense that the audience needs to choose to actively enter the world proposed by metaphor.
언어적 은유는 독자가 은유에 의해 제시된 세계에 적극적으로 들어가도록 선택할 필요가 있다는 점에서 수동적이다.

❸ In the Shakespearean metaphor "time is a beggar," the audience is unlikely to understand the metaphor without cognitive effort and without further engaging Shakespeare's prose.
"시간은 구걸하는 자다"라는 셰익스피어의 은유에서 독자는 인지적인 노력 없이 그리고 셰익스피어의 산문을 더 끌어들이지 않고는 은유를 이해할 것 같지 않다.

❹ Technological metaphors, on the other hand, are active and often imposing) in the sense that they are realized in digital artifacts that are actively doing things, forcefully changing a user's meaning horizon.
반면에 기술적 은유는 사용자의 의미의 지평을 강력하게 바꾸면서 능동적으로 일을 하는 디지털 인공물에서 그것이 실현된다는 점에서 능동적이다.

❺ Technological creators cannot generally afford to require their potential audience to wonder how the metaphor works; normally the selling point is that the usefulness of the technology is obvious at first glance.
기술적인 창작자는 일반적으로 그들의 잠재적인 독자에게 어떻게 은유가 작용하는지 궁금해하도록 요구할 여유가 없고, 일반적으로 매력은 기술의 유용성이 첫눈에 분명하다는 것이다.

❻ Shakespeare, on the other hand, is beloved in part because the meaning of his works is not immediately obvious and requires some thought on the part of the audience.
반면에 셰익스피어는 부분적으로는 그의 작품의 의미가 즉각적으로 분명하지 않고 독자 측에서 어느 정도의 생각을 요구하기 때문에 사랑받는다.

30 어휘

❶ Herbert Simon won his Nobel Prize for recognizing our limitations in information, time, and cognitive capacity.

Herbert Simon은 정보, 시간, 그리고 인지적인 능력에서 우리의 한계를 인지한 것으로 그의 노벨상을 받았다.

❷ As we lack the resources to compute answers independently, we distribute the computation across the population and solve the answer slowly, generation by generation.

우리는 독립적으로 해답을 계산하기 위한 자원이 부족하기 때문에 우리는 전체 인구에 걸쳐 복잡한 계산을 분배하고 세대에 걸쳐 해답을 천천히 풀어 낸다.

❸ Then all we have to do is socially learn the right answers. You don't need to understand how your computer or toilet works; you just need to be able to use the interface and flush.

그러면 우리가 해야 하는 모든 것은 올바른 해답을 사회적으로 배우는 것이다. 여러분은 여러분의 컴퓨터 혹은 변기가 어떻게 작동하는지 이해할 필요가 없고 여러분은 단지 인터페이스를 사용할 수 있고 (변기의) 물을 내릴 수 있기만 하면 된다.

❹ All that needs to be transmitted is which button to push —essentially how to interact with technologies rather than how they work.

전달될 필요가 있는 모든 것은 어떤 버튼을 눌러야 하는지, 근본적으로 어떻게 그것들이 작동하는지보다는 기술과 상호 작용하는 방법이다.

❺ And so instead of holding more information than we have mental capacity for and indeed need to know, we could dedicate our large brains to a small piece of a giant calculation.

그렇다면 우리가 정신적 수용을 할 수 있는 것보다 그리고 정말로 알아야 할 필요가 있는 것보다 더 많은 정보를 가지는 것 대신에 우리는 우리의 큰 두뇌를 거대한 계산의 작은 조각에 바칠 수 있다.

❻ We understand things well enough to benefit from them, but all the while we are making small calculations that contribute to a larger whole.

우리는 그것들로부터 이득을 얻기에 충분할 정도로 사물을 잘 이해하지만 그러면서 우리는 더 큰 전체에 기여하는 작은 계산을 하고 있다.

❼ We are just doing our part in a larger computation for our societies' collective brains.

우리는 우리 사회의 집합적인 두뇌를 위한 더 큰 복잡한 계산에서 단지 우리의 역할을 하고 있는 것이다.

31 빈칸

❶ The best defence most species of octopus have is to stay hidden as much as possible and do their own hunting at night.
대부분의 문어 종(種)이 가진 최고의 방어는 가능한 한 많이 숨어 있는 것과 밤에 그들 자신의 사냥을 하는 것이다.

❷ So to find one in full view in the shallows in daylight was a surprise for two Australian underwater photographers.
그래서 낮에 얕은 곳에서 전체가 보이는 문어를 발견한 것은 두 명의 호주 수중 사진작가들에게는 놀라운 일이었다.

❸ Actually, what they saw at first was a flounder.
사실 그들이 처음에 봤던 것은 넙치였다.

❹ It was only when they looked again that they saw a medium-sized octopus, with all eight of its arms folded and its two eyes staring upwards to create the illusion.
오직 그들이 다시 봤을 때서야 그들은 중 간 크기의 문어를 보았고 착시를 만들기 위해 그것의 여덟 개의 모든 팔이 접혀 있었고 그것의 두 눈이 위쪽으로 응시하고 있었다.

❺ An octopus has a big brain, excellent eyesight and the ability to change colour and pattern, and this one was using these assets to turn itself into a completely different creature.
문어는 큰 뇌, 뛰어난 시력과 색깔과 패턴을 바꾸는 능력을 지니고 있고, 이것은 스스로를 완전히 다른 생물체로 바꾸기 위해 이러한 이점을 사용하고 있었다.

❻ Many more of this species have been found since then, and there are now photographs of octopuses that could be said to be transforming into sea snakes.
이 종의 더 많은 것들이 그때 이후로 발견되어 왔으며 지금은 바다뱀으로 변신하는 중이라고 말해질 수 있는 문어의 사진이 있다.

❼ And while they mimic, they hunt —producing the spectacle of, say, a flounder suddenly developing an octopodian arm, sticking it down a hole and grabbing whatever's hiding there.
그리고 그들이 모방하는 동안에 그들은 사냥을 한다. 이것은 말하자면 넙치가 갑자기 문어 다리 같은 팔을 펼치며 그것을 구멍으로 찔러 넣어 그곳에 숨어 있는 무엇이든지 움켜잡는 광경을 만들어 낸다.

32 빈칸

❶ How much we suffer relates to how we frame the pain in our mind.

우리가 얼마나 고통받는지는 우리가 고통을 우리의 마음에서 어떻게 구성하는지와 관련된다.

❷ When 1500m runners push themselves into extreme pain to win a race—their muscles screaming and their lungs exploding with oxygen deficit, they don't psychologically suffer much.

1500미터 달리기 선수가 경주에서 이기기 위해 그들의 근육이 비명을 지르고 그들의 폐가 산소 부족으로 폭발하면서, 스스로를 극심한 고통으로 밀어붙일 때, 그들은 정신적으로 많이 고통받지 않는다.

❸ In fact, ultra-marathon runners—those people who are crazy enough to push themselves beyond the normal boundaries of human endurance, covering distances of 50-100km or more over many hours, talk about making friends with their pain.

사실 울트라 마라톤 선수들은 즉, 인간 인내력의 정상적 경계를 넘어서 스스로를 밀어붙일 만큼 충분히 열정적인 사람들은 많은 시간 동안 50에서 100킬로미터 혹은 그 이상의 거리를 가지만 그들의 고통과 친구가 되는 것에 대해 이야기한다.

❹ When a patient has paid for some form of passive back pain therapy and the practitioner pushes deeply into a painful part of a patient's back to mobilise it, the patient calls that good pain if he or she believes this type of deep pressure treatment will be of value, even though the practitioner is pushing right into the patient's sore tissues.

한 환자가 특정 형태의 수동적 등 통증 치료에 돈을 지불했고 의사가 그것을 풀어 주기 위해 환자 등의 아픈 부분을 깊게 눌렀을 때, 비록 의사가 환자의 아픈 조직을 직접적으로 누르고 있을지라도, 만약 그 또는 그녀가 이러한 종류의 깊은 압박 치료법이 가치가 있을 것이라고 믿는다면, 환자는 그것을 좋은 아픔이라고 부른다.

33 빈칸

❶ When I worked for a large electronics company that manufactured laser and inkjet-printers, I soon discovered why there are often three versions of many consumer goods.

내가 레이저와 잉크젯 프린터를 생산했던 큰 전자 회사에서 일했을 때 나는 많은 소비 상품의 세 가지 버전이 종종 있는 이유를 곧 발견했다.

❷ If the manufacturer makes only one version of its product, people who bought it might have been willing to spend more money, so the company is losing some income.

만약 생산자가 그 제품의 오직 한 가지 버전만 만든다면 그것을 구매했던 사람들은 기꺼이 더 많은 돈을 쓰려고 했을 수도 있어서 회사는 일부 수입을 잃을 것이다.

❸ If the company offers two versions, one with more features and more expensive than the other, people will compare the two models and still buy the less expensive one.

만약 그 회사가 두 버전을 제공하는데 한 버전이 나머지보다 더 많은 기능과 더 비싼 가격을 가진다면, 사람들은 두 모델을 비교하고 여전히 덜 비싼 것을 살 것이다.

❹ But if the company introduces a third model with even more features and more expensive than the other two, sales of the second model go up; many people like the features of the most expensive model, but not the price.

하지만 만약 그 회사가 나머지 두 개보다 훨씬 더 많은 기능과 더 비싼 가격을 가진 세 번째 모델을 출시한다면 두 번째 모델의 판매가 증가하는데, 왜냐하면 많은 사람들은 가장 비싼 모델의 기능을 좋아하지만 그것의 가격을 좋아하지는 않기 때문이다.

❺ The middle item has more features than the least expensive one, and it is less expensive than the fanciest model.

중간 제품은 가장 저렴한 제품보다 더 많은 기능이 있고 가장 고급 모델보다는 덜 비싸다.

❻ They buy the middle item, unaware that they have been manipulated by the presence of the higher-priced item.

그들은 자신이 더 비싼 가격의 제품의 존재에 의해 조종되었다는 것을 알지 못한 채 중간 제품을 구입한다.

34 빈칸

❶ On-screen, climate disaster is everywhere you look, but the scope of the world's climate transformation may just as quickly eliminate the climate-fiction genre — indeed eliminate any effort to tell the story of warming, which could grow too large and too obvious even for Hollywood.

영화상 기후 재난은 여러분이 보는 어디에나 있지만, 세계의 기후 변화의 범위는 그것만큼이나 빠르게 기후 픽션 장르를 없앨지도 모르고 실제로 온난화 이야기를 하고자 하는 노력도 없애 버리는데, 그것은 할리우드에서조차 너무 커지고 너무 명백해질 것이다.

❷ You can tell stories 'about' climate change while it still seems a marginal feature of human life.

기후 변화가 여전히 인간 삶의 주변적인 특징처럼 보이는 동안에 여러분은 그것에 '관한' 이야기를 할 수 있을 것이다.

❸ But when the temperature rises by three or four more degrees, hardly anyone will be able to feel isolated from its impacts.

하지만 기온이 3도 혹은 4도 이상 상승할 때는 아무도 그것의 영향으로부터 고립되었다고 느낄 수 없을 것이다.

❹ And so as climate change expands across the horizon, it may cease to be a story.

그리고 기후 변화가 지평선을 넘어 확장될 때 그것은 이야기가 되기를 멈출 것이다.

❺ Why watch or read climate fiction about the world you can see plainly out your own window? At the moment, stories illustrating global warming can still offer an escapist pleasure, even if that pleasure often comes in the form of horror.

왜 여러분 자신의 창문 밖으로 뚜렷하게 볼 수 있는 세상에 대한 기후 픽션을 보거나 읽겠는가? 비록 그 즐거움이 종종 공포의 형태로 올지라도 지금 당장은 지구 온난화를 묘사하는 이야기가 현실 도피적인 즐거움을 여전히 제공할 수 있다.

❻ But when we can no longer pretend that climate suffering is distant — in time or in place — we will stop pretending about it and start pretending within it.

하지만 우리가 더 이상 기후 고통이 시간적으로 또는 장소적으로 멀리 있다고 가장할 수 없을 때 우리는 그것에 대해 가장하는 것을 멈추고 그것 내에서 가장하기 시작할 것이다.

35 무관

❶ Today, the water crisis is political — which is to say, not inevitable or beyond our capacity to fix — and, therefore, functionally elective.

오늘날, 물 위기는 피할 수 없는 것이 아니며 우리의 바로잡을 수 있는 능력을 넘어서지 않는, 즉 정치적인 것이고 따라서 기능적으로 선택적이다.

❷ That is one reason it is nevertheless distressing: an abundant resource made scarce through governmental neglect and indifference, bad infrastructure and contamination, and careless urbanization.

그것은 그럼에도 불구하고 그것이 괴로운 한 가지 이유이다. 즉, 풍족한 자원이 정부의 소홀함과 무관심, 열악한 사회 기반 시설과 오염, 부주의한 도시화를 통해 부족하게 되었다.

❸ There is no need for a water crisis, in other words, but we have one anyway, and aren't doing much to address it.

다시 말해서 물 위기가 있어야 할 필요가 없지만 어쨌든 우리는 그것을 겪고 있고 그것을 해결하기 위해 많은 일을 하고 있지 않다.

❹ Some cities lose more water to leaks than they deliver to homes: even in the United States, leaks and theft account for an estimated loss of 16 percent of freshwater; in Brazil, the estimate is 40 percent.

일부 도시들은 그들이 주택으로 공급하는 것보다 누수로 인해 더 많은 물을 잃는다. 즉, 미국에서조차 누수와 도난은 담수의 16퍼센트의 추정된 손실을 차지하고 브라질에서는 그 추정치가 40퍼센트이다.

❺ Seen in both cases, as everywhere, the selective scarcity clearly highlights haveandhavenot inequities, leaving 2.1 billion people without safe drinking water and 4.5 billion without proper sanitation worldwide.

양쪽의 경우에서 보여지듯이 모든 곳에 서처럼 선택적 부족이 가진 자와 가지지 못한 자의 불평등을 분명히 강조하고 이것은 전 세계적으로 21억 명을 안전한 식수가 없고 45억 명을 적절한 위생이 없는 채로 둔다.

36 순서

❶ As individuals, our ability to thrive depended on how well we navigated relationships in a group.
개인으로서 성공하려는 우리의 능력은 우리가 집단 내에서 관계를 얼마나 잘 다루는지에 달려 있었다.

❷ If the group valued us, we could count on support, resources, and probably a mate. If it didn't, we might get none of these merits. It was a matter of survival, physically and genetically.
만약 그 집단이 우리를 가치 있게 여겼다면 우리는 지원, 자원, 그리고 아마도 짝을 기대할 수 있었을 것이다. 만약 그렇지 않았다면, 우리는 그러한 이점들 중 아무것도 얻지 못했을 것이다. 그것은 신체적으로 그리고 유전적으로 생존의 문제였다.

❸ Over millions of years, the pressure selected for people who are sensitive to and skilled at maximizing their standing. The result was the development of a tendency to unconsciously monitor how other people in our community perceive us.
수백만 년 동안 그러한 압박은 자신의 지위를 최대화하는 데 민감하고 능숙한 사람들을 선택했다. 그 결과는 우리 공동체의 다른 사람들이 우리를 어떻게 인식하는지 무의식적으로 관찰하는 경향의 발달이었다.

❹ We process that information in the form of self-esteem and such related emotions as pride, shame, or insecurity.
우리는 자존감 그리고 자존심, 수치심 또는 불안 같은 관련된 감정의 형태로 그 정보를 처리한다.

❺ These emotions compel us to do more of what makes our community value us and less of what doesn't.
이러한 감정들은 우리에게 우리의 공동체가 우리를 가치 있게 여기도록 만드는 것을 더 많이 하고 그렇지 않은 것을 덜 하도록 강요한다.

❻ And, crucially, they are meant to make that motivation feel like it is coming from within.
그리고 결정적으로 그것들은 그 동기가 내부에서 나오고 있는 것처럼 그것을 느끼게 만들도록 되어 있다.

❼ If we realized, on a conscious level, that we were responding to social pressure, our performance might come off as grudging or cynical, making it less persuasive.
우리가 사회적 압박에 반응하고 있었다는 것을 의식적인 수준에서 깨닫는다면, 우리의 행동은 그것(그 동기)을 설득력이 떨어지게 만들면서 투덜대거나 냉소적인 것으로 나타날 수 있다.

37 순서

❶ Conventional medicine has long believed that depression is caused by an imbalance of neurotransmitters in the brain.

전통적인 의학은 우울증이 뇌의 신경 전달 물질의 불균형으로 인해 발생한다고 오랫동안 믿어 왔다.

❷ However, there is a major problem with this explanation. This is because the imbalance of substances in the brain is a consequence of depression, not its cause.

그러나 이 설명에는 중대한 문제가 있다. 이것은 왜냐하면 뇌 속 물질의 불균형은 우울증의 원인이 아니라 그것의 결과이기 때문이다.

❸ In other words, depression causes a decrease in brain substances such as serotonin and noradrenaline, not a decrease in brain substances causes depression.

다시 말해서, 우울증이 세로토닌이나 노르아드레날린과 같은 뇌의 물질의 감소를 유발하는 것이지 뇌의 물질의 감소가 우울증을 유발하는 것이 아니다.

❹ In this revised cause-and-effect, the key is to reframe depression as a problem of consciousness.

이 수정된 인과 관계에서, 핵심은 우울증을 의식의 문제로 재구성하는 것이다.

❺ Our consciousness is a more fundamental entity that goes beyond the functioning of the brain. The brain is no more than an organ of consciousness.

우리의 의식은 뇌의 기능을 넘어서는 보다 근본적인 실체이다. 뇌는 의식의 기관에 지나지 않는다.

❻ If it is not consciousness itself, then the root cause of depression is also a distortion of our state of consciousness: a consciousness that has lost its sense of self and the meaning of life.

만약 그것이 의식 그 자체가 아니라면, 우울증의 근본 원인 역시 우리의 의식 상태의 왜곡이며 즉, 자아감과 삶의 의미를 상실한 의식이다.

❼ Such a disease of consciousness may manifest itself in the form of depression.

그러한 의식의 질환이 우울증의 형태로 명백히 나타날 수 있다.

38 삽입

❶ The common accounts of human nature that float around in society are generally a mixture of assumptions, tales and sometimes plain silliness. However, psychology is different.

사회에 떠도는 인간 본성에 대한 흔한 설명은 일반적으로 가정, 이야기, 그리고 때로는 순전한 어리석음의 혼합이다, 그러나, 심리학은 다르다.

❷ It is the branch of science that is devoted to understanding people: how and why we act as we do; why we see things as we do; and how we interact with one another.

그것은 사람들을 이해하는, 즉 우리가 어떻게 그리고 왜 행동하는 대로 행동하는지, 우리가 왜 보는 대로 사물을 보는 지, 그리고 우리가 어떻게 서로 상호 작용하는지를 이해하는 데 전념하는 과학 분야이다.

❸ The key word here is 'science.' Psychologists don't depend on opinions and hearsay, or the generally accepted views of society at the time, or even the considered opinions of deep thinkers.

여기서 핵심어는 '과학'이다. 심리학자들은 의견과 소문, 혹은 당대의 사회에서 일반적으로 받아들여지는 견해, 혹은 심지어 심오한 사상가들의 숙고된 의견에 의존하지 않는다.

❹ Instead, they look for evidence, to make sure that psychological ideas are firmly based, and not just derived from generally held beliefs or assumptions.

대신에 그들은 심리학적 개념이 단지 일반적으로 받아들여지는 신념이나 가정에서 도출된 것이 아니라, 확고하게 기반을 두고 있는지 확신하기 위해 증거를 찾는다.

❺ In addition to this evidence-based approach, psychology deals with fundamental processes and principles that generate our rich cultural and social diversity, as well as those shared by all human beings.

이러한 증거 기반 접근법에 더하여 심리학은 모든 인간에 의해 공유되는 근본적인 과정과 원리뿐만 아니라, 우리의 풍부한 문화적 사회적 다양성을 만들어 내는 것들을 다룬다.

❻ These are what modern psychology is all about.

이것들은 현대 심리학이 무엇인지 보여 준다.

39 삽입

❶ Life is what physicists might call a 'high-dimensional system,' which is their fancy way of saying that there's a lot going on.
생명은 물리학자들이 '고차원 시스템'이라고 부를 수 있는 것인데 이는 많은 일이 발생하고 있다고 말하는 그들의 멋진 방식이다.

❷ In just a single cell, the number of possible interactions between different molecules is enormous.
단 하나의 세포 내에서도 여러 분자 간의 가능한 상호 작용의 수는 매우 크다.

❸ Such a system can only hope to be stable if only a smaller number of collective ways of being may emerge.
이러한 시스템은 더 적은 수의 존재의 집합적인 방식이 나타날 때만 오직 안정적이기를 기대할 수 있다.

❹ For example, it is only a limited number of tissues and body shapes that may result from the development of a human embryo.
예를 들어 인간 배아의 발달로부터 나올 수 있는 것은 오직 제한된 수의 조직과 신체 형태이다.

❺ In 1942, the biologist Conrad Waddington called this drastic narrowing of outcomes *canalization*.
1942년에 생물학자 Conrad Waddington은 이러한 극적인 결과의 축소를 '운하화'라고 불렀다.

❻ The organism may switch between a small number of well-defined possible states, but can't exist in random states in between them, rather as a ball in a rough landscape must roll to the bottom of one valley or another.
오히려 울퉁불퉁한 경관에 있는 공이 이 계곡 혹은 또 다른 계곡의 바닥으로 반드시 굴러가야 하는 것처럼, 유기체는 적은 수의 명확하게 정의된 가능한 상태 사이에서 바뀔 수 있지만 그것들 사이에 있는 무작위의 상태로 존재할 수는 없다.

❼ We'll see that this is true also of health and disease: there are many causes of illness, but their manifestations at the physiological and symptomatic levels are often strikingly similar.
우리는 이것이 건강과 질병에도 적용된다는 것을 알게 될 것이다. 즉 질병의 많은 원인이 있지만, 그것들의 생리적이고 증상적인 수준에서의 발현은 종종 놀랍도록 유사하다.

40 요약

❶ Punishing a child may not be effective due to what Álvaro Bilbao, a neuropsychologist, calls 'trick-punishments.'

아이를 벌주는 것은 신경심리학자 Álvaro Bilbao가 '트릭 처벌'이라고 부르는 것으로 인해 효과적이지 않을 수 있다.

❷ A trick-punishment is a scolding, a moment of anger or a punishment in the most classic sense of the word.

트릭 처벌은 꾸짖음, 순간의 화 혹은 (처벌이라는) 단어의 가장 전형적인 의미에서의 처벌이다.

❸ Instead of discouraging the child from doing something, it encourages them to do it. For example, Hugh learns that when he hits his little brother, his mother scolds him.

아이가 무언가를 하는 것을 단념시키는 대신 트릭 처벌은 그들이 그것을 하도록 장려한다. 예를 들어 Hugh는 그가 자신의 남동생을 때릴 때 그의 어머니가 그를 꾸짖는다는 것을 배운다.

❹ For a child who feels lonely, being scolded is much better than feeling invisible, so he will continue to hit his brother.

외로움을 느끼는 아이에게는 꾸중을 듣는 것이 눈에 띄지 않는다고 느끼는 것보다 훨씬 나아서 그는 그의 남동생을 때리는 것을 계속할 것이다.

❺ In this case, his mother would be better adopting a different strategy.

이 경우에, 그의 어머니는 다른 전략을 채택하는 것이 보다 나을 것이다.

❻ For instance, she could congratulate Hugh when he has not hit his brother for a certain length of time.

예를 들어 그녀는 Hugh가 그의 남동생을 일정 기간 동안 때리지 않았을 때 그를 자랑스러워해 줄 수 있다.

❼ The mother clearly cannot allow the child to hit his little brother, but instead of constantly pointing out the negatives, she can choose to reward the positives. In this way, any parent can avoid trick-punishments.

어머니는 분명 아이가 그의 남동생을 때리는 것을 내버려둘 수 없고, 그녀는 부정적 측면을 계속 지적하는 대신에 긍정적 측면을 보상하는 것을 선택할 수 있다. 이렇게 어느 부모도 트릭 처벌을 피할 수 있다.

41~42 제목, 어휘

❶ From an early age, we assign purpose to objects and events, preferring this reasoning to random chance. Children assume, for instance, that pointy rocks are that way because they don't want you to sit on them.

어릴 때부터 우리는 사물과 사건에 목적을 부여하며, 무작위적인 우연보다 이러한 논리를 선호한다. 예를 들어 뾰족한 돌은 아이들이 그 위에 앉기를 원치 않기 때문에 그것이 그렇게 생겼다고 그들(아이들)은 가정한다.

❷ When we encounter something, we first need to determine what sort of thing it is. Inanimate objects and plants generally do not move and can be evaluated from physics alone. However, by attributing intention to animals and even objects, we are able to make fast decisions about the likely behaviour of that being.

우리가 무언가를 마주칠 때 우리는 먼저 그것이 어떤 종류의 것인지 결정할 필요가 있다. 무생물과 식물은 일반적으로 움직이지 않으며 물리적 현상만으로 평가될 수 있다. 그러나 동물과 심지어 사물도 의도가 있다고 생각함으로써 우리는 그 존재가 할 것 같은 행동에 대해 빠른 결정을 내릴 수 있다.

❸ This was essential in our hunter-gatherer days to avoid being eaten by predators. The anthropologist Stewart Guthrie made the point that survival in our evolutionary past meant that we interpret ambiguous objects as agents with human mental characteristics, as those are the mental processes which we understand.

이는 우리의 수렵 채집 시절에 포식자에게 잡아먹히는 것을 피하기 위해 필수적이었다. 인류학자 Stewart Guthrie는 인간의 정신적 특성이 우리가 이해하는 정신 과정이기 때문에, 우리의 진화상 과거에서 생존이란 우리가 모호한 사물을 인간의 정신적 특성을 가진 행위자로 해석하는 것을 의미한다고 주장했다.

❹ Ambiguous events are caused by such agents. This results in a perceptual system strongly biased towards anthropomorphism. Therefore, we tend to assume intention even where there is none. This would have arisen as a survival mechanism.

모호한 사건은 이러한 행위자에 의해 발생한다. 이는 의인화에 강하게 편향된 지각 체계로 귀결된다. 그러므로, 우리는 의도가 없는 곳에서도 의도를 가정하는 경향이 있다. 이는 생존 메커니즘으로 발생해 왔을 것이다.

❺ If a lion is about to attack you, you need to react quickly, given its probable intention to kill you. By the time you have realized that the design of its teeth and claws could kill you, you are dead. So, assuming intent, without detailed design analysis or understanding of the physics, has saved your life.

만약 사자가 당신을 막 공격하려 한다면 당신을 죽이려는 그것의 가능한 의도를 고려하여 당신은 빠르게 반응할 필요가 있다. 당신이 그것의 이빨과 발톱의 구조가 당신을 죽일 수 있다는 것을 깨달았을 즈음 당신은 죽어 있다. 따라서 상세한 구조 분석 또는 물리적 현상의 이해 없이 의도를 부여하는 것이 당신의 목숨을 구해 왔다.

43~45 순서, 지칭, 세부 내용

❶ Once long ago, deep in the Himalayas, there lived a little panda. He was as ordinary as all the other pandas. He was completely white from head to toe. His two big ears, his four furry feet and his cute round nose were all frosty white, leaving him feeling ordinary and sad.

옛날에 히말라야 산맥 깊숙한 곳에 작은 판다가 살았다. 그는 다른 모든 판다들만큼 평범했다. 그는 머리부터 발끝까지 전부 하얬다. 그의 두 개의 큰 귀, 네 개의 털 많은 발, 그리고 귀여운 둥근 코는 모두 서리처럼 하얘서 그가 평범하고 슬프게 느끼게 하였다.

❷ Unlike the cheerful and contented pandas around him, he desired to be distinctive, special, and unique. Driven by the desire for uniqueness, the little panda sought inspiration from his distant cousin, a giant white panda covered with heavenly black patches.

그의 주위에 있는 명랑하고 만족스러운 판다들과 달리 그는 특이하고 특별하며 독특해지기를 갈망했다. 독특함에 대한 열망에 사로잡혀 작은 판다는 그의 먼 사촌인 멋진 검은 반점으로 뒤덮인 거대한 흰 판다로부터 영감을 찾으려 했다.

❸ But the cousin revealed the patches were from an unintended encounter with mud, and he disliked them. Disappointed, the little panda walked home. On his way, he met a red-feathered peacock, who explained he turned red from eating wild berries.

그러나 사촌은 그 반점이 진흙과 의도치 않게 접촉한 결과이며, 그는 그것(반점)을 싫어한다고 밝혔다. 실망한 채로 작은 판다는 집으로 걸어갔다. 가는 길에 그는 붉은 깃털을 가진 공작새를 만났는데 그 공작새는 그가 야생 베리를 먹어서 붉게 변했다고 설명했다.

❹ The little panda changed his path and hurried to the nearest berry bush, greedily eating a mouthful of juicy red berries. However, they were so bitter he couldn't swallow even one. At dusk, he finally got home and slowly climbed his favorite bamboo tree.

작은 판다는 경로를 바꾸어 가장 가까운 베리 덤불로 서둘러 가서, 탐욕스럽게 한입 가득 즙이 많은 빨간 베리를 먹었다. 하지만 그것들은 너무 써서 그는 한 개도 삼킬 수 없었다. 해질 무렵 그는 마침내 집에 도착했고 그가 가장 좋아하는 대나무에 천천히 올라갔다.

❺ There, he discovered a strange black and red flower with a sweet scent that tempted him to eat all its blossoms. The following morning, under sunny skies, the little panda felt remarkably better. During breakfast, he found the other pandas chatting enthusiastically and asked why.

그곳에서 그가 그것의 모든 꽃을 먹도록 유혹하는 달콤한 향기를 가진 기묘한 검고 붉은 꽃을 발견하였다. 다음 날 아침 맑은 하늘 아래에서 작은 판다는 기분이 매우 좋아졌다. 아침 식사 중에 그는 다른 판다들이 신나게 수다를 떨고 있는 것을 발견하고 이유를 물어보았다.

❻ They burst into laughter, exclaiming, "Look at yourself!" Glancing down, he discovered his once white fur was now stained jet black and glowing red. He was overjoyed and realized that, rather than by imitating others, his wishes can come true from unexpected places and genuine experiences.

그들은 웃음을 터뜨리며 "네 자신을 좀 봐!"라고 외쳤다. 아래를 흘긋 보고, 그는 한때 하얬던 자신의 털이 이제 새까맣고 빛나는 붉은색으로 얼룩져 있다는 것을 발견했다. 그는 매우 기뻐했고 그의 소원이 남들을 모방하기보다는 예상치 못한 곳과 진정한 경험으로부터 실현될 수 있음을 깨달았다.

18

To the State Education Department,

I am writing with regard to the state's funding for the [**construction / destruction**]¹⁾ project at Fort Montgomery High School. Our school needs additional spaces to provide a fully functional Art and Library Media Center to serve our students in a more meaningful way. [**Although / Despite**]²⁾ submitting all required documentation for funding to your department in April 2024, we have not yet received any notification from your department. A delay in the process can carry [**considerable / considerate**]³⁾ consequences related to the school's budgetary constraints and schedule. Therefore, in order to proceed with our project, we request you [**notice / notify**]⁴⁾ us of the review result regarding the submitted documentation. I look forward to [**hear / hearing**]⁵⁾ from you.
Respectfully, Clara Smith Principal, Fort Montgomery High School

주 교육부 귀하, 저는 Fort Montgomery 고등학교의 건축 프로젝트를 위한 주 예산과 관련하여 편지를 씁니다. 저희 학교는 보다 의미 있는 방식으로 학생들을 만족시키기 위해 완전하게 제 기능을 하는 Art and Library Media Center를 제공하기 위한 추가 공간이 필요합니다. 2024년 4월에 귀하의 부서로 예산에 필요한 모든 서류를 제출했음에도 불구하고, 저희는 아직 귀하의 부서로부터 어떠한 통지도 받지 못했습니다. 과정상 지연은 학교의 예산 제한 및 일정과 관련하여 상당한 결과를 초래할 수 있습니다. 그러므로, 저희의 프로젝트를 진행하기 위해 제출 서류와 관련한 검토 결과를 저희에게 통지해 줄 것을 요청합니다. 귀하로부터의 답변을 고대합니다. Fort Montgomery 고등학교 교장, Clara Smith 드림

19

As I waited outside the locker room after a hard-fought basketball game, the coach called out to me, "David, walk with me." I figured he was going to tell me something important. He was going to select me to be the captain of the team, the leader I had always [**want / wanted**]⁶⁾ to be. My heart was racing with [**anticipation / disappointment**]⁷⁾. But when his next words hit my ears, [**everything / nothing**]⁸⁾ changed. "We're going to have to send you home," he said [**cold / coldly**]⁹⁾. "I don't think you are going to make it." I couldn't believe his decision. I tried to hold it together, but inside I was falling apart. A car would be waiting tomorrow morning to take me home. And just like that, it was over.

내가 치열하게 싸운 농구 경기 후에 라커 룸 밖에서 기다릴 때, 코치가 "David, 나와 함께 걷자."라며 나를 크게 불렀다. 나는 그가 나에게 무언가 중요한 것을 말해 줄 거라고 생각했다. 그는 내가 항상 되기를 원했던 리더인 팀의 주장으로 나를 뽑으려 할 것이라고 (생각했다). 나의 심장이 기대감으로 빠르게 뛰었다. 그러나 그의 다음 말이 내 귀를 쳤을 때, 모든 것이 변했다. "우리는 너를 집으로 보내야만 해."라고 그가 차갑게 말했다. "나는 네가 해낼 거라고 생각하지 않아." 나는 그의 결정을 믿을 수 없었다. 나는 마음을 가다듬으려고 했지만, 내면에서 나는 산산이 무너지고 있었다. 내일 아침에 나를 집에 데려갈 차가 기다리고 있을 것이다. 그리고 그렇게, 끝이 났다.

20

For many of us, making time for exercise is a continuing challenge. Between work commitments and family obligations, it often feels like there's no room in our [**packed** / relaxed]10) schedules for a dedicated workout. But what if the workout came [**from** / to]11) you, right in the midst of your daily routine? That's [when / **where**]12) the beauty of integrating mini-exercises into household chores comes into play. Let's be realistic; chores are [**inevitable** / inevitably]13). Whether it's washing dishes or [take / **taking**]14) out the trash, these tasks are an [**essential** / unnecessary]15) part of daily life. But rather than viewing chores as [pure / **purely**]16) obligatory activities, why not seize these moments as opportunities for [mental / **physical**]17) activity? For instance, practice squats or engage in some wall push-ups as you wait for your morning kettle to boil. [Incorporate / **Incorporating**]18) quick exercises into your daily chores can [approve / **improve**]19) your health.

우리 중 다수에게 운동할 시간을 내는 것은 계속되는 도전이다. 업무에 대한 전념과 가족 의무 사이에서, 우리의 빡빡한 일정들에는 운동에 전념할 여유가 없는 것처럼 종종 느껴진다. 그러나 만약 여러분의 일상 바로 한가운데에서 운동이 여러분을 찾아온다면 어떨까? 그것이 바로 간단한 운동을 집안일에 통합시키는 아름다움이 작동하는 지점이다. 현실적이 되자. 집안일은 불가피하다. 그것이 설거지하는 것이든 쓰레기를 내다 버리는 것이든지 간에, 이런 일들은 일상생활의 필수적인 부분이다. 하지만 집안일을 순전히 의무적인 행위로 간주하기보다는, 이런 순간들을 신체 활동을 위한 기회로 잘 이용하는 것이 어떨까? 예를 들어, 여러분의 아침 주전자가 끓기를 기다리면서 스쿼트를 연습하거나 벽에 대고 하는 팔 굽혀 펴기 몇 개를 시작해 보라. 짧은 운동을 여러분의 일상적인 집안일에 포함시키는 것이 여러분의 건강을 향상시킬 수 있다.

21

When we see something, we naturally and automatically break it up into shapes, colors, and concepts [**that** / what]20) we have learned through education. We recode [that / **what**]21) we see through the lens of everything we know. We reconstruct memories rather than retrieving the video from memory. This is a [**useful** / usefully]22) trait. It's a more [**efficient** / efficiently]23) way to store information — a bit like an optimal image compression algorithm such as JPG, rather than storing a raw bitmap image file. People who lack this ability and [remember / **remembering**]24) everything in perfect detail struggle to generalize, learn, and make connections between [that / **what**]25) they have learned. But [represent / **representing**]26) the world as abstract ideas and features comes at a cost of seeing the world as it is. Instead, we see the world through our assumptions, motivations, and past experiences. The discovery that our memories [**are reconstructed** / reconstructed]27) through [**abstract** / concrete]28) representations rather than played back like a movie completely undermined the legal primacy of eyewitness testimony. Seeing is not believing.

우리가 무언가를 볼 때, 우리는 그것을 자연스럽게 그리고 자동적으로 우리가 교육을 통해 배운 모양, 색깔, 그리고 개념들로 해체한다. 우리는 우리가 알고 있는 모든 것의 렌즈를 통해 우리가 보는 것을 재부 호화한다. 우리는 기억에서 영상을 생각해 내기보다 기억을 재구성한다. 이것은 유용한 특성이다. 그것은 가공되지 않은 비트맵 이미지 파일을 저장하기보다 JPG 와 같은 최적의 이미지 압축 알고리즘과 약간 비슷하게 정보를 저장하기 위한 더 효율적인 방법이다. 이런 능력이 부족하고 완벽히 세세하게 모든 것을 기억하는 사람들은 일반화하고, 학습하고, 자신들이 학습한 것들 사이를 연결하려고 고군분투한다. 그러나 세상을 추상적 생각과 특징으로 재현하는 것은 세상을 있는 그대로 보는 것을 희생하여 나온다. 대신에, 우리는 우리의 가정, 동기 그리고 과거 경험을 통해 세상을 바라본다. 우리의 기억이 영화처럼 재생되기보다는 추상적 재현을 통해 재구성된다는 발견은 목격자 증언의 법적 우위성을 완전히 손상시켰다. 보는 것이 믿는 것은 아니다.

22

In his Cornell laboratory, David Dunning [**conducted** / **deducted**]²⁹⁾ experimental tests of eyewitness testimony and found evidence [**that** / **what**]³⁰⁾ a careful deliberation of facial features and a detailed discussion of selection procedures can actually be a sign of an *inaccurate* identification. It's when people find [**them** / **themselves**]³¹⁾ unable to explain why they recognize the person, saying things like "his face just popped out at me," that they tend to [**be** / **being**]³²⁾ accurate more often. Sometimes our first, immediate, [**automatic** / **automatically**]³³⁾ reaction to a situation is the truest interpretation of [**that** / **what**]³⁴⁾ our mind is telling us. That very first [**expression** / **impression**]³⁵⁾ can also be more [**accurate** / **inaccurate**]³⁶⁾ about the world than the deliberative, reasoned self-narrative can be. In his book *Blink*, Malcolm Gladwell describes a variety of studies in psychology and behavioral economics that [**demonstrate** / **demonstrates**]³⁷⁾ the superior performance of [**relative** / **relatively**]³⁸⁾ unconscious first guesses compared to logical step-by-step justifications for a decision.

David Dunning의 코넬 대학의 실험실에서, 그는 목격자 증언에 대한 실험을 수행했고, 얼굴 특징에 대한 신중한 숙고와 선택 절차에 대한 상세한 논의가 실제로는 '부정확한' 식별의 징후일 수 있다는 증거를 발견했다. 사람들이 "그의 얼굴이 그냥 나에게 탁 떠올랐다"라는 식으로 말하면서 왜 그 사람을 알아보는지 설명할 수 없는 스스로를 발견하는 바로 그때 그들은 더 자주 정확한 경향이 있다. 때때로 상황에 대한 우리의 최초의, 즉각적인, 자동적인 반응이 우리 마음이 우리에게 말하고 있는 것에 대한 가장 정확한 해석이다. 바로 그 첫인상이 또한 신중하고 논리적인 자기 서사보다 세상에 대해 더 정확할 수 있다. Malcolm Gladwell은 그의 저서 'Blink'에서, 결정에 대한 논리적인 단계적 정당화에 비해서 상대적으로 무의식적인 최초 추측의 우수성을 보여 주는 심리학 및 행동 경제학의 다양한 연구를 기술한다.

23

Many forms of research lead naturally to [**qualitative** / **quantitative**]³⁹⁾ data. A study of happiness might measure the number of times someone smiles [**during** / **while**]⁴⁰⁾ an interaction, and a study of memory might measure [**a number of** / **the number of**]⁴¹⁾ items an individual can recall after one, five, and ten minutes. Asking people how many times in a year they are sad will also yield [**qualitative** / **quantitative**]⁴²⁾ data, but it might not be reliable. Respondents' [**collections** / **recollections**]⁴³⁾ may be inaccurate, and their definitions of 'sad' could vary widely. But asking "How many times in the past year were you [**enough sad** / **sad enough**]⁴⁴⁾ to call in sick to work?" [**prompt** / **prompts**]⁴⁵⁾ a concrete answer. Similarly, instead of asking people to rate how bad a procrastinator they are, ask, "How many of your utility bills are you currently late in paying, even though you can afford to [**pay** / **paying**]⁴⁶⁾ them?" Questions that seek concrete responses help make [**abstract** / **concrete**]⁴⁷⁾ concepts clearer and [**ensure** / **ensuring**]⁴⁸⁾ consistency from one study to the next.

많은 종류의 연구는 자연스럽게 양적 데이터로 이어진다. 행복에 관한 연구는 누군가가 상호 작용 중에 미소 짓는 횟수를 측정할 수 있고, 기억에 관한 연구는 개인이 1분, 5분, 그리고 10분 후에 회상할 수 있는 항목의 수를 측정할 수 있다. 사람들에게 자신이 일년에 몇 번 슬픈지 물어보는 것 또한 양적 데이터를 산출할 수 있지만, 이는 신뢰할 만하지 않을 수도 있다. 응답자의 회상은 부정확할 수 있고, '슬픈'에 대한 그들의 정의는 크게 다를 수 있다. 그러나 "지난 1년 동안 직장에 병가를 낼 만큼 슬펐던 적이 몇 번 있었습니까?"라고 묻는 것은 구체적인 답변을 유발한다. 마찬가지로, 사람들에게 그들이 얼마나 심하게 미루는 사람인지를 평가하도록 묻는 대신, "당신이 지불할 여유가 있음에도 불구하고 얼마나 많은 공과금 고지서의 납부가 현재 늦었나요?"라고 물어보라. 구체적인 응답을 요구하는 질문은 추상적인 개념을 더 명확하게 만들고 한 연구에서 다음 연구 간의 일관성을 보장하는 것을 돕는다.

24

The [**evolution / revolution**]⁴⁹⁾ of AI is often associated with the concept of singularity. Singularity refers to the point [**at / in**]⁵⁰⁾ which AI exceeds human intelligence. After that point, it is predicted that AI will repeatedly improve [**it / itself**]⁵¹⁾ and evolve at an accelerated pace. When AI becomes self-aware and [**pursue / pursues**]⁵²⁾ its own goals, it will be a conscious being, not just a machine. AI and human consciousness will then begin to [**evolve / involve**]⁵³⁾ together. Our consciousness will evolve to new dimensions through our interactions with AI, [**that / which**]⁵⁴⁾ will provide us with intellectual stimulation and [**inspire / inspires**]⁵⁵⁾ new insights and creativity. Conversely, our consciousness also has a significant impact on the evolution of AI. The direction of AI's evolution will depend greatly on [**that / what**]⁵⁶⁾ values and ethics we incorporate into AI. We need to see our relationship with AI as a [**mutual / mutually**]⁵⁷⁾ coexistence of conscious beings, recognizing its rights and [**support / supporting**]⁵⁸⁾ the evolution of its consciousness.

AI의 진화는 종종 특이점의 개념과 연관된다. 특이점은 AI가 인간의 지능을 넘어서는 지점을 의미한다. 그 지점 이후, AI는 스스로를 반복적으로 개선하고 가속화된 속도로 진화할 것으로 예측된다. AI가 스스로를 인식하게 되고 자기 자신의 목표를 추구할 때, 그것은 단지 기계가 아니라 의식이 있는 존재가 될 것이다. AI와 인간의 의식은 그러면 함께 진화하기 시작할 것이다. 우리의 의식은 우리의 AI와의 상호 작용을 통해 새로운 차원으로 진화할 것이며, 이는 우리에게 지적 자극을 제공하고 새로운 통찰력과 창의성을 불어넣을 것이다. 반대로, 우리의 의식 또한 AI의 진화에 중대한 영향을 끼친다. AI 진화의 방향은 우리가 어떤 가치와 윤리를 AI에 통합시키는지에 크게 좌우될 것이다. 우리는 AI의 권리를 인식하고 그것의 의식의 진화를 지지하면서, 우리와 AI와의 관계를 의식 있는 존재들의 상호 공존으로 볼 필요가 있다.

29

Digital technologies are essentially related to metaphors, but digital metaphors are different from linguistic [**one / ones**]⁵⁹⁾ in important ways. Linguistic metaphors are [**active / passive**]⁶⁰⁾, in the sense that the audience needs to choose to actively enter the world proposed by metaphor. In the Shakespearean metaphor "time is a beggar," the audience is [**likely / unlikely**]⁶¹⁾ to understand the metaphor without cognitive effort and without further [**engage / engaging**]⁶²⁾ Shakespeare's prose. Technological metaphors, on the other hand, [**are / is**]⁶³⁾ active and often imposing) in the sense that they [**are realized / realized**]⁶⁴⁾ in digital artifacts that are actively doing things, forcefully changing a user's meaning horizon. Technological creators cannot generally afford to [**require / requiring**]⁶⁵⁾ their [**potential / potentially**]⁶⁶⁾ audience to wonder how the metaphor works; normally the selling point is that the usefulness of the technology is [**obvious / obviously**]⁶⁷⁾ at first glance. Shakespeare, on the other hand, is beloved in part [**because / because of**]⁶⁸⁾ the meaning of his works is not immediately obvious and [**require / requires**]⁶⁹⁾ some thought on the part of the audience.

디지털 기술은 근본적으로 은유와 관련되어 있지만, 디지털 은유는 중요한 면에서 언어적 은유와 다르다. 언어적 은유는 독자가 은유에 의해 제시된 세계에 적극적으로 들어가도록 선택할 필요가 있다는 점에서 수동적이다. "시간은 구걸하는 자다"라는 셰익스피어의 은유에서 독자는 인지적인 노력 없이 그리고 셰익스피어의 산문을 더 끌어들이지 않고는 은유를 이해할 것 같지 않다. 반면에 기술적 은유는 사용자의 의미의 지평을 강력하게 바꾸면서 능동적으로 일을 하는 디지털 인공물에서 그것이 실현된다는 점에서 능동적이다. (그리고 종종 강요적이다.) 기술적인 창작자는 일반적으로 그들의 잠재적인 독자에게 어떻게 은유가 작용하는지 궁금해하도록 요구할 여유가 없고, 일반적으로 매력은 기술의 유용성이 첫눈에 분명하다는 것이다. 반면에 셰익스피어는 부분적으로는 그의 작품의 의미가 즉각적으로 분명하지 않고 독자 측에서 어느 정도의 생각을 요구하기 때문에 사랑받는다.

30

Herbert Simon won his Nobel Prize for recognizing our limitations in information, time, and [**cognitive** / **cognitively**]70) capacity. As we lack the resources to compute answers independently, we distribute the computation across the population and [**solve** / **solving**]71) the answer slowly, generation by generation. Then all we have to do is socially learn the right answers. You don't need to understand how your computer or toilet works; you just need to be able to use the interface and flush. All that needs to be transmitted is [**what** / **which**]72) button to push — essentially how to interact with technologies rather than how they work. And so instead of [**hold** / **holding**]73) more information than we have [**mental** / **physical**]74) capacity for and indeed need to know, we could [**dedicate** / **withhold**]75) our large brains to a small piece of a giant calculation. We understand things [**enough well** / **well enough**]76) to benefit from them, but all the while we are making small calculations [**that** / **what**]77) contribute to a larger whole. We are just doing our part in a [**larger** / **smaller**]78) computation for our societies' collective brains.

Herbert Simon은 정보, 시간, 그리고 인지적인 능력에서 우리의 한계를 인지한 것으로 그의 노벨상을 받았다. 우리는 독립적으로 해답을 계산하기 위한 자원이 부족하기 때문에 우리는 전체 인구에 걸쳐 복잡한 계산을 분배하고 세대에 걸쳐 해답을 천천히 풀어 낸다. 그러면 우리가 해야 하는 모든 것은 올바른 해답을 사회적으로 배우는 것이다. 여러분은 여러분의 컴퓨터 혹은 변기가 어떻게 작동하는지 이해할 필요가 없고 여러분은 단지 인터페이스를 사용할 수 있고 (변기의) 물을 내릴 수 있기만 하면 된다. 전달될 필요가 있는 모든 것은 어떤 버튼을 눌러야 하는지, 근본적으로 어떻게 그것들이 작동하는지보다는 기술과 상호 작용하는 방법이다. 그렇다면 우리가 정신적 수용을 할 수 있는 것보다 그리고 정말로 알아야 할 필요가 있는 것보다 더 많은 정보를 가지는 것 대신에 우리는 우리의 큰 두뇌를 거대한 계산의 작은 조각에 바칠 수 있다. 우리는 그것들로부터 이득을 얻기에 충분할 정도로 사물을 잘 이해하지만 그러면서 우리는 더 큰 전체에 기여하는 작은 계산을 하고 있다. 우리는 우리 사회의 집합적인 두뇌를 위한 더 큰 복잡한 계산에서 단지 우리의 역할을 하고 있는 것이다.

31

The best defence most species of octopus [**has** / **have**]79) is to stay hidden as much as possible and [**do** / **doing**]80) their own hunting at night. So to find one in full view in the shallows in daylight was a surprise for two Australian underwater photographers. Actually, [**that** / **what**]81) they saw at first was a flounder. It was only when they looked again that they saw a medium-sized octopus, with all eight of its arms folded and its two eyes staring upwards [**creating** / **to create**]82) the illusion. An octopus has a big brain, excellent eyesight and the ability to change colour and pattern, and this one was using these assets to turn [**it** / **itself**]83) into a completely different creature. Many more of this species [**have been found** / **have found**]84) since then, and there are now photographs of octopuses that could be said to be transforming into sea snakes. And [**during** / **while**]85) they mimic, they hunt — producing the spectacle of, say, a flounder suddenly developing an octopodian arm, [**sticking down it** / **sticking it down**]86) a hole and [**grab** / **grabbing**]87) whatever's hiding there.

대부분의 문어 종(種)이 가진 최고의 방어는 가능한 한 많이 숨어 있는 것과 밤에 그들 자신의 사냥을 하는 것이다. 그래서 낮에 얕은 곳에서 전체가 보이는 문어를 발견한 것은 두 명의 호주 수중 사진작가들에게는 놀라운 일이었다. 사실 그들이 처음에 봤던 것은 넙치였다. 오직 그들이 다시 봤을 때서야 그들은 중 간 크기의 문어를 보았고 착시를 만들기 위해 그것의 여덟 개의 모든 팔이 접혀 있었고 그것의 두 눈이 위쪽으로 응시하고 있었다. 문어는 큰 뇌, 뛰어난 시력과 색깔과 패턴을 바꾸는 능력을 지니고 있고, 이것은 스스로를 완전히 다른 생물체로 바꾸기 위해 이러한 이점을 사용하고 있었다. 이 종의 더 많은 것들이 그때 이후로 발견되어 왔으며 지금은 바다뱀으로 변신하는 중이라고 말해질 수 있는 문어의 사진이 있다. 그리고 그들이 모방하는 동안에 그들은 사냥을 한다. 이것은 말하자면 넙치가 갑자기 문어 다리 같은 팔을 펼치며 그것을 구멍으로 찔러 넣어 그곳에 숨어 있는 무엇이든지 움켜잡는 광경을 만들어 낸다.

32

How much we suffer [**relate** / **relates**]⁸⁸⁾ to how we frame the pain in our mind. When 1500m runners push [**them** / **themselves**]⁸⁹⁾ into [**extreme** / **extremely**]⁹⁰⁾ pain to win a race—their muscles screaming and their lungs [**explode** / **exploding**]⁹¹⁾ with oxygen [**abundance** / **deficit**]⁹²⁾, they don't psychologically suffer much. In fact, ultra-marathon runners—those people who are crazy enough to push [**them** / **themselves**]⁹³⁾ beyond the normal boundaries of human endurance, covering distances of 50-100km or more over many hours, talk about making friends with their pain. When a patient has paid for some form of passive back pain therapy and the practitioner pushes [**deep** / **deeply**]⁹⁴⁾ into a painful part of a patient's back to mobilise it, the patient calls [**that** / **what**]⁹⁵⁾ good pain if he or she believes this type of deep pressure treatment will be of value, even though the practitioner is pushing right into the patient's sore tissues.

우리가 얼마나 고통받는지는 우리가 고통을 우리의 마음에서 어떻게 구성하는지와 관련된다. 1500미터 달리기 선수가 경주에서 이기기 위해 그들의 근육이 비명을 지르고 그들의 폐가 산소 부족으로 폭발하면서, 스스로를 극심한 고통으로 밀어붙일 때, 그들은 정신적으로 많이 고통받지 않는다. 사실 울트라 마라톤 선수들은 즉, 인간 인내력의 정상적 경계를 넘어서 스스로를 밀어붙일 만큼 충분히 열정적인 사람들은 많은 시간 동안 50에서 100킬로미터 혹은 그 이상의 거리를 가지만 그들의 고통과 친구가 되는 것에 대해 이야기한다. 한 환자가 특정 형태의 수동적 등 통증 치료에 돈을 지불했고 의사가 그것을 풀어 주기 위해 환자 등의 아픈 부분을 깊게 눌렀을 때, 비록 의사가 환자의 아픈 조직을 직접적으로 누르고 있을지라도, 만약 그 또는 그녀가 이러한 종류의 깊은 압박 치료법이 가치가 있을 것이라고 믿는다면, 환자는 그것을 좋은 아픔이라고 부른다.

33

When I worked for a large electronics company [**that** / **what**]⁹⁶⁾ manufactured laser and inkjet-printers, I soon discovered why there are often three versions of many consumer goods. If the manufacturer makes only one version of [**its** / **their**]⁹⁷⁾ product, people who bought it might have been willing to spend [**less** / **more**]⁹⁸⁾ money, so the company is [**gaining** / **losing**]⁹⁹⁾ some income. If the company offers two versions, one with more features and more expensive than [**another** / **the other**]¹⁰⁰⁾ , people will compare the two models and still buy the less expensive one. But if the company introduces a third model with even more features and more expensive than [**another** / **the other**]¹⁰¹⁾ two, sales of the second model go up; many people like the features of the most expensive model, but not the price. The middle item has more features than the [**least** / **most**]¹⁰²⁾ expensive one, and it is less expensive than the fanciest model. They buy the middle item, [**aware** / **unaware**]¹⁰³⁾ that they [**have been manipulated** / **have manipulated**]¹⁰⁴⁾ by the presence of the higher-priced item.

내가 레이저와 잉크젯 프린터를 생산했던 큰 전자 회사에서 일했을 때 나는 많은 소비 상품의 세 가지 버전이 종종 있는 이유를 곧 발견했다. 만약 생산자가 그 제품의 오직 한 가지 버전만 만든다면 그것을 구매했던 사람들은 기꺼이 더 많은 돈을 쓰려고 했을 수도 있어서 회사는 일부 수입을 잃을 것이다. 만약 그 회사가 두 버전을 제공하는데 한 버전이 나머지보다 더 많은 기능과 더 비싼 가격을 가진다면, 사람들은 두 모델을 비교하고 여전히 덜 비싼 것을 살 것이다. 하지만 만약 그 회사가 나머지 두 개보다 훨씬 더 많은 기능과 더 비싼 가격을 가진 세 번째 모델을 출시한다면 두 번째 모델의 판매가 증가하는데, 왜냐하면 많은 사람들은 가장 비싼 모델의 기능을 좋아하지만 그것의 가격을 좋아하지는 않기 때문이다. 중간 제품은 가장 저렴한 제품보다 더 많은 기능이 있고 가장 고급 모델보다는 덜 비싸다. 그들은 자신이 더 비싼 가격의 제품의 존재에 의해 조종되었다는 것을 알지 못한 채 중간 제품을 구입한다.

34

On-screen, climate disaster is everywhere you look, but the scope of the world's climate transformation may just as quickly eliminate the climate-fiction genre — indeed eliminate any effort to tell the story of warming, which could grow too large and too obvious even for Hollywood. You can tell stories 'about' climate change [**during / while**]105) it still seems a [**marginal / marginally**]106) feature of human life. But when the temperature [**raises / rises**]107) by three or four more degrees, hardly anyone will be able to feel [**isolated / isolating**]108) from its impacts. And so as climate change expands across the horizon, it may [**cease / continue**]109) to be a story. Why watch or read climate fiction about the world you can see plainly out your own window? At the moment, stories [**illustrated / illustrating**]110) global warming can still offer an escapist pleasure, even if that pleasure often comes in the form of horror. But when we can no longer pretend [**that / what**]111) climate suffering is distant — in time or in place — we will stop [**pretending / to pretend**]112) about it and start pretending within it.

영화상 기후 재난은 여러분이 보는 어디에나 있지만, 세계의 기후 변화의 범위는 그것만큼이나 빠르게 기후 픽션 장르를 없앨지도 모르고 실제로 온난화 이야기를 하고자 하는 노력도 없애 버리는데, 그것은 할리우드에서조차 너무 커지고 너무 명백해질 것이다. 기후 변화가 여전히 인간 삶의 주변적인 특징처럼 보이는 동안에 여러분은 그것에 '관한' 이야기를 할 수 있을 것이다. 하지만 기온이 3도 혹은 4도 이상 상승할 때는 아무도 그것의 영향으로부터 고립되었다고 느낄 수 없을 것이다. 그리고 기후 변화가 지평선을 넘어 확장될 때 그것은 이야기가 되기를 멈출 것이다. 왜 여러분 자신의 창문 밖으로 뚜렷하게 볼 수 있는 세상에 대한 기후 픽션을 보거나 읽겠는가? 비록 그 즐거움이 종종 공포의 형태로 올지라도 지금 당장은 지구 온난화를 묘사하는 이야기가 현실 도피적인 즐거움을 여전히 제공할 수 있다. 하지만 우리가 더 이상 기후 고통이 시간적으로 또는 장소적으로 멀리 있다고 가장할 수 없을 때 우리는 그것에 대해 가장하는 것을 멈추고 그것 내에서 가장하기 시작할 것이다.

35

Today, the water crisis is political — [**what / which**]113) is to say, not [**evitable / inevitable**]114) or beyond our capacity to fix — and, therefore, functionally elective. That is one reason it is nevertheless [**distressed / distressing**]115): an abundant resource made scarce through governmental neglect and indifference, bad infrastructure and contamination, and [**careless / carelessly**]116) urbanization. There is no need for a water crisis, in other words, but we have one anyway, and aren't doing much to address [**it / them**]117). Some cities lose more water to leaks than they deliver to homes: even in the United States, leaks and theft [**account for / accounts for**]118) an estimated loss of 16 percent of freshwater; in Brazil, the estimate is 40 percent. [**Seeing / Seen**]119) in both cases, as everywhere, the selective scarcity clearly [**highlight / highlights**]120) haveandhavenot inequities, [**leaving / left**]121) 2.1 billion people without safe drinking water and 4.5 billion without proper sanitation worldwide.

오늘날, 물 위기는 피할 수 없는 것이 아니며 우리의 바로잡을 수 있는 능력을 넘어서지 않는, 즉 정치적인 것이고 따라서 기능적으로 선택적이다. 그것은 그럼에도 불구하고 그것이 괴로운 한 가지 이유이다. 즉, 풍족한 자원이 정부의 소홀함과 무관심, 열악한 사회 기반 시설과 오염, 부주의한 도시화를 통해 부족하게 되었다. 다시 말해서 물 위기가 있어야 할 필요가 없지만 어쨌든 우리는 그것을 겪고 있고 그것을 해결하기 위해 많은 일을 하고 있지 않다. 일부 도시들은 그들이 주택으로 공급하는 것보다 누수로 인해 더 많은 물을 잃는다. 즉, 미국에서조차 누수와 도난은 담수의 16퍼센트의 추정된 손실을 차지하고 브라질에서는 그 추정치가 40퍼센트이다. 양쪽의 경우에서 보여지듯이 모든 곳에 서처럼 선택적 부족이 가진 자와 가지지 못한 자의 불평등을 분명히 강조하고 이것은 전 세계적으로 21억 명을 안전한 식수가 없고 45억 명을 적절한 위생이 없는 채로 둔다.

36

As individuals, our ability [**thriving / to thrive**]122) depended on how well we navigated relationships in a group. If the group valued us, we could count on support, resources, and probably a mate. If it didn't, we might get [**none / some**]123) of these merits. It was a matter of survival, physically and genetically. Over millions of years, the pressure selected for people who are [**sensitive / sensitively**]124) to and skilled at [**maximize / maximizing**]125) their standing. The result was the development of a tendency to [**unconscious / unconsciously**]126) monitor how other people in our community perceive us. We process that information in the form of self-esteem and such [**related / relating**]127) emotions as pride, shame, or insecurity. These emotions compel us [**do / to do**]128) more of what makes our community value us and less of what doesn't. And, crucially, they are meant to make that motivation feel like it is coming from within. If we realized, on a conscious level, that we were responding to [**social / socially**]129) pressure, our performance might come off as grudging or cynical, [**make / making**]130) it [**less / more**]131) persuasive.

개인으로서 성공하려는 우리의 능력은 우리가 집단 내에서 관계를 얼마나 잘 다루는지에 달려 있었다. 만약 그 집단이 우리를 가치 있게 여겼다면 우리는 지원, 자원, 그리고 아마도 짝을 기대할 수 있었을 것이다. 만약 그렇지 않았다면, 우리는 그러한 이점들 중 아무것도 얻지 못했을 것이다. 그것은 신체적으로 그리고 유전적으로 생존의 문제였다. 수백만 년 동안 그러한 압박은 자신의 지위를 최대화하는 데 민감하고 능숙한 사람들을 선택했다. 그 결과는 우리 공동체의 다른 사람들이 우리를 어떻게 인식하는지 무의식적으로 관찰하는 경향의 발달이었다. 우리는 자존감 그리고 자존심, 수치심 또는 불안 같은 관련된 감정의 형태로 그 정보를 처리한다. 이러한 감정들은 우리에게 우리의 공동체가 우리를 가치 있게 여기도록 만드는 것을 더 많이 하고 그렇지 않은 것을 덜 하도록 강요한다. 그리고 결정적으로 그것들은 그 동기가 내부에서 나오고 있는 것처럼 그것을 느끼게 만들도록 되어 있다. 우리가 사회적 압박에 반응하고 있었다는 것을 의식적인 수준에서 깨닫는다면, 우리의 행동은 그것(그 동기)을 설득력이 떨어지게 만들면서 투덜대거나 냉소적인 것으로 나타날 수 있다.

37

Conventional medicine has long believed that depression [**caused / is caused**]132) by an imbalance of neurotransmitters in the brain. However, there is a [**major / minor**]133) problem with this explanation. [**This is because / This is why**]134) the imbalance of substances in the brain is a consequence of depression, not its cause. In other words, depression causes a decrease in brain substances such as serotonin and noradrenaline, not a decrease in brain substances causes depression. In this [**revised / revising**]135) cause-and-effect, the key is to reframe depression as a problem of consciousness. Our consciousness is a more [**fundamental / fundamentally**]136) entity that goes [**beyond / within**]137) the functioning of the brain. The brain is no more than an organ of consciousness. If it is not consciousness itself, then the root cause of depression [**are / is**]138) also a distortion of our state of consciousness: a consciousness [**that / what**]139) has lost its sense of self and the meaning of life. Such a disease of consciousness may manifest [**it / itself**]140) in the form of depression.

전통적인 의학은 우울증이 뇌의 신경 전달 물질의 불균형으로 인해 발생한다고 오랫동안 믿어 왔다. 그러나 이 설명에는 중대한 문제가 있다. 이것은 왜냐하면 뇌 속 물질의 불균형은 우울증의 원인이 아니라 그것의 결과이기 때문이다. 다시 말해서, 우울증이 세로토닌이나 노르아드레날린과 같은 뇌의 물질의 감소를 유발하는 것이지 뇌의 물질의 감소가 우울증을 유발하는 것이 아니다. 이 수정된 인과 관계에서, 핵심은 우울증을 의식의 문제로 재구성하는 것이다. 우리의 의식은 뇌의 기능을 넘어서는 보다 근본적인 실체이다. 뇌는 의식의 기관에 지나지 않는다. 만약 그것이 의식 그 자체가 아니라면, 우울증의 근본 원인 역시 우리의 의식 상태의 왜곡이며 즉, 자아감과 삶의 의미를 상실한 의식이다. 그러한 의식의 질환이 우울증의 형태로 명백히 나타날 수 있다.

38

The common accounts of human nature [**that / what**]141) float around in society are generally a mixture of assumptions, tales and sometimes plain silliness. However, psychology is different. It is the branch of science [**that / what**]142) is devoted to understanding people: how and why we act as we do; why we see things as we do; and how we interact with one another. The key word here is 'science.' Psychologists don't depend on opinions and hearsay, or the generally [**accepted / accepting**]143) views of society at the time, or even the [**considered / considering**]144) opinions of deep thinkers. Instead, they [**look at / look for**]145) evidence, to make sure that psychological ideas are [**firm / firmly**]146) based, and not just derived from generally held beliefs or assumptions. In addition to this evidence-based approach, psychology deals with fundamental processes and principles that [**generate / generates**]147) our rich cultural and social diversity, as well as those [**shared / sharing**]148) by all human beings. These are [**that / what**]149) modern psychology is all about.

사회에 떠도는 인간 본성에 대한 흔한 설명은 일반적으로 가정, 이야기, 그리고 때로는 순전한 어리석음의 혼합이다. 그러나, 심리학은 다르다. 그것은 사람들을 이해하는, 즉 우리가 어떻게 그리고 왜 행동하는 대로 행동하는지, 우리가 왜 보는 대로 사물을 보는 지, 그리고 우리가 어떻게 서로 상호 작용하는지를 이해하는 데 전념하는 과학 분야이다. 여기서 핵심어는 '과학'이다. 심리학자들은 의견과 소문, 혹은 당대의 사회에서 일반적으로 받아들여지는 견해, 혹은 심지어 심오한 사상가들의 숙고된 의견에 의존하지 않는다. 대신에 그들은 심리학적 개념이 단지 일반적으로 받아들여지는 신념이나 가정에서 도출된 것이 아니라, 확고하게 기반을 두고 있는지 확신하기 위해 증거를 찾는다. 이러한 증거 기반 접근법에 더하여 심리학은 모든 인간에 의해 공유되는 근본적인 과정과 원리뿐만 아니라, 우리의 풍부한 문화적 사회적 다양성을 만들어 내는 것들을 다룬다. 이것들은 현대 심리학이 무엇인지 보여 준다.

39

Life is [**that / what**]150) physicists might call a 'high-dimensional system,' [**that / which**]151) is their fancy way of saying that there's a lot going on. In just a single cell, the number of possible interactions between different molecules [**are / is**]152) enormous. Such a system can only hope to be stable if only a smaller number of collective ways of being may [**disappear / emerge**]153). For example, it is only a limited number of tissues and body shapes that may [**result from / result in**]154) the development of a human embryo. In 1942, the biologist Conrad Waddington called this [**drastic / drastically**]155) narrowing of outcomes *canalization*. The organism may switch between a small number of well-defined possible states, but can't exist in [**random / randomly**]156) states in between them, rather as a ball in a rough landscape must roll to the bottom of one valley or [**another / other**]157). We'll see that this is true also of health and disease: there are many causes of illness, but their manifestations at the physiological and symptomatic levels [**are / is**]158) often strikingly similar.

생명은 물리학자들이 '고차원 시스템'이라고 부를 수 있는 것인데 이는 많은 일이 발생하고 있다고 말하는 그들의 멋진 방식이다. 단 하나의 세포 내에서도 여러 분자 간의 가능한 상호 작용의 수는 매우 크다. 이러한 시스템은 더 적은 수의 존재의 집합적인 방식이 나타날 때만 오직 안정적이기를 기대할 수 있다. 예를 들어 인간 배아의 발달로부터 나올 수 있는 것은 오직 제한된 수의 조직과 신체 형태이다. 1942년에 생물학자 Conrad Waddington은 이러한 극적인 결과의 축소를 '운하화'라고 불렀다. 오히려 울퉁불퉁한 경관에 있는 공이 이 계곡 혹은 또 다른 계곡의 바닥으로 반드시 굴러가야 하는 것처럼, 유기체는 적은 수의 명확하게 정의된 가능한 상태 사이에서 바뀔 수 있지만 그것들 사이에 있는 무작위의 상태로 존재할 수는 없다. 우리는 이것이 건강과 질병에도 적용된다는 것을 알게 될 것이다. 즉 질병의 많은 원인이 있지만, 그것들의 생리적이고 증상적인 수준에서의 발현은 종종 놀랍도록 유사하다.

40

Punishing a child may not be [**affective / effective**]¹⁵⁹⁾ due to what Álvaro Bilbao, a neuropsychologist, calls 'trick-punishments.' A trick-punishment is a scolding, a moment of anger or a punishment in the most classic sense of the word. Instead of [**discourage / discouraging**]¹⁶⁰⁾ the child from doing something, it encourages them [**doing / to do**]¹⁶¹⁾ it. For example, Hugh learns that when he hits his little brother, his mother scolds him. For a child who feels lonely, being scolded is much [**better / worse**]¹⁶²⁾ than feeling invisible, so he will continue to hit his brother. In this case, his mother would be better [**adapting / adopting**]¹⁶³⁾ a different strategy. For instance, she could congratulate Hugh [**when / where**]¹⁶⁴⁾ he has not hit his brother for a certain length of time. The mother clearly cannot allow the child [**hit / to hit**]¹⁶⁵⁾ his little brother, but instead of constantly [**point / pointing**]¹⁶⁶⁾ out the negatives, she can choose to [**award / reward**]¹⁶⁷⁾ the positives. In this way, any parent can avoid trick-punishments.

아이를 벌주는 것은 신경심리학자 Álvaro Bilbao가 '트릭 처벌'이라고 부르는 것으로 인해 효과적이지 않을 수 있다. 트릭 처벌은 꾸짖음, 순간의 화 혹은 (처벌이라는) 단어의 가장 전형적인 의미에서의 처벌이다. 아이가 무언가를 하는 것을 단념시키는 대신 트릭 처벌은 그들이 그것을 하도록 장려한다. 예를 들어 Hugh는 그가 자신의 남동생을 때릴 때 그의 어머니가 그를 꾸짖는다는 것을 배운다. 외로움을 느끼는 아이에게는 꾸중을 듣는 것이 눈에 띄지 않는다고 느끼는 것보다 훨씬 나아서 그는 그의 남동생을 때리는 것을 계속할 것이다. 이 경우에, 그의 어머니는 다른 전략을 채택하는 것이 보다 나을 것이다. 예를 들어 그녀는 Hugh가 그의 남동생을 일정 기간 동안 때리지 않았을 때 그를 자랑스러워해 줄 수 있다. 어머니는 분명 아이가 그의 남동생을 때리는 것을 내버려둘 수 없고, 그녀는 부정적 측면을 계속 지적하는 대신에 긍정적 측면을 보상하는 것을 선택할 수 있다. 이렇게 어느 부모도 트릭 처벌을 피할 수 있다.

41, 42

From an early age, we assign purpose to objects and events, [**prefer / preferring**]¹⁶⁸⁾ this reasoning [**in / to**]¹⁶⁹⁾ random chance. Children assume, for instance, that pointy rocks are that way [**because / because of**]¹⁷⁰⁾ they don't want you to sit on them. When we encounter something, we first need to determine [**that / what**]¹⁷¹⁾ sort of thing it is. [**Animate / Inanimate**]¹⁷²⁾ objects and plants generally do not move and can be evaluated from physics alone. However, by [**attribute / attributing**]¹⁷³⁾ intention to animals and even objects, we are able to [**make / making**]¹⁷⁴⁾ fast decisions about the likely behaviour of that being. This was essential in our hunter-gatherer days to avoid [**be eaten / being eaten**]¹⁷⁵⁾ by predators.

The anthropologist Stewart Guthrie made the point [**that / what**]¹⁷⁶⁾ survival in our evolutionary past meant that we interpret [**ambiguous / clear**]¹⁷⁷⁾ objects as agents with human mental characteristics, as those are the mental processes which we understand. Ambiguous events [**are caused / caused**]¹⁷⁸⁾ by such agents. This [**results from / results in**]¹⁷⁹⁾ a perceptual system strongly biased towards anthropomorphism. Therefore, we tend to [**assume / assuming**]¹⁸⁰⁾ intention even where there is none. This would have arisen as a survival mechanism. If a lion is about to [**attack / attacking**]¹⁸¹⁾ you, you need to react [**quick / quickly**]¹⁸²⁾, given its probable intention to kill you. By the time you have realized [**that / what**]¹⁸³⁾ the design of its teeth and claws could kill you, you are dead. So, [**assume / assuming**]¹⁸⁴⁾ intent, without detailed design analysis or understanding of the physics, has saved your life.

어릴 때부터 우리는 사물과 사건에 목적을 부여하며, 무작위적인 우연보다 이러한 논리를 선호한다. 예를 들어 뾰족한 돌은 아이들이 그 위에 앉기를 원치 않기 때문에 그것이 그렇게 생겼다고 그들(아이들)은 가정한다. 우리가 무언가를 마주칠 때 우리는 먼저 그것이 어떤 종류의 것인지 결정할 필요가 있다. 무생물과 식물은 일반적으로 움직이지 않으며 물리적 현상만으로 평가될 수 있다. 그러나 동물과 심지어 사물도 의도가 있다고 생각함으로써 우리는 그 존재가 할 것 같은 행동에 대해 빠른 결정을 내릴 수 있다. 이는 우리의 수렵 채집 시절에 포식자에게 잡아먹히는 것을 피하기 위해 필수적이었다.

인류학자 Stewart Guthrie는 인간의 정신적 특성이 우리가 이해하는 정신 과정이기 때문에, 우리의 진화상 과거에서 생존이란 우리가 모호한 사물을 인간의 정신적 특성을 가진 행위자로 해석하는 것을 의미한다고 주장했다. 모호한 사건은 이러한 행위자에 의해 발생한다. 이는 의인화에 강하게 편향된 지각 체계로 귀결된다. 그러므로, 우리는 의도가 없는 곳에서도 의도를 가정하는 경향이 있다. 이는 생존 메커니즘으로 발생해 왔을 것이다. 만약 사자가 당신을 막 공격하려 한다면 당신을 죽이려는 그것의 가능한 의도를 고려하여 당신은 빠르게 반응할 필요가 있다. 당신이 그것의 이빨과 발톱의 구조가 당신을 죽일 수 있다는 것을 깨달았을 즈음 당신은 죽어 있다. 따라서 상세한 구조 분석 또는 물리적 현상의 이해 없이 의도를 부여하는 것이 당신의 목숨을 구해 왔다.

43 ~ 45

Once long ago, deep in the Himalayas, there lived a little panda. He was as [**extraordinary / ordinary**]185) as all the other pandas. He was completely white from head to toe. His two big ears, his four furry feet and his cute round nose were all frosty white, leaving him feeling ordinary and sad. Unlike the cheerful and [**contented / contenting**]186) pandas around him, he desired to be [**distinctive / distinctively**]187), Once long ago, deep in the Himalayas, there lived a little panda. He was as ordinary as all the [**another / other**]188) pandas. He was completely white from head to toe. His two big ears, his four furry feet and his cute round nose were all frosty white, leaving him feeling ordinary and sad. [**Like / Unlike**]189) the cheerful and contented pandas around him, he desired to be distinctive, special, and unique. [**Driven / Driving**]190) by the desire for uniqueness, the little panda sought inspiration from his distant cousin, a giant white panda covered with heavenly black patches. But the cousin [**concealed / revealed**]191) the patches were from an unintended encounter with mud, and he [**disliked / liked**]192) them. Disappointed, the little panda walked home. On his way, he met a red-feathered peacock, who explained he turned red from [**eat / eating**]193) wild berries. The little panda changed his path and [**hurried / hurrying**]194) to the nearest berry bush, greedily eating a mouthful of juicy red berries. However, they were so bitter he couldn't swallow even one. At dusk, he finally got home and slowly [**climbed / climbing**]195) his favorite bamboo tree. There, he discovered a strange black and red flower with a sweet scent [**that / what**]196) tempted him to eat all its blossoms. The following morning, under sunny skies, the little panda felt remarkably better. [**During / While**]197) breakfast, he found the other pandas chatting [**enthusiastic / enthusiastically**]198) and asked why. They burst into laughter, exclaiming, "Look at yourself!" Glancing down, he discovered his once white fur was now stained jet black and glowing red. He was overjoyed and [**realize / realized**]199) that, rather than by imitating [**others / the others**]200) , his wishes can come true from unexpected places and genuine experiences.

옛날에 히말라야 산맥 깊숙한 곳에 작은 판다가 살았다. 그는 다른 모든 판다들만큼 평범했다. 그는 머리부터 발끝까지 전부 하얬다. 그의 두 개의 큰 귀, 네 개의 털 많은 발, 그리고 귀여운 둥근 코는 모두 서리처럼 하얘서 그가 평범하고 슬프게 느끼게 하였다. 그의 주위에 있는 명랑하고 만족스러운 판다들과 달리 그는 특이하고 특별하며 독특해지기를 갈망했다. 독특함에 대한 열망에 사로잡혀 작은 판다는 그의 먼 사촌인 멋진 검은 반점으로 뒤덮인 거대한 흰 판다로부터 영감을 찾으려 했다. 그러나 사촌은 그 반점이 진흙과 의도치 않게 접촉한 결과이며, 그는 그것(반점)을 싫어한다고 밝혔다. 실망한 채로 작은 판다는 집으로 걸어갔다. 가는 길에 그는 붉은 깃털을 가진 공작새를 만났는데 그 공작새는 그가 야생 베리를 먹어서 붉게 변했다고 설명했다. 작은 판다는 경로를 바꾸어 가장 가까운 베리 덤불로 서둘러 가서, 탐욕스럽게 한입 가득 즙이 많은 빨간 베리를 먹었다. 하지만 그것들은 너무 써서 그는 한 개도 삼킬 수 없었다. 해질 무렵 그는 마침내 집에 도착했고 그가 가장 좋아하는 대나무에 천천히 올라갔다. 그곳에서 그가 그것의 모든 꽃을 먹도록 유혹하는 달콤한 향기를 가진 기묘한 검고 붉은 꽃을 발견하였다. 다음 날 아침 맑은 하늘 아래에서 작은 판다는 기분이 매우 좋아졌다. 아침 식사 중에 그는 다른 판다들이 신나게 수다를 떨고 있는 것을 발견하고 이유를 물어보았다. 그들은 웃음을 터뜨리며 "네 자신을 좀 봐!"라고 외쳤다. 아래를 흘긋 보고, 그는 한때 하얬던 자신의 털이 이제 새까맣고 빛나는 붉은색으로 얼룩져 있다는 것을 발견했다. 그는 매우 기뻐했고 그의 소원이 남들을 모방하기보다는 예상치 못한 곳과 진정한 경험으로부터 실현될 수 있음을 깨달았다.

18

To the State Education Department,
I am writing with regard to the state's funding for the [**construction / destruction**]1) project at Fort Montgomery High School. Our school needs additional spaces to provide a fully functional Art and Library Media Center to serve our students in a more meaningful way. [**Although / Despite**]2) submitting all required documentation for funding to your department in April 2024, we have not yet received any notification from your department. A delay in the process can carry [**considerable / considerate**]3) consequences related to the school's budgetary constraints and schedule. Therefore, in order to proceed with our project, we request you [**notice / notify**]4) us of the review result regarding the submitted documentation. I look forward to [**hear / hearing**]5) from you.
Respectfully, Clara Smith Principal, Fort Montgomery High School

19

As I waited outside the locker room after a hard-fought basketball game, the coach called out to me, "David, walk with me." I figured he was going to tell me something important. He was going to select me to be the captain of the team, the leader I had always [**want / wanted**]6) to be. My heart was racing with [**anticipation / disappointment**]7). But when his next words hit my ears, [**everything / nothing**]8) changed. "We're going to have to send you home," he said [**cold / coldly**]9). "I don't think you are going to make it." I couldn't believe his decision. I tried to hold it together, but inside I was falling apart. A car would be waiting tomorrow morning to take me home. And just like that, it was over.

20

For many of us, making time for exercise is a continuing challenge. Between work commitments and family obligations, it often feels like there's no room in our [**packed / relaxed**]10) schedules for a dedicated workout. But what if the workout came [**from / to**]11) you, right in the midst of your daily routine? That's [**when / where**]12) the beauty of integrating mini-exercises into household chores comes into play. Let's be realistic; chores are [**inevitable / inevitably**]13). Whether it's washing dishes or [**take / taking**]14) out the trash, these tasks are an [**essential / unnecessary**]15) part of daily life. But rather than viewing chores as [**pure / purely**]16) obligatory activities, why not seize these moments as opportunities for [**mental / physical**]17) activity? For instance, practice squats or engage in some wall push-ups as you wait for your morning kettle to boil. [**Incorporate / Incorporating**]18) quick exercises into your daily chores can [**approve / improve**]19) your health.

21

When we see something, we naturally and automatically break it up into shapes, colors, and concepts [**that / what**]20) we have learned through education. We recode [**that / what**]21) we see through the lens of everything we know. We reconstruct memories rather than retrieving the video from memory. This is a [**useful / usefully**]22) trait. It's a more [**efficient / efficiently**]23) way to store information — a bit like an optimal image compression algorithm such as JPG, rather than storing a raw bitmap image file. People who lack this ability and [**remember / remembering**]24) everything in perfect detail struggle to generalize, learn, and make connections between [**that / what**]25) they have learned. But [**represent /**

representing]26) the world as abstract ideas and features comes at a cost of seeing the world as it is. Instead, we see the world through our assumptions, motivations, and past experiences. The discovery that our memories [**are reconstructed / reconstructed**]27) through [**abstract / concrete**]28) representations rather than played back like a movie completely undermined the legal primacy of eyewitness testimony. Seeing is not believing.

22

In his Cornell laboratory, David Dunning [**conducted / deducted**]29) experimental tests of eyewitness testimony and found evidence [**that / what**]30) a careful deliberation of facial features and a detailed discussion of selection procedures can actually be a sign of an *inaccurate* identification. It's when people find [**them / themselves**]31) unable to explain why they recognize the person, saying things like "his face just popped out at me," that they tend to [**be / being**]32) accurate more often. Sometimes our first, immediate, [**automatic / automatically**]33) reaction to a situation is the truest interpretation of [**that / what**]34) our mind is telling us. That very first [**expression / impression**]35) can also be more [**accurate / inaccurate**]36) about the world than the deliberative, reasoned self-narrative can be. In his book *Blink*, Malcolm Gladwell describes a variety of studies in psychology and behavioral economics that [**demonstrate / demonstrates**]37) the superior performance of [**relative / relatively**]38) unconscious first guesses compared to logical step-by-step justifications for a decision.

23

Many forms of research lead naturally to [**qualitative / quantitative**]39) data. A study of happiness might measure the number of times someone smiles [**during / while**]40) an interaction, and a study of memory might measure [**a number of / the number of**]41) items an individual can recall after one, five, and ten minutes. Asking people how many times in a year they are sad will also yield [**qualitative / quantitative**]42) data, but it might not be reliable. Respondents' [**collections / recollections**]43) may be inaccurate, and their definitions of 'sad' could vary widely. But asking "How many times in the past year were you [**enough sad / sad enough**]44) to call in sick to work?" [**prompt / prompts**]45) a concrete answer. Similarly, instead of asking people to rate how bad a procrastinator they are, ask, "How many of your utility bills are you currently late in paying, even though you can afford to [**pay / paying**]46) them?" Questions that seek concrete responses help make [**abstract / concrete**]47) concepts clearer and [**ensure / ensuring**]48) consistency from one study to the next.

24

The [**evolution / revolution**]49) of AI is often associated with the concept of singularity. Singularity refers to the point [**at / in**]50) which AI exceeds human intelligence. After that point, it is predicted that AI will repeatedly improve [**it / itself**]51) and evolve at an accelerated pace. When AI becomes self-aware and [**pursue / pursues**]52) its own goals, it will be a conscious being, not just a machine. AI and human consciousness will then begin to [**evolve / involve**]53) together. Our consciousness will evolve to new dimensions through our interactions with AI, [**that / which**]54) will provide us with intellectual stimulation and [**inspire / inspires**]55) new insights and creativity. Conversely, our consciousness also has a significant impact on the evolution of AI. The direction of AI's evolution will depend greatly on [**that / what**]56) values and ethics we incorporate into AI. We need to see our relationship with AI as a [**mutual / mutually**]57) coexistence of conscious beings, recognizing its rights and [**support / supporting**]58) the evolution of its consciousness.

29

Digital technologies are essentially related to metaphors, but digital metaphors are different from linguistic [**one / ones**]59) in important ways. Linguistic metaphors are [**active / passive**]60), in the sense that the audience needs to choose to actively enter the world proposed by metaphor. In the Shakespearean metaphor "time is a beggar," the audience is [**likely / unlikely**]61) to understand the metaphor without cognitive effort and without further [**engage / engaging**]62) Shakespeare's prose. Technological metaphors, on the other hand, [**are / is**]63) active and often imposing) in the sense that they [**are realized / realized**]64) in digital artifacts that are actively doing things, forcefully changing a user's meaning horizon. Technological creators cannot generally afford to [**require / requiring**]65) their [**potential / potentially**]66) audience to wonder how the metaphor works; normally the selling point is that the usefulness of the technology is [**obvious / obviously**]67) at first glance. Shakespeare, on the other hand, is beloved in part [**because / because of**]68) the meaning of his works is not immediately obvious and [**require / requires**]69) some thought on the part of the audience.

30

Herbert Simon won his Nobel Prize for recognizing our limitations in information, time, and [**cognitive / cognitively**]70) capacity. As we lack the resources to compute answers independently, we distribute the computation across the population and [**solve / solving**]71) the answer slowly, generation by generation. Then all we have to do is socially learn the right answers. You don't need to understand how your computer or toilet works; you just need to be able to use the interface and flush. All that needs to be transmitted is [**what / which**]72) button to push — essentially how to interact with technologies rather than how they work. And so instead of [**hold / holding**]73) more information than we have [**mental / physical**]74) capacity for and indeed need to know, we could [**dedicate / withhold**]75) our large brains to a small piece of a giant calculation. We understand things [**enough well / well enough**]76) to benefit from them, but all the while we are making small calculations [**that / what**]77) contribute to a larger whole. We are just doing our part in a [**larger / smaller**]78) computation for our societies' collective brains.

31

The best defence most species of octopus [**has / have**]79) is to stay hidden as much as possible and [**do / doing**]80) their own hunting at night. So to find one in full view in the shallows in daylight was a surprise for two Australian underwater photographers. Actually, [**that / what**]81) they saw at first was a flounder. It was only when they looked again that they saw a medium-sized octopus, with all eight of its arms folded and its two eyes staring upwards [**creating / to create**]82) the illusion. An octopus has a big brain, excellent eyesight and the ability to change colour and pattern, and this one was using these assets to turn [**it / itself**]83) into a completely different creature. Many more of this species [**have been found / have found**]84) since then, and there are now photographs of octopuses that could be said to be transforming into sea snakes. And [**during / while**]85) they mimic, they hunt — producing the spectacle of, say, a flounder suddenly developing an octopodian arm, [**sticking down it / sticking it down**]86) a hole and [**grab / grabbing**]87) whatever's hiding there.

32

How much we suffer [**relate / relates**]⁸⁸⁾ to how we frame the pain in our mind. When 1500m runners push [**them / themselves**]⁸⁹⁾ into [**extreme / extremely**]⁹⁰⁾ pain to win a race—their muscles screaming and their lungs [**explode / exploding**]⁹¹⁾ with oxygen [**abundance / deficit**]⁹²⁾, they don't psychologically suffer much. In fact, ultra-marathon runners—those people who are crazy enough to push [**them / themselves**]⁹³⁾ beyond the normal boundaries of human endurance, covering distances of 50-100km or more over many hours, talk about making friends with their pain. When a patient has paid for some form of passive back pain therapy and the practitioner pushes [**deep / deeply**]⁹⁴⁾ into a painful part of a patient's back to mobilise it, the patient calls [**that / what**]⁹⁵⁾ good pain if he or she believes this type of deep pressure treatment will be of value, even though the practitioner is pushing right into the patient's sore tissues.

33

When I worked for a large electronics company [**that / what**]⁹⁶⁾ manufactured laser and inkjet-printers, I soon discovered why there are often three versions of many consumer goods. If the manufacturer makes only one version of [**its / their**]⁹⁷⁾ product, people who bought it might have been willing to spend [**less / more**]⁹⁸⁾ money, so the company is [**gaining / losing**]⁹⁹⁾ some income. If the company offers two versions, one with more features and more expensive than [**another / the other**]¹⁰⁰⁾ , people will compare the two models and still buy the less expensive one. But if the company introduces a third model with even more features and more expensive than [**another / the other**]¹⁰¹⁾ two, sales of the second model go up; many people like the features of the most expensive model, but not the price. The middle item has more features than the [**least / most**]¹⁰²⁾ expensive one, and it is less expensive than the fanciest model. They buy the middle item, [**aware / unaware**]¹⁰³⁾ that they [**have been manipulated / have manipulated**]¹⁰⁴⁾ by the presence of the higher-priced item.

34

On-screen, climate disaster is everywhere you look, but the scope of the world's climate transformation may just as quickly eliminate the climate-fiction genre — indeed eliminate any effort to tell the story of warming, which could grow too large and too obvious even for Hollywood. You can tell stories 'about' climate change [**during / while**]¹⁰⁵⁾ it still seems a [**marginal / marginally**]¹⁰⁶⁾ feature of human life. But when the temperature [**raises / rises**]¹⁰⁷⁾ by three or four more degrees, hardly anyone will be able to feel [**isolated / isolating**]¹⁰⁸⁾ from its impacts. And so as climate change expands across the horizon, it may [**cease / continue**]¹⁰⁹⁾ to be a story. Why watch or read climate fiction about the world you can see plainly out your own window? At the moment, stories [**illustrated / illustrating**]¹¹⁰⁾ global warming can still offer an escapist pleasure, even if that pleasure often comes in the form of horror. But when we can no longer pretend [**that / what**]¹¹¹⁾ climate suffering is distant — in time or in place — we will stop [**pretending / to pretend**]¹¹²⁾ about it and start pretending within it.

35

Today, the water crisis is political — [**what / which**]113) is to say, not [**evitable / inevitable**]114) or beyond our capacity to fix — and, therefore, functionally elective. That is one reason it is nevertheless [**distressed / distressing**]115): an abundant resource made scarce through governmental neglect and indifference, bad infrastructure and contamination, and [**careless / carelessly**]116) urbanization. There is no need for a water crisis, in other words, but we have one anyway, and aren't doing much to address [**it / them**]117). Some cities lose more water to leaks than they deliver to homes: even in the United States, leaks and theft [**account for / accounts for**]118) an estimated loss of 16 percent of freshwater; in Brazil, the estimate is 40 percent. [**Seeing / Seen**]119) in both cases, as everywhere, the selective scarcity clearly [**highlight / highlights**]120) haveandhavenot inequities, [**leaving / left**]121) 2.1 billion people without safe drinking water and 4.5 billion without proper sanitation worldwide.

36

As individuals, our ability [**thriving / to thrive**]122) depended on how well we navigated relationships in a group. If the group valued us, we could count on support, resources, and probably a mate. If it didn't, we might get [**none / some**]123) of these merits. It was a matter of survival, physically and genetically. Over millions of years, the pressure selected for people who are [**sensitive / sensitively**]124) to and skilled at [**maximize / maximizing**]125) their standing. The result was the development of a tendency to [**unconscious / unconsciously**]126) monitor how other people in our community perceive us. We process that information in the form of self-esteem and such [**related / relating**]127) emotions as pride, shame, or insecurity. These emotions compel us [**do / to do**]128) more of what makes our community value us and less of what doesn't. And, crucially, they are meant to make that motivation feel like it is coming from within. If we realized, on a conscious level, that we were responding to [**social / socially**]129) pressure, our performance might come off as grudging or cynical, [**make / making**]130) it [**less / more**]131) persuasive.

37

Conventional medicine has long believed that depression [**caused / is caused**]132) by an imbalance of neurotransmitters in the brain. However, there is a [**major / minor**]133) problem with this explanation. [**This is because / This is why**]134) the imbalance of substances in the brain is a consequence of depression, not its cause. In other words, depression causes a decrease in brain substances such as serotonin and noradrenaline, not a decrease in brain substances causes depression. In this [**revised / revising**]135) cause-and-effect, the key is to reframe depression as a problem of consciousness. Our consciousness is a more [**fundamental / fundamentally**]136) entity that goes [**beyond / within**]137) the functioning of the brain. The brain is no more than an organ of consciousness. If it is not consciousness itself, then the root cause of depression [**are / is**]138) also a distortion of our state of consciousness: a consciousness [**that / what**]139) has lost its sense of self and the meaning of life. Such a disease of consciousness may manifest [**it / itself**]140) in the form of depression.

38

The common accounts of human nature [**that / what**]¹⁴¹⁾ float around in society are generally a mixture of assumptions, tales and sometimes plain silliness. However, psychology is different. It is the branch of science [**that / what**]¹⁴²⁾ is devoted to understanding people: how and why we act as we do; why we see things as we do; and how we interact with one another. The key word here is 'science.' Psychologists don't depend on opinions and hearsay, or the generally [**accepted / accepting**]¹⁴³⁾ views of society at the time, or even the [**considered / considering**]¹⁴⁴⁾ opinions of deep thinkers. Instead, they [**look at / look for**]¹⁴⁵⁾ evidence, to make sure that psychological ideas are [**firm / firmly**]¹⁴⁶⁾ based, and not just derived from generally held beliefs or assumptions. In addition to this evidence-based approach, psychology deals with fundamental processes and principles that [**generate / generates**]¹⁴⁷⁾ our rich cultural and social diversity, as well as those [**shared / sharing**]¹⁴⁸⁾ by all human beings. These are [**that / what**]¹⁴⁹⁾ modern psychology is all about.

39

Life is [**that / what**]¹⁵⁰⁾ physicists might call a 'high-dimensional system,' [**that / which**]¹⁵¹⁾ is their fancy way of saying that there's a lot going on. In just a single cell, the number of possible interactions between different molecules [**are / is**]¹⁵²⁾ enormous. Such a system can only hope to be stable if only a smaller number of collective ways of being may [**disappear / emerge**]¹⁵³⁾. For example, it is only a limited number of tissues and body shapes that may [**result from / result in**]¹⁵⁴⁾ the development of a human embryo. In 1942, the biologist Conrad Waddington called this [**drastic / drastically**]¹⁵⁵⁾ narrowing of outcomes *canalization*. The organism may switch between a small number of well-defined possible states, but can't exist in [**random / randomly**]¹⁵⁶⁾ states in between them, rather as a ball in a rough landscape must roll to the bottom of one valley or [**another / other**]¹⁵⁷⁾. We'll see that this is true also of health and disease: there are many causes of illness, but their manifestations at the physiological and symptomatic levels [**are / is**]¹⁵⁸⁾ often strikingly similar.

40

Punishing a child may not be [**affective / effective**]¹⁵⁹⁾ due to what Álvaro Bilbao, a neuropsychologist, calls 'trick-punishments.' A trick-punishment is a scolding, a moment of anger or a punishment in the most classic sense of the word. Instead of [**discourage / discouraging**]¹⁶⁰⁾ the child from doing something, it encourages them [**doing / to do**]¹⁶¹⁾ it. For example, Hugh learns that when he hits his little brother, his mother scolds him. For a child who feels lonely, being scolded is much [**better / worse**]¹⁶²⁾ than feeling invisible, so he will continue to hit his brother. In this case, his mother would be better [**adapting / adopting**]¹⁶³⁾ a different strategy. For instance, she could congratulate Hugh [**when / where**]¹⁶⁴⁾ he has not hit his brother for a certain length of time. The mother clearly cannot allow the child [**hit / to hit**]¹⁶⁵⁾ his little brother, but instead of constantly [**point / pointing**]¹⁶⁶⁾ out the negatives, she can choose to [**award / reward**]¹⁶⁷⁾ the positives. In this way, any parent can avoid trick-punishments.

41, 42

From an early age, we assign purpose to objects and events, [**prefer / preferring**]168) this reasoning [**in / to**]169) random chance. Children assume, for instance, that pointy rocks are that way [**because / because of**]170) they don't want you to sit on them. When we encounter something, we first need to determine [**that / what**]171) sort of thing it is. [**Animate / Inanimate**]172) objects and plants generally do not move and can be evaluated from physics alone. However, by [**attribute / attributing**]173) intention to animals and even objects, we are able to [**make / making**]174) fast decisions about the likely behaviour of that being. This was essential in our hunter-gatherer days to avoid [**be eaten / being eaten**]175) by predators.

  The anthropologist Stewart Guthrie made the point [**that / what**]176) survival in our evolutionary past meant that we interpret [**ambiguous / clear**]177) objects as agents with human mental characteristics, as those are the mental processes which we understand. Ambiguous events [**are caused / caused**]178) by such agents. This [**results from / results in**]179) a perceptual system strongly biased towards anthropomorphism. Therefore, we tend to [**assume / assuming**]180) intention even where there is none. This would have arisen as a survival mechanism. If a lion is about to [**attack / attacking**]181) you, you need to react [**quick / quickly**]182), given its probable intention to kill you. By the time you have realized [**that / what**]183) the design of its teeth and claws could kill you, you are dead. So, [**assume / assuming**]184) intent, without detailed design analysis or understanding of the physics, has saved your life.

43 ~ 45

Once long ago, deep in the Himalayas, there lived a little panda. He was as [**extraordinary / ordinary**]185) as all the other pandas. He was completely white from head to toe. His two big ears, his four furry feet and his cute round nose were all frosty white, leaving him feeling ordinary and sad. Unlike the cheerful and [**contented / contenting**]186) pandas around him, he desired to be [**distinctive / distinctively**]187), Once long ago, deep in the Himalayas, there lived a little panda. He was as ordinary as all the [**another / other**]188) pandas. He was completely white from head to toe. His two big ears, his four furry feet and his cute round nose were all frosty white, leaving him feeling ordinary and sad. [**Like / Unlike**]189) the cheerful and contented pandas around him, he desired to be distinctive, special, and unique. [**Driven / Driving**]190) by the desire for uniqueness, the little panda sought inspiration from his distant cousin, a giant white panda covered with heavenly black patches. But the cousin [**concealed / revealed**]191) the patches were from an unintended encounter with mud, and he [**disliked / liked**]192) them. Disappointed, the little panda walked home. On his way, he met a red-feathered peacock, who explained he turned red from [**eat / eating**]193) wild berries. The little panda changed his path and [**hurried / hurrying**]194) to the nearest berry bush, greedily eating a mouthful of juicy red berries. However, they were so bitter he couldn't swallow even one. At dusk, he finally got home and slowly [**climbed / climbing**]195) his favorite bamboo tree. There, he discovered a strange black and red flower with a sweet scent [**that / what**]196) tempted him to eat all its blossoms. The following morning, under sunny skies, the little panda felt remarkably better. [**During / While**]197) breakfast, he found the other pandas chatting [**enthusiastic / enthusiastically**]198) and asked why. They burst into laughter, exclaiming, "Look at yourself!" Glancing down, he discovered his once white fur was now stained jet black and glowing red. He was overjoyed and [**realize / realized**]199) that, rather than by imitating [**others / the others**]200) , his wishes can come true from unexpected places and genuine experiences.

2024 고1 11월 모의고사 ❶ 회차 : 점 / 300점

2024_H1_11_18

To the State Education Department,
I am writing with r_____1) to the state's f_____2) for the construction project at Fort Montgomery High School. Our school needs a_____3) spaces to p_____4) a fully functional Art and Library Media Center to serve our students in a more meaningful way. D_____5) s_____6) all required documentation for funding to your department in April 2024, we have not yet received any n_____7) from your department. A d_____8) in the process can carry considerable consequences related to the school's budgetary c_____9) and schedule. Therefore, in order to p_____10) with our project, we request you n_____11) us of the review result r_____12) the s_____13) documentation. I look forward to hearing from you.
Respectfully, Clara Smith Principal, Fort Montgomery High School

주 교육부 귀하, 저는 Fort Montgomery 고등학교의 건축 프로젝트를 위한 주 예산과 관련하여 편지를 씁니다. 저희 학교는 보다 의미 있는 방식으로 학생들을 만족시키기 위해 완전하게 제 기능을 하는 Art and Library Media Center를 제공하기 위한 추가 공간이 필요합니다. 2024년 4월에 귀하의 부서로 예산에 필요한 모든 서류를 제출했음에도 불구하고, 저희는 아직 귀하의 부서로부터 어떠한 통지도 받지 못했습니다. 과정상 지연은 학교의 예산 제한 및 일정과 관련하여 상당한 결과를 초래할 수 있습니다. 그러므로, 저희의 프로젝트를 진행하기 위해 제출 서류와 관련한 검토 결과를 저희에게 통지해 줄 것을 요청합니다. 귀하로부터의 답변을 고대합니다. Fort Montgomery 고등학교 교장, Clara Smith 드림

2024_H1_11_19

As I waited outside the locker room after a h_____14) basketball game, the coach called out to me, "David, walk with me." I f_____15) he was going to tell me something important. He was going to select me to be the captain of the team, the leader I had always wanted to be. My heart was racing with a_____16) . But when his next words hit my ears, everything changed. "We're going to have to send you home," he said c_____17) . "I don't think you are going to make it." I couldn't believe his decision. I tried to hold it together, but inside I was falling apart. A car would be waiting tomorrow morning to take me home. And just like that, it was over.

내가 치열하게 싸운 농구 경기 후에 라커 룸 밖에서 기다릴 때, 코치가 "David, 나와 함께 걷자."라며 나를 크게 불렀다. 나는 그가 나에게 무언가 중요한 것을 말해 줄 거라고 생각했다. 그는 내가 항상 되기를 원했던 리더인 팀의 주장으로 나를 뽑으려 할 것이라고 (생각했다). 나의 심장이 기대감으로 빠르게 뛰었다. 그러나 그의 다음 말이 내 귀를 쳤을 때, 모든 것이 변했다. "우리는 너를 집으로 보내야만 해."라고 그가 차갑게 말했다. "나는 네가 해낼 거라고 생각하지 않아." 나는 그의 결정을 믿을 수 없었다. 나는 마음을 가다듬으려고 했지만, 내면에서 나는 산산이 무너지고 있었다. 내일 아침에 나를 집에 데려갈 차가 기다리고 있을 것이다. 그리고 그렇게, 끝이 났다.

2024_H1_11_20

For many of us, making time for exercise is a continuing challenge. Between work c_____ 18) and family o_____ 19) , it often feels like there's no room in our packed schedules for a d_____ _20) workout. But what if the workout came to you, right in the m_____ 21) of your daily r_____ 22) ? That's where the beauty of i_____ 23) mini-exercises into household chores comes into play. Let's be r_____ 24) ; chores are i_____ 25) . Whether it's washing dishes or taking out the trash, these tasks are an e_____ 26) part of daily life. But rather than viewing chores as p_____ 27) o_____ 28) activities, why not s_____ 29) these moments as opportunities for p_____ 30) activity? For instance, practice squats or e_____ 31) in some wall push-ups as you wait for your morning kettle to boil. I_____ 32) quick exercises into your daily chores can improve your health.

우리 중 다수에게 운동할 시간을 내는 것은 계속되는 도전이다. 업무에 대한 전념과 가족 의무 사이에서, 우리의 빡빡한 일정들에는 운동에 전념할 여유가 없는 것처럼 종종 느껴진다. 그러나 만약 여러분의 일상 바로 한가운데에서 운동이 여러분을 찾아온다면 어떨까? 그것이 바로 간단한 운동을 집안일에 통합시키는 아름다움이 작동하는 지점이다. 현실적이 되자. 집안일은 불가피하다. 그것이 설거지하는 것이든 쓰레기를 내다 버리는 것이든지 간에, 이런 일들은 일상생활의 필수적인 부분이다. 하지만 집안일을 순전히 의무적인 행위로 간주하기보다는, 이런 순간들을 신체 활동을 위한 기회로 잘 이용하는 것이 어떨까? 예를 들어, 여러분의 아침 주전자가 끓기를 기다리면서 스쿼트를 연습하거나 벽에 대고 하는 팔 굽혀 펴기 몇 개를 시작해 보라. 짧은 운동을 여러분의 일상적인 집안일에 포함시키는 것이 여러분의 건강을 향상시킬 수 있다.

2024_H1_11_21

When we see something, we n_____ 33) and a_____ 34) break it up into shapes, colors, and c_____ 35) that we have learned through education. We r_____ 36) what we see through the lens of everything we know. We r_____ 37) memories rather than r_____ 38) the video from memory. This is a useful t_____ 39) . It's a more efficient way to store information—a bit like an o_____ 40) image c_____ 41) algorithm such as JPG, rather than storing a raw b_____ 42) image file. People who l_____ 43) this ability and remember everything in perfect detail struggle to g_____ 44) , learn, and make connections between what they have learned. But r_____ 45) the world as a_____ 46) ideas and features comes at a cost of seeing the world as it is. Instead, we see the world through our a_____ 47) , motivations, and past experiences. The discovery that our memories are reconstructed through a_____ 48) representations rather than played back like a movie completely undermined the legal p_____ 49) of eyewitness t_____ 50) . Seeing is not believing.

우리가 무언가를 볼 때, 우리는 그것을 자연스럽게 그리고 자동적으로 우리가 교육을 통해 배운 모양, 색깔, 그리고 개념들로 해체한다. 우리는 우리가 알고 있는 모든 것의 렌즈를 통해 우리가 보는 것을 재부 호화한다. 우리는 기억에서 영상을 생각해 내기보다 기억을 재구성한다. 이것은 유용한 특성이다. 그것은 가공되지 않은 비트맵 이미지 파일을 저장하기보다 JPG 와 같은 최적의 이미지 압축 알고리즘과 약간 비슷하게 정보를 저장하기 위한 더 효율적인 방법이다. 이런 능력이 부족하고 완벽히 세세하게 모든 것을 기억하는 사람들은 일반화하고, 학습하고, 자신들이 학습한 것들 사이를 연결하려고 고군분투한다. 그러나 세상을 추상적 생각과 특징으로 재현하는 것은 세상을 있는 그대로 보는 것을 희생하여 나온다. 대신에, 우리는 우리의 가정, 동기 그리고 과거 경험을 통해 세상을 바라본다. 우리의 기억이 영화처럼 재생되기보다는 추상적 재현을 통해 재구성된다는 발견은 목격자 증언의 법적 우위성을 완전히 손상시켰다. 보는 것이 믿는 것은 아니다.

2024_H1_11_22

In his Cornell laboratory, David Dunning c_____51) experimental tests of eyewitness t_____52) and found evidence that a careful d_____53) of f_____54) features and a detailed discussion of selection p_____55) can actually be a sign of an *inaccurate* identification. It's when people find themselves u_____56) to explain why they r_____57) the person, saying things like "his face just popped out at me," that they t_____58) to be accurate more often. Sometimes our first, i_____59) , a_____60) reaction to a situation is the truest interpretation of what our mind is telling us. That very first impression can also be more a_____61) about the world than the d_____62) , reasoned self-narrative can be. In his book *Blink*, Malcolm Gladwell describes a variety of studies in psychology and behavioral economics that d_____63) the superior performance of relatively u_____64) first guesses compared to logical step-by-step j_____65) for a decision.

David Dunning의 코넬 대학의 실험실에서, 그는 목격자 증언에 대한 실험을 수행했고, 얼굴 특징에 대한 신중한 숙고와 선택 절차에 대한 상세한 논의가 실제로는 '부정확한' 식별의 징후일 수 있다는 증거를 발견했다. 사람들이 "그의 얼굴이 그냥 나에게 탁 떠올랐다"라는 식으로 말하면서 왜 그 사람을 알아보는지 설명할 수 없는 스스로를 발견하는 바로 그때 그들은 더 자주 정확한 경향이 있다. 때때로 상황에 대한 우리의 최초의, 즉각적인, 자동적인 반응이 우리 마음이 우리에게 말하고 있는 것에 대한 가장 정확한 해석이다. 바로 그 첫인상이 또한 신중하고 논리적인 자기 서사보다 세상에 대해 더 정확할 수 있다. Malcolm Gladwell은 그의 저서 'Blink'에서, 결정에 대한 논리적인 단계적 정당화에 비해서 상대적으로 무의식적인 최초 추측의 우수성을 보여 주는 심리학 및 행동 경제학의 다양한 연구를 기술한다.

2024_H1_11_23

Many forms of research lead naturally to q_____66) data. A study of happiness might measure the number of times someone smiles during an i_____67) , and a study of memory might measure the number of items an individual can r_____68) after one, five, and ten minutes. Asking people how many times in a year they are sad will also y_____69) q_____70) data, but it might not be r_____71) . Respondents' r_____72) may be inaccurate, and their definitions of 'sad' could v_____73) widely. But asking "How many times in the past year were you sad enough to call in sick to work?" p_____74) a c_____75) answer. Similarly, instead of asking people to rate how bad a p_____76) they are, ask, "How many of your u_____77) bills are you currently late in paying, even though you can afford to pay them?" Questions that seek concrete responses help make a_____78) concepts clearer and e_____79) c_____80) from one study to the next.

많은 종류의 연구는 자연스럽게 양적 데이터로 이어진다. 행복에 관한 연구는 누군가가 상호 작용 중에 미소 짓는 횟수를 측정할 수 있고, 기억에 관한 연구는 개인이 1분, 5분, 그리고 10분 후에 회상할 수 있는 항목의 수를 측정할 수 있다. 사람들에게 자신이 일년에 몇 번 슬픈지 물어보는 것 또한 양적 데이터를 산출할 수 있지만, 이는 신뢰할 만하지 않을 수도 있다. 응답자의 회상은 부정확할 수 있고, '슬픈'에 대한 그들의 정의는 크게 다를 수 있다. 그러나 "지난 1년 동안 직장에 병가를 낼 만큼 슬펐던 적이 몇 번 있었습니까?"라고 묻는 것은 구체적인 답변을 유발한다. 마찬가지로, 사람들에게 그들이 얼마나 심하게 미루는 사람인지를 평가하도록 묻는 대신, "당신이 지불할 여유가 있음에도 불구하고 얼마나 많은 공과금 고지서의 납부가 현재 늦었나요?"라고 물어보라. 구체적인 응답을 요구하는 질문은 추상적인 개념을 더 명확하게 만들고 한 연구에서 다음 연구 간의 일관성을 보장하는 것을 돕는다.

2024_H1_11_24

The e_____81) of AI is often a_____82) with the concept of s_____83) . S_____84) refers to the point at which AI e_____85) human intelligence. After that point, it is predicted that AI will repeatedly improve itself and e_____86) at an accelerated p_____87) . When AI becomes self-aware and p_____88) its own goals, it will be a c_____89) being, not just a machine. AI and human c_____90) will then begin to evolve together. Our c_____91) will evolve to new d_____92) through our i_____93) with AI, which will provide us with i_____94) stimulation and inspire new i_____95) and creativity. C_____96) , our consciousness also has a s_____97) impact on the evolution of AI. The direction of AI's evolution will depend greatly on what values and e_____98) we i_____99) into AI. We need to see our relationship with AI as a mutual c_____100) of conscious beings, recognizing its rights and supporting the evolution of its consciousness.

AI의 진화는 종종 특이점의 개념과 연관된다. 특이점은 AI가 인간의 지능을 넘어서는 지점을 의미한다. 그 지점 이후, AI는 스스로를 반복적으로 개선하고 가속화된 속도로 진화할 것으로 예측된다. AI가 스스로를 인식하게 되고 자기 자신의 목표를 추구할 때, 그것은 단지 기계가 아니라 의식이 있는 존재가 될 것이다. AI와 인간의 의식은 그러면 함께 진화하기 시작할 것이다. 우리의 의식은 우리의 AI와의 상호 작용을 통해 새로운 차원으로 진화할 것이며, 이는 우리에게 지적 자극을 제공하고 새로운 통찰력과 창의성을 불어넣을 것이다. 반대로, 우리의 의식 또한 AI의 진화에 중대한 영향을 끼친다. AI 진화의 방향은 우리가 어떤 가치와 윤리를 AI에 통합시키는지에 크게 좌우될 것이다. 우리는 AI의 권리를 인식하고 그것의 의식의 진화를 지지하면서, 우리와 AI와의 관계를 의식 있는 존재들의 상호 공존으로 볼 필요가 있다.

2024_H1_11_29

Digital technologies are e_____101) related to metaphors, but d_____102) metaphors are different from l_____103) ones in important ways. Linguistic metaphors are p_____104) , in the sense that the audience needs to choose to actively enter the world p_____105) by m_____106) . In the Shakespearean metaphor "time is a beggar," the audience is u_____107) to understand the metaphor without c_____108) effort and without further engaging Shakespeare's p_____109) . Technological metaphors, on the other hand, are active and often imposing) in the sense that they are realized in digital a_____110) that are actively doing things, forcefully changing a user's meaning h_____111) . Technological creators cannot generally a_____112) to require their p_____113) audience to wonder how the metaphor works; normally the selling point is that the usefulness of the technology is obvious at first glance. Shakespeare, on the other hand, is beloved in part because the meaning of his works is not immediately obvious and requires some thought on the part of the audience.

디지털 기술은 근본적으로 은유와 관련되어 있지만, 디지털 은유는 중요한 면에서 언어적 은유와 다르다. 언어적 은유는 독자가 은유에 의해 제시된 세계에 적극적으로 들어가도록 선택할 필요가 있다는 점에서 수동적이다. "시간은 구걸하는 자다"라는 셰익스피어의 은유에서 독자는 인지적인 노력 없이는 그리고 셰익스피어의 산문을 더 끌어들이지 않고는 은유를 이해할 것 같지 않다. 반면에 기술적 은유는 사용자의 의미의 지평을 강력하게 바꾸면서 능동적으로 일을 하는 디지털 인공물에서 그것이 실현된다는 점에서 능동적이다. (그리고 종종 강요적이다.) 기술적인 창작자는 일반적으로 그들의 잠재적인 독자에게 어떻게 은유가 작용하는지 궁금해하도록 요구할 여유가 없고, 일반적으로 매력은 기술의 유용성이 첫눈에 분명하다는 것이다. 반면에 셰익스피어는 부분적으로는 그의 작품의 의미가 즉각적으로 분명하지 않고 독자 측에서 어느 정도의 생각을 요구하기 때문에 사랑받는다.

2024_H1_11_30

Herbert Simon won his Nobel Prize for recognizing our l_____114) in information, time, and c_____115) capacity. As we lack the resources to compute answers independently, we d_____116) the c_____117) across the population and solve the answer slowly, generation by generation. Then all we have to do is socially learn the right answers. You don't need to understand how your computer or toilet works; you just need to be able to use the i_____118) and flush. All that needs to be t_____119) is which button to push —essentially how to interact with technologies rather than how they work. And so instead of holding more information than we have mental c_____120) for and indeed need to know, we could d_____121) our large brains to a small piece of a giant calculation. We understand things well enough to b_____122) from them, but all the while we are making small calculations that c_____123) to a larger whole. We are just doing our part in a larger computation for our societies' collective brains.

Herbert Simon은 정보, 시간, 그리고 인지적인 능력에서 우리의 한계를 인지한 것으로 그의 노벨상을 받았다. 우리는 독립적으로 해답을 계산하기 위한 자원이 부족하기 때문에 우리는 전체 인구에 걸쳐 복잡한 계산을 분배하고 세대에 걸쳐 해답을 천천히 풀어 낸다. 그러면 우리가 해야 하는 모든 것은 올바른 해답을 사회적으로 배우는 것이다. 여러분은 여러분의 컴퓨터 혹은 변기가 어떻게 작동하는지 이해할 필요가 없고 여러분은 단지 인터페이스를 사용할 수 있고 (변기의) 물을 내릴 수 있기만 하면 된다. 전달될 필요가 있는 모든 것은 어떤 버튼을 눌러야 하는지, 근본적으로 어떻게 그것들이 작동하는지 보다는 기술과 상호 작용하는 방법이다. 그렇다면 우리가 정신적 수용을 할 수 있는 것보다 그리고 정말로 알아야 할 필요가 있는 것보다 더 많은 정보를 가지는 것 대신에 우리는 우리의 큰 두뇌를 거대한 계산의 작은 조각에 바칠 수 있다. 우리는 그것들로부터 이득을 얻기에 충분할 정도로 사물을 잘 이해하지만 그러면서 우리는 더 큰 전체에 기여하는 작은 계산을 하고 있다. 우리는 우리 사회의 집합적인 두뇌를 위한 더 큰 복잡한 계산에서 단지 우리의 역할을 하고 있는 것이다.

2024_H1_11_31

The best d_____124) most species of octopus have is to stay hidden as much as possible and do their own hunting at night. So to find one in full view in the shallows in daylight was a surprise for two Australian underwater photographers. Actually, what they saw at first was a f_____125) . It was only when they looked again that they saw a medium-sized octopus, with all eight of its arms folded and its two eyes staring upwards to create the i_____126) . An octopus has a big brain, excellent eyesight and the ability to change colour and pattern, and this one was using these a_____127) to turn itself into a completely different creature. Many more of this species have been found since then, and there are now photographs of octopuses that could be said to be t_____128) into sea snakes. And while they m_____129) , they hunt —producing the s_____130) of, say, a f_____131) suddenly developing an octopodian arm, sticking it down a hole and grabbing whatever's hiding there.

대부분의 문어 종(種)이 가진 최고의 방어는 가능한 한 많이 숨어 있는 것과 밤에 그들 자신의 사냥을 하는 것이다. 그래서 낮에 얕은 곳에서 전체가 보이는 문어를 발견한 것은 두 명의 호주 수중 사진작가들에게는 놀라운 일이었다. 사실 그들이 처음에 봤던 것은 넙치였다. 오직 그들이 다시 봤을 때서야 그들은 중 간 크기의 문어를 보았고 착시를 만들기 위해 그것의 여덟 개의 모든 팔이 접혀 있었고 그것의 두 눈이 위쪽으로 응시하고 있었다. 문어는 큰 뇌, 뛰어난 시력과 색깔과 패턴을 바꾸는 능력을 지니고 있고, 이것은 스스로를 완전히 다른 생물체로 바꾸기 위해 이러한 이점을 사용하고 있었다. 이 종의 더 많은 것들이 그때 이후로 발견되어 왔으며 지금은 바다뱀으로 변신하는 중이라고 말해질 수 있는 문어의 사진이 있다. 그리고 그들이 모방하는 동안에 그들은 사냥을 한다. 이것은 말하자면 넙치가 갑자기 문어 다리 같은 팔을 펼치며 그것을 구멍으로 찔러 넣어 그곳에 숨어 있는 무엇이든지 움켜잡는 광경을 만들어 낸다.

2024_H1_11_32

How much we **s**_____ **132)** relates to how we **f**_____ **133)** the pain in our mind. When 1500m runners push themselves into extreme pain to win a race—their muscles screaming and their lungs exploding with oxygen **d**_____ **134)** , they don't **p**_____ **135)** suffer much. In fact, ultra-marathon runners—those people who are crazy enough to push themselves beyond the normal **b**_____ **136)** of human **e**_____ **137)** , covering distances of 50-100km or more over many hours, talk about making friends with their pain. When a patient has paid for some form of passive back pain **t**_____ **138)** and the **p**_____ **139)** pushes deeply into a painful part of a patient's back to **m**_____ **140)** it, the patient calls that good pain if he or she believes this type of deep pressure treatment will be of value, even though the practitioner is pushing right into the patient's **s**_____ **141)** tissues.

우리가 얼마나 고통받는지는 우리가 고통을 우리의 마음에서 어떻게 구성하는지와 관련된다. 1500미터 달리기 선수가 경주에서 이기기 위해 그들의 근육이 비명을 지르고 그들의 폐가 산소 부족으로 폭발하면서, 스스로를 극심한 고통으로 밀어붙일 때, 그들은 정신적으로 많이 고통받지 않는다. 사실 울트라 마라톤 선수들은 즉, 인간 인내력의 정상적 경계를 넘어서 스스로를 밀어붙일 만큼 충분히 열정적인 사람들은 많은 시간 동안 50에서 100킬로미터 혹은 그 이상의 거리를 가지만 그들의 고통과 친구가 되는 것에 대해 이야기한다. 한 환자가 특정 형태의 수동적 등 통증 치료에 돈을 지불했고 의사가 그것을 풀어 주기 위해 환자 등의 아픈 부분을 깊게 눌렀을 때, 비록 의사가 환자의 아픈 조직을 직접적으로 누르고 있을지라도, 만약 그 또는 그녀가 이러한 종류의 깊은 압박 치료법이 가치가 있을 것이라고 믿는다면, 환자는 그것을 좋은 아픔이라고 부른다.

2024_H1_11_33

When I worked for a large electronics company that manufactured laser and inkjet-printers, I soon discovered why there are often three **v**_____ **142)** of many consumer goods. If the **m**_____ **143)** makes only one version of its product, people who bought it might have been **w**_____ **144)** to spend more money, so the company is losing some **i**_____ **145)** . If the company offers two versions, one with more **f**_____ **146)** and more expensive than the other, people will compare the two models and still buy the less expensive one. But if the company **i**_____ **147)** a third model with even more features and more expensive than the other two, sales of the second model go up; many people like the features of the most expensive model, but not the price. The middle item has more features than the least expensive one, and it is less expensive than the fanciest model. They buy the middle item, **u**_____ **148)** that they have been **m**_____ **149)** by the **p**_____ **150)** of the higher-priced item.

내가 레이저와 잉크젯 프린터를 생산했던 큰 전자 회사에서 일했을 때 나는 많은 소비 상품의 세 가지 버전이 종종 있는 이유를 곧 발견했다. 만약 생산자가 그 제품의 오직 한 가지 버전만 만든다면 그것을 구매했던 사람들은 기꺼이 더 많은 돈을 쓰려고 했을 수도 있어서 회사는 일부 수입을 잃을 것이다. 만약 그 회사가 두 버전을 제공하는데 한 버전이 나머지보다 더 많은 기능과 더 비싼 가격을 가진다면, 사람들은 두 모델을 비교하고 여전히 덜 비싼 것을 살 것이다. 하지만 만약 그 회사가 나머지 두 개보다 훨씬 더 많은 기능과 더 비싼 가격을 가진 세 번째 모델을 출시한다면 두 번째 모델의 판매가 증가하는데, 왜냐하면 많은 사람들은 가장 비싼 모델의 기능을 좋아하지만 그것의 가격을 좋아하지는 않기 때문이다. 중간 제품은 가장 저렴한 제품보다 더 많은 기능이 있고 가장 고급 모델보다는 덜 비싸다. 그들은 자신이 더 비싼 가격의 제품의 존재에 의해 조종되었다는 것을 알지 못한 채 중간 제품을 구입한다.

2024_H1_11_34

On-screen, climate disaster is everywhere you look, but the s_____151) of the world's climate transformation may just as quickly e_____152) the climate-fiction g_____153) — indeed eliminate any effort to tell the story of warming, which could grow too large and too o_____154) even for Hollywood. You can tell stories 'about' climate change while it still seems a m_____155) feature of human life. But when the temperature rises by three or four more degrees, hardly anyone will be able to feel i_____156) from its impacts. And so as climate change e_____157) across the horizon, it may c_____158) to be a story. Why watch or read climate fiction about the world you can see p_____159) out your own window? At the moment, stories illustrating global warming can still offer an e_____160) pleasure, even if that p_____161) often comes in the form of horror. But when we can no longer pretend that climate suffering is d_____162) — in time or in place — we will stop pretending about it and start pretending within it.

영화상 기후 재난은 여러분이 보는 어디에나 있지만, 세계의 기후 변화의 범위는 그것만큼이나 빠르게 기후 픽션 장르를 없앨지도 모르고 실제로 온난화 이야기를 하고자 하는 노력도 없애 버리는데, 그것은 할리우드에서조차 너무 커지고 너무 명백해질 것이다. 기후 변화가 여전히 인간 삶의 주변적인 특징처럼 보이는 동안에 여러분은 그것에 '관한' 이야기를 할 수 있을 것이다. 하지만 기온이 3도 혹은 4도 이상 상승할 때는 아무도 그것의 영향으로부터 고립되었다고 느낄 수 없을 것이다. 그리고 기후 변화가 지평선을 넘어 확장될 때 그것은 이야기가 되기를 멈출 것이다. 왜 여러분 자신의 창문 밖으로 뚜렷하게 볼 수 있는 세상에 대한 기후 픽션을 보거나 읽겠는가? 비록 그 즐거움이 종종 공포의 형태로 올지라도 지금 당장은 지구 온난화를 묘사하는 이야기가 현실 도피적인 즐거움을 여전히 제공할 수 있다. 하지만 우리가 더 이상 기후 고통이 시간적으로 또는 장소적으로 멀리 있다고 가장할 수 없을 때 우리는 그것에 대해 가장하는 것을 멈추고 그것 내에서 가장하기 시작할 것이다.

2024_H1_11_35

Today, the water c_____163) is p_____164) — which is to say, not i_____165) or beyond our capacity to fix — and, therefore, functionally e_____166). That is one reason it is nevertheless d_____167): an a_____168) resource made scarce through governmental n_____169) and indifference, bad i_____170) and c_____171), and careless u_____172). There is no need for a water crisis, in other words, but we have one anyway, and aren't doing much to a_____173) it. Some cities lose more water to l_____174) than they deliver to homes: even in the United States, leaks and theft a_____175) for an estimated loss of 16 percent of freshwater; in Brazil, the estimate is 40 percent. Seen in both cases, as everywhere, the s_____176) s_____177) clearly highlights have and have not i_____178), leaving 2.1 billion people without safe drinking water and 4.5 billion without proper s_____179) worldwide.

오늘날, 물 위기는 피할 수 없는 것이 아니며 우리의 바로잡을 수 있는 능력을 넘어서지 않는, 즉 정치적인 것이고 따라서 기능적으로 선택적이다. 그것은 그럼에도 불구하고 그것이 괴로운 한 가지 이유이다. 즉, 풍족한 자원이 정부의 소홀함과 무관심, 열악한 사회 기반 시설과 오염, 부주의한 도시화를 통해 부족하게 되었다. 다시 말해서 물 위기가 있어야 할 필요가 없지만 어쨌든 우리는 그것을 겪고 있고 그것을 해결하기 위해 많은 일을 하고 있지 않다. 일부 도시들은 그들이 주택으로 공급하는 것보다 누수로 인해 더 많은 물을 잃는다. 즉, 미국에서조차 누수와 도난은 담수의 16퍼센트의 추정된 손실을 차지하고 브라질에서는 그 추정치가 40퍼센트이다. 양쪽의 경우에서 보여지듯이 모든 곳에 서처럼 선택적 부족이 가진 자와 가지지 못한 자의 불평등을 분명히 강조하고 이것은 전 세계적으로 21억 명을 안전한 식수가 없고 45억 명을 적절한 위생이 없는 채로 둔다.

2024_H1_11_36

As individuals, our ability to t_____180) depended on how well we navigated relationships in a group. If the group v_____181) us, we could c_____182) on support, resources, and probably a m_____183) . If it didn't, we might get none of these m_____184) . It was a matter of survival, physically and g_____185) . Over millions of years, the p_____186) selected for people who are s_____187) to and skilled at m_____188) their s_____189) . The result was the development of a t_____190) to u_____191) monitor how other people in our community p_____192) us. We process that information in the form of s_____193) and such related emotions as pride, shame, or i_____194) . These emotions c_____195) us to do more of what makes our community value us and less of what doesn't. And, c_____196) , they are meant to make that motivation feel like it is coming from within. If we realized, on a conscious level, that we were responding to social pressure, our performance might come off as g_____197) or c_____198) , making it less p_____199) .

개인으로서 성공하려는 우리의 능력은 우리가 집단 내에서 관계를 얼마나 잘 다루는지에 달려 있었다. 만약 그 집단이 우리를 가치 있게 여겼다면 우리는 지원, 자원, 그리고 아마도 짝을 기대할 수 있었을 것이다. 만약 그렇지 않았다면, 우리는 그러한 이점들 중 아무것도 얻지 못했을 것이다. 그것은 신체적으로 그리고 유전적으로 생존의 문제였다. 수백만 년 동안 그러한 압박은 자신의 지위를 최대화하는 데 민감하고 능숙한 사람들을 선택했다. 그 결과는 우리 공동체의 다른 사람들이 우리를 어떻게 인식하는지 무의식적으로 관찰하는 경향의 발달이었다. 우리는 자존감 그리고 자존심, 수치심 또는 불안 같은 관련된 감정의 형태로 그 정보를 처리한다. 이러한 감정들은 우리에게 우리의 공동체가 우리를 가치 있게 여기도록 만드는 것을 더 많이 하고 그렇지 않은 것을 덜 하도록 강요한다. 그리고 결정적으로 그것들은 그 동기가 내부에서 나오고 있는 것처럼 그것을 느끼게 만들도록 되어 있다. 우리가 사회적 압박에 반응하고 있었다는 것을 의식적인 수준에서 깨닫는다면, 우리의 행동은 그것(그 동기)을 설득력이 떨어지게 만들면서 투덜대거나 냉소적인 것으로 나타날 수 있다.

2024_H1_11_37

C_____200) medicine has long believed that d_____201) is caused by an i_____202) of n_____203) in the brain. However, there is a major problem with this explanation. This is because the imbalance of s_____204) in the brain is a consequence of depression, not its cause. In other words, depression causes a decrease in brain substances such as s_____205) and n_____206) , not a decrease in brain substances causes depression. In this r_____207) cause-and-effect, the key is to r_____208) depression as a problem of consciousness. Our consciousness is a more f_____209) e_____210) that goes beyond the functioning of the brain. The brain is no more than an o_____211) of consciousness. If it is not consciousness itself, then the r_____212) cause of depression is also a d_____213) of our state of consciousness: a consciousness that has lost its sense of self and the meaning of life. Such a d_____214) of consciousness may m_____215) itself in the form of depression.

전통적인 의학은 우울증이 뇌의 신경 전달 물질의 불균형으로 인해 발생한다고 오랫동안 믿어 왔다. 그러나 이 설명에는 중대한 문제가 있다. 이것은 왜냐하면 뇌 속 물질의 불균형은 우울증의 원인이 아니라 그것의 결과이기 때문이다. 다시 말해서, 우울증이 세로토닌이나 노르아드레날린과 같은 뇌의 물질의 감소를 유발하는 것이지 뇌의 물질의 감소가 우울증을 유발하는 것이 아니다. 이 수정된 인과 관계에서, 핵심은 우울증을 의식의 문제로 재구성하는 것이다. 우리의 의식은 뇌의 기능을 넘어서는 보다 근본적인 실체이다. 뇌는 의식의 기관에 지나지 않는다. 만약 그것이 의식 그 자체가 아니라면, 우울증의 근본 원인 역시 우리의 의식 상태의 왜곡이며 즉, 자아감과 삶의 의미를 상실한 의식이다. 그러한 의식의 질환이 우울증의 형태로 명백히 나타날 수 있다.

2024_H1_11_38

The common a_____216) of human nature that f_____217) around in society are generally a m_____218) of a_____219) , tales and sometimes p_____220) silliness. However, p_____221) is different. It is the b_____222) of science that is d_____223) to understanding people: how and why we act as we do; why we see things as we do; and how we i_____224) with one another. The key word here is 'science.' Psychologists don't depend on o_____225) and h_____226) , or the generally accepted views of society at the time, or even the considered opinions of deep thinkers. Instead, they look for evidence, to make sure that psychological ideas are f_____227) based, and not just d_____228) from generally held beliefs or assumptions. In addition to this e_____229) approach, psychology deals with f_____230) processes and principles that g_____231) our rich cultural and social d_____232) , as well as those shared by all human beings. These are what m_____233) psychology is all about.

사회에 떠도는 인간 본성에 대한 흔한 설명은 일반적으로 가정, 이야기, 그리고 때로는 순전한 어리석음의 혼합이다, 그러나, 심리학은 다르다. 그것은 사람들을 이해하는, 즉 우리가 어떻게 그리고 왜 행동하는 대로 행동하는지, 우리가 왜 보는 대로 사물을 보는 지, 그리고 우리가 어떻게 서로 상호 작용하는지를 이해하는 데 전념하는 과학 분야이다. 여기서 핵심어는 '과학'이다. 심리학자들은 의견과 소문, 혹은 당대의 사회에서 일반적으로 받아들여지는 견해, 혹은 심지어 심오한 사상가들의 숙고된 의견에 의존하지 않는다. 대신에 그들은 심리학적 개념이 단지 일반적으로 받아들여지는 신념이나 가정에서 도출된 것이 아니라, 확고하게 기반을 두고 있는지 확신하기 위해 증거를 찾는다. 이러한 증거 기반 접근법에 더하여 심리학은 모든 인간에 의해 공유되는 근본적인 과정과 원리뿐만 아니라, 우리의 풍부한 문화적 사회적 다양성을 만들어 내는 것들을 다룬다. 이것들은 현대 심리학이 무엇인지 보여 준다.

2024_H1_11_39

Life is what p_____234) might call a 'high-dimensional system,' which is their f_____235) way of saying that there's a lot going on. In just a single cell, the number of possible interactions between different m_____236) is enormous. Such a system can only hope to be s_____237) if only a smaller number of c_____238) ways of being may e_____239) . For example, it is only a limited number of tissues and body shapes that may result from the development of a human e_____240) . In 1942, the b_____241) Conrad Waddington called this d_____242) narrowing of outcomes c_____243) . The o_____244) may switch between a small number of well-defined possible s_____245) , but can't exist in r_____246) states in between them, rather as a ball in a r_____247) landscape must roll to the bottom of one v_____248) or another. We'll see that this is true also of health and d_____249) : there are many causes of illness, but their m_____250) at the physiological and s_____251) levels are often s_____252) similar.

생명은 물리학자들이 '고차원 시스템'이라고 부를 수 있는 것인데 이는 많은 일이 발생하고 있다고 말하는 그들의 멋진 방식이다. 단 하나의 세포 내에서도 여러 분자 간의 가능한 상호 작용의 수는 매우 크다. 이러한 시스템은 더 적은 수의 존재의 집합적인 방식이 나타날 때만 오직 안정적이기를 기대할 수 있다. 예를 들어 인간 배아의 발달로부터 나올 수 있는 것은 오직 제한된 수의 조직과 신체 형태이다. 1942년에 생물학자 Conrad Waddington은 이러한 극적인 결과의 축소를 '운하화'라고 불렀다. 오히려 울퉁불퉁한 경관에 있는 공이 이 계곡 혹은 또 다른 계곡의 바닥으로 반드시 굴러가야 하는 것처럼, 유기체는 적은 수의 명확하게 정의된 가능한 상태 사이에서 바뀔 수 있지만 그것들 사이에 있는 무작위의 상태로 존재할 수는 없다. 우리는 이것이 건강과 질병에도 적용된다는 것을 알게 될 것이다. 즉 질병의 많은 원인이 있지만, 그것들의 생리적이고 증상적인 수준에서의 발현은 종종 놀랍도록 유사하다.

2024_H1_11_40

P_____253) a child may not be effective due to what Álvaro Bilbao, a neuropsychologist, calls 'trick-punishments.' A trick-punishment is a s_____254), a moment of anger or a punishment in the most classic sense of the word. Instead of d_____255) the child from doing something, it encourages them to do it. For example, Hugh learns that when he hits his little brother, his mother scolds him. For a child who feels lonely, being scolded is much better than feeling i_____256), so he will continue to hit his brother. In this case, his mother would be better a_____257) a different s_____258). For instance, she could c_____259) Hugh when he has not hit his brother for a certain length of time. The mother clearly cannot allow the child to hit his little brother, but instead of constantly pointing out the negatives, she can choose to reward the p_____260). In this way, any parent can a_____261) trick-punishments.

아이를 벌주는 것은 신경심리학자 Álvaro Bilbao가 '트릭 처벌'이라고 부르는 것으로 인해 효과적이지 않을 수 있다. 트릭 처벌은 꾸짖음, 순간의 화 혹은 (처벌이라는) 단어의 가장 전형적인 의미에서의 처벌이다. 아이가 무언가를 하는 것을 단념시키는 대신 트릭 처벌은 그들이 그것을 하도록 장려한다. 예를 들어 Hugh는 그가 자신의 남동생을 때릴 때 그의 어머니가 그를 꾸짖는다는 것을 배운다. 외로움을 느끼는 아이에게는 꾸중을 듣는 것이 눈에 띄지 않는다고 느끼는 것보다 훨씬 나아서 그는 그의 남동생을 때리는 것을 계속할 것이다. 이 경우에, 그의 어머니는 다른 전략을 채택하는 것이 보다 나을 것이다. 예를 들어 그녀는 Hugh가 그의 남동생을 일정 기간 동안 때리지 않았을 때 그를 자랑스러워해 줄 수 있다. 어머니는 분명 아이가 그의 남동생을 때리는 것을 내버려둘 수 없고, 그녀는 부정적 측면을 계속 지적하는 대신에 긍정적 측면을 보상하는 것을 선택할 수 있다. 이렇게 어느 부모도 트릭 처벌을 피할 수 있다.

2024_H1_11_41,42

From an early age, we a_____262) purpose to objects and events, p_____263) this reasoning to r_____264) chance. Children a_____265), for instance, that p_____266) rocks are that way because they don't want you to sit on them. When we e_____267) something, we first need to d_____268) what sort of thing it is. I_____269) objects and plants g_____270) do not move and can be e_____271) from physics alone. However, by a_____272) i_____273) to animals and even objects, we are able to make fast decisions about the likely behaviour of that being. This was e_____274) in our hunter-gatherer days to avoid being eaten by predators.

The a_____275) Stewart Guthrie made the point that survival in our e_____276) past meant that we interpret a_____277) objects as agents with human mental characteristics, as those are the mental processes which we understand. Ambiguous events are caused by such a_____278). This results in a p_____279) system strongly b_____280) towards a_____281). Therefore, we tend to assume i_____282) even where there is none. This would have arisen as a survival m_____283). If a lion is about to attack you, you need to react quickly, given its p_____284) intention to kill you. By the time you have realized that the design of its teeth and claws could kill you, you are dead. So, assuming i_____285), without detailed design a_____286) or understanding of the physics, has saved your life.

어릴 때부터 우리는 사물과 사건에 목적을 부여하며, 무작위적인 우연보다 이러한 논리를 선호한다. 예를 들어 뾰족한 돌은 아이들이 그 위에 앉기를 원치 않기 때문에 그것이 그렇게 생겼다고 그들(아이들)은 가정한다. 우리가 무언가를 마주칠 때 우리는 먼저 그것이 어떤 종류의 것인지 결정할 필요가 있다. 무생물과 식물은 일반적으로 움직이지 않으며 물리적 현상만으로 평가될 수 있다. 그러나 동물과 심지어 사물도 의도가 있다고 생각함으로써 우리는 그 존재가 할 것 같은 행동에 대해 빠른 결정을 내릴 수 있다. 이는 우리의 수렵 채집 시절에 포식자에게 잡아먹히는 것을 피하기 위해 필수적이었다.
인류학자 Stewart Guthrie는 인간의 정신적 특성이 우리가 이해하는 정신 과정이기 때문에, 우리의 진화상 과거에서 생존이란 우리가 모호한 사물을 인간의 정신적 특성을 가진 행위자로 해석하는 것을 의미한다고 주장했다. 모호한 사건은 이러한 행위자에 의해 발생한다. 이는 의인화에 강하게 편향된 지각 체계로 귀결된다. 그러므로, 우리는 의도가 없는 곳에서도 의도를 가정하는 경향이 있다. 이는 생존 메커니즘으로 발생해 왔을 것이다. 만약 사자가 당신을 막 공격하려 한다면 당신을 죽이려는 그것의 가능한 의도를 고려하여 당신은 빠르게 반응할 필요가 있다. 당신이 그것의 이빨과 발톱의 구조가 당신을 죽일 수 있다는 것을 깨달았을 즈음 당신은 죽어 있다. 따라서 상세한 구조 분석 또는 물리적 현상의 이해 없이 의도를 부여하는 것이 당신의 목숨을 구해 왔다.

2024_H1_43,44,45

Once long ago, deep in the Himalayas, there lived a little panda. He was as ordinary as all the other pandas. He was completely white from head to toe. His two big ears, his four furry feet and his cute round nose were all frosty white, leaving him feeling ordinary and sad. Unlike the cheerful and c_____287) pandas around him, he desired to be d_____288) , special, and unique. Driven by the desire for uniqueness, the little panda sought i_____289) from his distant cousin, a giant white panda covered with heavenly black p_____290) . But the cousin revealed the patches were from an u_____291) encounter with mud, and he disliked them. Disappointed, the little panda walked home. On his way, he met a red-feathered p_____292) , who explained he turned red from eating wild berries. The little panda changed his path and hurried to the nearest berry bush, g_____293) eating a mouthful of juicy red berries. However, they were so bitter he couldn't swallow even one. At dusk, he finally got home and slowly climbed his favorite bamboo tree. There, he discovered a strange black and red flower with a sweet s_____294) that t_____295) him to eat all its blossoms. The following morning, under sunny skies, the little panda felt r_____296) better. During breakfast, he found the other pandas chatting e_____297) and asked why. They burst into laughter, exclaiming, "Look at yourself!" Glancing down, he discovered his once white fur was now stained jet black and glowing red. He was o_____298) and realized that, rather than by i_____299) others, his wishes can come true from unexpected places and g_____300) experiences.

옛날에 히말라야 산맥 깊숙한 곳에 작은 판다가 살았다. 그는 다른 모든 판다들만큼 평범했다. 그는 머리부터 발끝까지 전부 하얬다. 그의 두 개의 큰 귀, 네 개의 털 많은 발, 그리고 귀여운 둥근 코는 모두 서리처럼 하얘서 그가 평범하고 슬프게 느끼게 하였다. 그의 주위에 있는 명랑하고 만족스러운 판다들과 달리 그는 특이하고 특별하며 독특해지기를 갈망했다. 독특함에 대한 열망에 사로잡혀 작은 판다는 그의 먼 사촌인 멋진 검은 반점으로 뒤덮인 거대한 흰 판다로부터 영감을 찾으려 했다. 그러나 사촌은 그 반점이 진흙과 의도치 않게 접촉한 결과이며, 그는 그것(반점)을 싫어한다고 밝혔다. 실망한 채로 작은 판다는 집으로 걸어갔다. 가는 길에 그는 붉은 깃털을 가진 공작새를 만났는데 그 공작새는 그가 야생 베리를 먹어서 붉게 변했다고 설명했다. 작은 판다는 경로를 바꾸어 가장 가까운 베리 덤불로 서둘러 가서, 탐욕스럽게 한입 가득 즙이 많은 빨간 베리를 먹었다. 하지만 그것들은 너무 써서 그는 한 개도 삼킬 수 없었다. 해질 무렵 그는 마침내 집에 도착했고 그가 가장 좋아하는 대나무에 천천히 올라갔다. 그곳에서 그가 그것의 모든 꽃을 먹도록 유혹하는 달콤한 향기를 가진 기묘한 검고 붉은 꽃을 발견하였다. 다음 날 아침 맑은 하늘 아래에서 작은 판다는 기분이 매우 좋아졌다. 아침 식사 중에 그는 다른 판다들이 신나게 수다를 떨고 있는 것을 발견하고 이유를 물어보았다. 그들은 웃음을 터뜨리며 "네 자신을 좀 봐!"라고 외쳤다. 아래를 흘긋 보고, 그는 한때 하얬던 자신의 털이 이제 새까맣고 빛나는 붉은색으로 얼룩져 있다는 것을 발견했다. 그는 매우 기뻐했고 그의 소원이 남들을 모방하기보다는 예상치 못한 곳과 진정한 경험으로부터 실현될 수 있음을 깨달았다.

2024 고1 11월 모의고사   ❷ 회차 :   점 / 300점

❶ voca   ❷ text   ❸ [/]   ④ _____   ❺ quiz 1   ❻ quiz 2   ❼ quiz 3   ❽ quiz 4   ❾ quiz 5

2024_H1_11_18

To the State Education Department,
I am writing with r_____1) to the state's f_____2) for the construction project at Fort Montgomery High School. Our school needs a_____3) spaces to p_____4) a fully functional Art and Library Media Center to serve our students in a more meaningful way. D_____5) s_____6) all required documentation for funding to your department in April 2024, we have not yet received any n_____7) from your department. A d_____8) in the process can carry considerable consequences related to the school's budgetary c_____9) and schedule. Therefore, in order to p_____10) with our project, we request you n_____11) us of the review result r_____12) the s_____13) documentation. I look forward to hearing from you.
Respectfully, Clara Smith Principal, Fort Montgomery High School

2024_H1_11_19

As I waited outside the locker room after a h_____14) basketball game, the coach called out to me, "David, walk with me." I f_____15) he was going to tell me something important. He was going to select me to be the captain of the team, the leader I had always wanted to be. My heart was racing with a_____16) . But when his next words hit my ears, everything changed. "We're going to have to send you home," he said c_____17) . "I don't think you are going to make it." I couldn't believe his decision. I tried to hold it together, but inside I was falling apart. A car would be waiting tomorrow morning to take me home. And just like that, it was over.

2024_H1_11_20

For many of us, making time for exercise is a continuing challenge. Between work c_____18) and family o_____19) , it often feels like there's no room in our packed schedules for a d_____ _20) workout. But what if the workout came to you, right in the m_____21) of your daily r_____22) ? That's where the beauty of i_____23) mini-exercises into household chores comes into play. Let's be r_____24) ; chores are i_____25) . Whether it's washing dishes or taking out the trash, these tasks are an e_____26) part of daily life. But rather than viewing chores as p_____27) o_____28) activities, why not s_____29) these moments as opportunities for p_____30) activity? For instance, practice squats or e_____31) in some wall push-ups as you wait for your morning kettle to boil. I_____32) quick exercises into your daily chores can improve your health.

2024_H1_11_21

When we see something, we **n**_____ 33) and **a**_____ 34) break it up into shapes, colors, and **c**_____ 35) that we have learned through education. We **r**_____ 36) what we see through the lens of everything we know. We **r**_____ 37) memories rather than **r**_____ 38) the video from memory. This is a useful **t**_____ 39) . It's a more efficient way to store information—a bit like an **o**_____ 40) image **c**_____ 41) algorithm such as JPG, rather than storing a raw **b**_____ 42) image file. People who **l**_____ 43) this ability and remember everything in perfect detail struggle to **g**_____ 44) , learn, and make connections between what they have learned. But **r**_____ 45) the world as **a**_____ 46) ideas and features comes at a cost of seeing the world as it is. Instead, we see the world through our **a**_____ 47) , motivations, and past experiences. The discovery that our memories are reconstructed through **a**_____ 48) representations rather than played back like a movie completely undermined the legal **p**_____ 49) of eyewitness **t**_____ 50) . Seeing is not believing.

2024_H1_11_22

In his Cornell laboratory, David Dunning **c**_____ 51) experimental tests of eyewitness **t**_____ 52) and found evidence that a careful **d**_____ 53) of **f**_____ 54) features and a detailed discussion of selection **p**_____ 55) can actually be a sign of an *inaccurate* identification. It's when people find themselves **u**_____ 56) to explain why they **r**_____ 57) the person, saying things like "his face just popped out at me," that they **t**_____ 58) to be accurate more often. Sometimes our first, **i**_____ 59) , **a**_____ 60) reaction to a situation is the truest interpretation of what our mind is telling us. That very first impression can also be more **a**_____ 61) about the world than the **d**_____ 62) , reasoned self-narrative can be. In his book *Blink*, Malcolm Gladwell describes a variety of studies in psychology and behavioral economics that **d**_____ 63) the superior performance of relatively **u**_____ 64) first guesses compared to logical step-by-step **j**_____ 65) for a decision.

2024_H1_11_23

Many forms of research lead naturally to **q**_____ 66) data. A study of happiness might measure the number of times someone smiles during an **i**_____ 67) , and a study of memory might measure the number of items an individual can **r**_____ 68) after one, five, and ten minutes. Asking people how many times in a year they are sad will also **y**_____ 69) **q**_____ 70) data, but it might not be **r**_____ 71) . Respondents' **r**_____ 72) may be inaccurate, and their definitions of 'sad' could **v**_____ 73) widely. But asking "How many times in the past year were you sad enough to call in sick to work?" **p**_____ 74) a **c**_____ 75) answer. Similarly, instead of asking people to rate how bad a **p**_____ 76) they are, ask, "How many of your **u**_____ 77) bills are you currently late in paying, even though you can afford to pay them?" Questions that seek concrete responses help make **a**_____ 78) concepts clearer and **e**_____ 79) **c**_____ 80) from one study to the next.

2024_H1_11_24

The **e**_____81) of AI is often **a**_____82) with the concept of **s**_____83) . **S**_____84) refers to the point at which AI **e**_____85) human intelligence. After that point, it is predicted that AI will repeatedly improve itself and **e**_____86) at an accelerated **p**_____87) . When AI becomes self-aware and **p**_____88) its own goals, it will be a **c**_____89) being, not just a machine. AI and human **c**_____90) will then begin to evolve together. Our **c**_____91) will evolve to new **d**_____92) through our **i**_____93) with AI, which will provide us with **i**_____94) stimulation and inspire new **i**_____95) and creativity. **C**_____96) , our consciousness also has a **s**_____97) impact on the evolution of AI. The direction of AI's evolution will depend greatly on what values and **e**_____98) we **i**_____99) into AI. We need to see our relationship with AI as a mutual **c**_____100) of conscious beings, recognizing its rights and supporting the evolution of its consciousness.

2024_H1_11_29

Digital technologies are **e**_____101) related to metaphors, but **d**_____102) metaphors are different from **l**_____103) ones in important ways. Linguistic metaphors are **p**_____104) , in the sense that the audience needs to choose to actively enter the world **p**_____105) by **m**_____106) . In the Shakespearean metaphor "time is a beggar," the audience is **u**_____107) to understand the metaphor without **c**_____108) effort and without further engaging Shakespeare's **p**_____109) . Technological metaphors, on the other hand, are active and often imposing) in the sense that they are realized in digital **a**_____110) that are actively doing things, forcefully changing a user's meaning **h**_____111) . Technological creators cannot generally **a**_____112) to require their **p**_____113) audience to wonder how the metaphor works; normally the selling point is that the usefulness of the technology is obvious at first glance. Shakespeare, on the other hand, is beloved in part because the meaning of his works is not immediately obvious and requires some thought on the part of the audience.

2024_H1_11_30

Herbert Simon won his Nobel Prize for recognizing our **l**_____114) in information, time, and **c**_____115) capacity. As we lack the resources to compute answers independently, we **d**_____116) the **c**_____117) across the population and solve the answer slowly, generation by generation. Then all we have to do is socially learn the right answers. You don't need to understand how your computer or toilet works; you just need to be able to use the **i**_____118) and flush. All that needs to be **t**_____119) is which button to push —essentially how to interact with technologies rather than how they work. And so instead of holding more information than we have mental **c**_____120) for and indeed need to know, we could **d**_____121) our large brains to a small piece of a giant calculation. We understand things well enough to **b**_____122) from them, but all the while we are making small calculations that **c**_____123) to a larger whole. We are just doing our part in a larger computation for our societies' collective brains.

2024_H1_11_31

The best **d**_____ ¹²⁴⁾ most species of octopus have is to stay hidden as much as possible and do their own hunting at night. So to find one in full view in the shallows in daylight was a surprise for two Australian underwater photographers. Actually, what they saw at first was a **f**_____ ¹²⁵⁾ . It was only when they looked again that they saw a medium-sized octopus, with all eight of its arms folded and its two eyes staring upwards to create the **i**_____ ¹²⁶⁾ . An octopus has a big brain, excellent eyesight and the ability to change colour and pattern, and this one was using these **a**_____ ¹²⁷⁾ to turn itself into a completely different creature. Many more of this species have been found since then, and there are now photographs of octopuses that could be said to be **t**_____ ¹²⁸⁾ into sea snakes. And while they **m**_____ ¹²⁹⁾ , they hunt —producing the **s**_____ ¹³⁰⁾ of, say, a **f**_____ ¹³¹⁾ suddenly developing an octopodian arm, sticking it down a hole and grabbing whatever's hiding there.

2024_H1_11_32

How much we **s**_____ ¹³²⁾ relates to how we **f**_____ ¹³³⁾ the pain in our mind. When 1500m runners push themselves into extreme pain to win a race—their muscles screaming and their lungs exploding with oxygen **d**_____ ¹³⁴⁾ , they don't **p**_____ ¹³⁵⁾ suffer much. In fact, ultra-marathon runners—those people who are crazy enough to push themselves beyond the normal **b**_____ ¹³⁶⁾ of human **e**_____ ¹³⁷⁾ , covering distances of 50-100km or more over many hours, talk about making friends with their pain. When a patient has paid for some form of passive back pain **t**_____ ¹³⁸⁾ and the **p**_____ ¹³⁹⁾ pushes deeply into a painful part of a patient's back to **m**_____ ¹⁴⁰⁾ it, the patient calls that good pain if he or she believes this type of deep pressure treatment will be of value, even though the practitioner is pushing right into the patient's **s**_____ _¹⁴¹⁾ tissues.

2024_H1_11_33

When I worked for a large electronics company that manufactured laser and inkjet-printers, I soon discovered why there are often three **v**_____ ¹⁴²⁾ of many consumer goods. If the **m**_____ ¹⁴³⁾ makes only one version of its product, people who bought it might have been **w**_____ ¹⁴⁴⁾ to spend more money, so the company is losing some **i**_____ ¹⁴⁵⁾ . If the company offers two versions, one with more **f**_____ ¹⁴⁶⁾ and more expensive than the other, people will compare the two models and still buy the less expensive one. But if the company **i**_____ ¹⁴⁷⁾ a third model with even more features and more expensive than the other two, sales of the second model go up; many people like the features of the most expensive model, but not the price. The middle item has more features than the least expensive one, and it is less expensive than the fanciest model. They buy the middle item, **u**_____ ¹⁴⁸⁾ that they have been **m**_____ ¹⁴⁹⁾ by the **p**_____ ¹⁵⁰⁾ of the higher-priced item.

2024_H1_11_34

On-screen, climate disaster is everywhere you look, but the s_____151) of the world's climate transformation may just as quickly e_____152) the climate-fiction g_____153) — indeed eliminate any effort to tell the story of warming, which could grow too large and too o_____154) even for Hollywood. You can tell stories 'about' climate change while it still seems a m_____155) feature of human life. But when the temperature rises by three or four more degrees, hardly anyone will be able to feel i_____156) from its impacts. And so as climate change e_____157) across the horizon, it may c_____158) to be a story. Why watch or read climate fiction about the world you can see p_____159) out your own window? At the moment, stories illustrating global warming can still offer an e_____160) pleasure, even if that p_____161) often comes in the form of horror. But when we can no longer pretend that climate suffering is d_____162) — in time or in place — we will stop pretending about it and start pretending within it.

2024_H1_11_35

Today, the water c_____163) is p_____164) — which is to say, not i_____165) or beyond our capacity to fix — and, therefore, functionally e_____166) . That is one reason it is nevertheless d_____167) : an a_____168) resource made scarce through governmental n_____169) and indifference, bad i_____170) and c_____171) , and careless u_____172) . There is no need for a water crisis, in other words, but we have one anyway, and aren't doing much to a_____173) it. Some cities lose more water to l_____174) than they deliver to homes: even in the United States, leaks and theft a_____175) for an estimated loss of 16 percent of freshwater; in Brazil, the estimate is 40 percent. Seen in both cases, as everywhere, the s_____176) s_____177) clearly highlights have and have not i_____178) , leaving 2.1 billion people without safe drinking water and 4.5 billion without proper s_____179) worldwide.

2024_H1_11_36

As individuals, our ability to t_____180) depended on how well we navigated relationships in a group. If the group v_____181) us, we could c_____182) on support, resources, and probably a m_____183) . If it didn't, we might get none of these m_____184) . It was a matter of survival, physically and g_____185) . Over millions of years, the p_____186) selected for people who are s_____187) to and skilled at m_____188) their s_____189) . The result was the development of a t_____190) to u_____191) monitor how other people in our community p_____192) us. We process that information in the form of s_____193) and such related emotions as pride, shame, or i_____194) . These emotions c_____195) us to do more of what makes our community value us and less of what doesn't. And, c_____196) , they are meant to make that motivation feel like it is coming from within. If we realized, on a conscious level, that we were responding to social pressure, our performance might come off as g_____197) or c_____198) , making it less p_____199) .

2024_H1_11_37

C_____²⁰⁰⁾ medicine has long believed that d_____²⁰¹⁾ is caused by an i_____²⁰²⁾ of n_____²⁰³⁾ in the brain. However, there is a major problem with this explanation. This is because the imbalance of s_____²⁰⁴⁾ in the brain is a consequence of depression, not its cause. In other words, depression causes a decrease in brain substances such as s_____²⁰⁵⁾ and n_____²⁰⁶⁾, not a decrease in brain substances causes depression. In this r_____²⁰⁷⁾ cause-and-effect, the key is to r_____²⁰⁸⁾ depression as a problem of consciousness. Our consciousness is a more f_____²⁰⁹⁾ e_____²¹⁰⁾ that goes beyond the functioning of the brain. The brain is no more than an o_____²¹¹⁾ of consciousness. If it is not consciousness itself, then the r_____²¹²⁾ cause of depression is also a d_____²¹³⁾ of our state of consciousness: a consciousness that has lost its sense of self and the meaning of life. Such a d_____²¹⁴⁾ of consciousness may m_____²¹⁵⁾ itself in the form of depression.

2024_H1_11_38

The common a_____²¹⁶⁾ of human nature that f_____²¹⁷⁾ around in society are generally a m_____²¹⁸⁾ of a_____²¹⁹⁾, tales and sometimes p_____²²⁰⁾ silliness. However, p_____²²¹⁾ is different. It is the b_____²²²⁾ of science that is d_____²²³⁾ to understanding people: how and why we act as we do; why we see things as we do; and how we i_____²²⁴⁾ with one another. The key word here is 'science.' Psychologists don't depend on o_____²²⁵⁾ and h_____²²⁶⁾, or the generally accepted views of society at the time, or even the considered opinions of deep thinkers. Instead, they look for evidence, to make sure that psychological ideas are f_____²²⁷⁾ based, and not just d_____²²⁸⁾ from generally held beliefs or assumptions. In addition to this e_____²²⁹⁾ approach, psychology deals with f_____²³⁰⁾ processes and principles that g_____²³¹⁾ our rich cultural and social d_____²³²⁾, as well as those shared by all human beings. These are what m_____²³³⁾ psychology is all about.

2024_H1_11_39

Life is what p_____²³⁴⁾ might call a 'high-dimensional system,' which is their f_____²³⁵⁾ way of saying that there's a lot going on. In just a single cell, the number of possible interactions between different m_____²³⁶⁾ is enormous. Such a system can only hope to be s_____²³⁷⁾ if only a smaller number of c_____²³⁸⁾ ways of being may e_____²³⁹⁾. For example, it is only a limited number of tissues and body shapes that may result from the development of a human e_____²⁴⁰⁾. In 1942, the b_____²⁴¹⁾ Conrad Waddington called this d_____²⁴²⁾ narrowing of outcomes c_____²⁴³⁾. The o_____²⁴⁴⁾ may switch between a small number of well-defined possible s_____²⁴⁵⁾, but can't exist in r_____²⁴⁶⁾ states in between them, rather as a ball in a r_____²⁴⁷⁾ landscape must roll to the bottom of one v_____²⁴⁸⁾ or another. We'll see that this is true also of health and d_____²⁴⁹⁾: there are many causes of illness, but their m_____²⁵⁰⁾ at the physiological and s_____²⁵¹⁾ levels are often s_____²⁵²⁾ similar.

2024_H1_11_40

P_____253) a child may not be effective due to what Álvaro Bilbao, a neuropsychologist, calls 'trick-punishments.' A trick-punishment is a s_____254) , a moment of anger or a punishment in the most classic sense of the word. Instead of d_____255) the child from doing something, it encourages them to do it. For example, Hugh learns that when he hits his little brother, his mother scolds him. For a child who feels lonely, being scolded is much better than feeling i_____256) , so he will continue to hit his brother. In this case, his mother would be better a_____257) a different s_____258) . For instance, she could c_____259) Hugh when he has not hit his brother for a certain length of time. The mother clearly cannot allow the child to hit his little brother, but instead of constantly pointing out the negatives, she can choose to reward the p_____260) . In this way, any parent can a_____261) trick-punishments.

2024_H1_11_41,42

From an early age, we a_____262) purpose to objects and events, p_____263) this reasoning to r_____264) chance. Children a_____265) , for instance, that p_____266) rocks are that way because they don't want you to sit on them. When we e_____267) something, we first need to d_____268) what sort of thing it is. I_____269) objects and plants g_____270) do not move and can be e_____271) from physics alone. However, by a_____272) i_____273) to animals and even objects, we are able to make fast decisions about the likely behaviour of that being. This was e_____274) in our hunter-gatherer days to avoid being eaten by predators.

The a_____275) Stewart Guthrie made the point that survival in our e_____276) past meant that we interpret a_____277) objects as agents with human mental characteristics, as those are the mental processes which we understand. Ambiguous events are caused by such a_____278) . This results in a p_____279) system strongly b_____280) towards a_____281) . Therefore, we tend to assume i_____282) even where there is none. This would have arisen as a survival m_____283) . If a lion is about to attack you, you need to react quickly, given its p_____284) intention to kill you. By the time you have realized that the design of its teeth and claws could kill you, you are dead. So, assuming i_____285) , without detailed design a_____286) or understanding of the physics, has saved your life.

2024_H1_43,44,45

Once long ago, deep in the Himalayas, there lived a little panda. He was as ordinary as all the other pandas. He was completely white from head to toe. His two big ears, his four furry feet and his cute round nose were all frosty white, leaving him feeling ordinary and sad. Unlike the cheerful and c_____287) pandas around him, he desired to be d_____288) , special, and unique. Driven by the desire for uniqueness, the little panda sought i_____289) from his distant cousin, a giant white panda covered with heavenly black p_____290) . But the cousin revealed the patches were from an u_____291) encounter with mud, and he disliked them. Disappointed, the little panda walked home. On his way, he met a red-feathered p_____292) , who explained he turned red from eating wild berries. The little panda changed his path and hurried to the nearest berry bush, g_____293) eating a mouthful of juicy red berries. However, they were so bitter he couldn't swallow even one. At dusk, he finally got home and slowly climbed his favorite bamboo tree. There, he discovered a strange black and red flower with a sweet s_____294) that t_____295) him to eat all its blossoms. The following morning, under sunny skies, the little panda felt r_____296) better. During breakfast, he found the other pandas chatting e_____297) and asked why. They burst into laughter, exclaiming, "Look at yourself!" Glancing down, he discovered his once white fur was now stained jet black and glowing red. He was o_____298) and realized that, rather than by i_____299) others, his wishes can come true from unexpected places and g_____300) experiences.

2024 고1 11월 모의고사

☑ 다음 문맥 상 문장들의 적절한 순서를 쓰시오.

1. 18[1)]

(A) A delay in the process can carry considerable consequences related to the school's budgetary constraints and schedule. Therefore, in order to proceed with our project, we request you notify us of the review result regarding the submitted documentation.

(B) I look forward to hearing from you. Respectfully, Clara Smith Principal, Fort Montgomery High School

(C) Our school needs additional spaces to provide a fully functional Art and Library Media Center to serve our students in a more meaningful way. Despite submitting all required documentation for funding to your department in April 2024, we have not yet received any notification from your department.

(D) To the State Education Department,

(E) I am writing with regard to the state's funding for the construction project at Fort Montgomery High School.

2. 19[2)]

(A) But when his next words hit my ears, everything changed. "We're going to have to send you home," he said coldly.

(B) He was going to select me to be the captain of the team, the leader I had always wanted to be. My heart was racing with anticipation.

(C) "I don't think you are going to make it." I couldn't believe his decision.

(D) As I waited outside the locker room after a hard-fought basketball game, the coach called out to me, "David, walk with me." I figured he was going to tell me something important.

(E) I tried to hold it together, but inside I was falling apart. A car would be waiting tomorrow morning to take me home. And just like that, it was over.

3. 20[3)]

(A) Whether it's washing dishes or taking out the trash, these tasks are an essential part of daily life. But rather than viewing chores as purely obligatory activities, why not seize these moments as opportunities for physical activity?

(B) That's where the beauty of integrating mini-exercises into household chores comes into play. Let's be realistic; chores are inevitable.

(C) For many of us, making time for exercise is a continuing challenge.

(D) Between work commitments and family obligations, it often feels like there's no room in our packed schedules for a dedicated workout. But what if the workout came to you, right in the midst of your daily routine?

(E) For instance, practice squats or engage in some wall push-ups as you wait for your morning kettle to boil. Incorporating quick exercises into your daily chores can improve your health.

4. 21[4]

(A) It's a more efficient way to store information — a bit like an optimal image compression algorithm such as JPG, rather than storing a raw bitmap image file. People who lack this ability and remember everything in perfect detail struggle to generalize, learn, and make connections between what they have learned.

(B) When we see something, we naturally and automatically break it up into shapes, colors, and concepts that we have learned through education. We recode what we see through the lens of everything we know.

(C) But representing the world as abstract ideas and features comes at a cost of seeing the world as it is. Instead, we see the world through our assumptions, motivations, and past experiences.

(D) The discovery that our memories are reconstructed through abstract representations rather than played back like a movie completely undermined the legal primacy of eyewitness testimony. Seeing is not believing.

(E) We reconstruct memories rather than retrieving the video from memory. This is a useful trait.

5. 22[5]

(A) It's when people find themselves unable to explain why they recognize the person, saying things like "his face just popped out at me," that they tend to be accurate more often.

(B) That very first impression can also be more accurate about the world than the deliberative, reasoned self-narrative can be.

(C) In his book Blink, Malcolm Gladwell describes a variety of studies in psychology and behavioral economics that demonstrate the superior performance of relatively unconscious first guesses compared to logical step-by-step justifications for a decision.

(D) In his Cornell laboratory, David Dunning conducted experimental tests of eyewitness testimony and found evidence that a careful deliberation of facial features and a detailed discussion of selection procedures can actually be a sign of an inaccurate identification.

(E) Sometimes our first, immediate, automatic reaction to a situation is the truest interpretation of what our mind is telling us.

6. 23[6]

(A) A study of happiness might measure the number of times someone smiles during an interaction, and a study of memory might measure the number of items an individual can recall after one, five, and ten minutes.

(B) Asking people how many times in a year they are sad will also yield quantitative data, but it might not be reliable.

(C) Similarly, instead of asking people to rate how bad a procrastinator they are, ask, "How many of your utility bills are you currently late in paying, even though you can afford to pay them?" Questions that seek concrete responses help make abstract concepts clearer and ensure consistency from one study to the next.

(D) Many forms of research lead naturally to quantitative data.

(E) Respondents' recollections may be inaccurate, and their definitions of 'sad' could vary widely. But asking "How many times in the past year were you sad enough to call in sick to work?" prompts a concrete answer.

7. 24⁷⁾

(A) The direction of AI's evolution will depend greatly on what values and ethics we incorporate into AI. We need to see our relationship with AI as a mutual coexistence of conscious beings, recognizing its rights and supporting the evolution of its consciousness.

(B) Singularity refers to the point at which AI exceeds human intelligence. After that point, it is predicted that AI will repeatedly improve itself and evolve at an accelerated pace.

(C) Our consciousness will evolve to new dimensions through our interactions with AI, which will provide us with intellectual stimulation and inspire new insights and creativity. Conversely, our consciousness also has a significant impact on the evolution of AI.

(D) When AI becomes self-aware and pursues its own goals, it will be a conscious being, not just a machine. AI and human consciousness will then begin to evolve together.

(E) The evolution of AI is often associated with the concept of singularity.

8. 26⁸⁾

(A) Kirkland spent his weeks shooting day-to-day life across the United States and his weekends in exotic locations. His photo essays could run up to a dozen pages and were seen by more than half of all Americans.

(B) When he was young, he eagerly awaited the weekly arrival of Life magazine and discussed the photographs the magazine contained with his father.

(C) Believing that he would have better career prospects, Kirkland moved to the United States after graduating from high school and found work at a photography studio.

(D) Douglas Kirkland, known for his highly artistic portraits of Hollywood celebrities, was born in Toronto, Canada.

(E) When Look magazine hired him at age 24, he became their second-youngest photographer ever. His photos taken of Marilyn Monroe in 1961 became iconic almost instantly.

9. 29⁹⁾

(A) Technological metaphors, on the other hand, are active (and often imposing) in the sense that they are realized in digital artifacts that are actively doing things, forcefully changing a user's meaning horizon.

(B) Linguistic metaphors are passive, in the sense that the audience needs to choose to actively enter the world proposed by metaphor.

(C) Digital technologies are essentially related to metaphors, but digital metaphors are different from linguistic ones in important ways.

(D) Technological creators cannot generally afford to require their potential audience to wonder how the metaphor works; normally the selling point is that the usefulness of the technology is obvious at first glance. Shakespeare, on the other hand, is beloved in part because the meaning of his works is not immediately obvious and requires some thought on the part of the audience.

(E) In the Shakespearean metaphor "time is a beggar," the audience is unlikely to understand the metaphor without cognitive effort and without further engaging Shakespeare's prose.

10. 30[10)

(A) We understand things well enough to benefit from them, but all the while we are making small calculations that contribute to a larger whole. We are just doing our part in a larger computation for our societies' collective brains.

(B) As we lack the resources to compute answers independently, we distribute the computation across the population and solve the answer slowly, generation by generation.

(C) Then all we have to do is socially learn the right answers. You don't need to understand how your computer or toilet works; you just need to be able to use the interface and flush.

(D) All that needs to be transmitted is which button to push — essentially how to interact with technologies rather than how they work. And so instead of holding more information than we have mental capacity for and indeed need to know, we could dedicate our large brains to a small piece of a giant calculation.

(E) Herbert Simon won his Nobel Prize for recognizing our limitations in information, time, and cognitive capacity.

11. 31[11)

(A) Actually, what they saw at first was a flounder.

(B) It was only when they looked again that they saw a medium-sized octopus, with all eight of its arms folded and its two eyes staring upwards to create the illusion. An octopus has a big brain, excellent eyesight and the ability to change colour and pattern, and this one was using these assets to turn itself into a completely different creature.

(C) So to find one in full view in the shallows in daylight was a surprise for two Australian underwater photographers.

(D) The best defence most species of octopus have is to stay hidden as much as possible and do their own hunting at night.

(E) Many more of this species have been found since then, and there are now photographs of octopuses that could be said to be transforming into sea snakes. And while they mimic, they hunt — producing the spectacle of, say, a flounder suddenly developing an octopodian arm, sticking it down a hole and grabbing whatever's hiding there.

12. 32[12)

(A) In fact, ultramarathon runners — those people who are crazy enough to push themselves beyond the normal boundaries of human endurance, covering distances of 50-100km or more over many hours, talk about making friends with their pain.

(B) When a patient has paid for some form of passive back pain therapy and the practitioner pushes deeply into a painful part of a patient's back to mobilise it, the patient calls that good pain if he or she believes this type of deep pressure treatment will be of value, even though the practitioner is pushing right into the patient's sore tissues.

(C) When 1500m runners push themselves into extreme pain to win a race — their muscles screaming and their lungs exploding with oxygen deficit, they don't psychologically suffer much.

(D) How much we suffer relates to how we frame the pain in our mind.

13. 33¹³⁾

(A) The middle item has more features than the least expensive one, and it is less expensive than the fanciest model. They buy the middle item, unaware that they have been manipulated by the presence of the higher-priced item.

(B) If the company offers two versions, one with more features and more expensive than the other, people will compare the two models and still buy the less expensive one.

(C) If the manufacturer makes only one version of its product, people who bought it might have been willing to spend more money, so the company is losing some income.

(D) But if the company introduces a third model with even more features and more expensive than the other two, sales of the second model go up; many people like the features of the most expensive model, but not the price.

(E) When I worked for a large electronics company that manufactured laser and inkjet printers, I soon discovered why there are often three versions of many consumer goods.

14. 34¹⁴⁾

(A) You can tell stories 'about' climate change while it still seems a marginal feature of human life.

(B) But when the temperature rises by three or four more degrees, hardly anyone will be able to feel isolated from its impacts.

(C) And so as climate change expands across the horizon, it may cease to be a story. Why watch or read climate fiction about the world you can see plainly out your own window?

(D) At the moment, stories illustrating global warming can still offer an escapist pleasure, even if that pleasure often comes in the form of horror. But when we can no longer pretend that climate suffering is distant — in time or in place — we will stop pretending about it and start pretending within it.

(E) Onscreen, climate disaster is everywhere you look, but the scope of the world's climate transformation may just as quickly eliminate the climate-fiction genre — indeed eliminate any effort to tell the story of warming, which could grow too large and too obvious even for Hollywood.

15. 35¹⁵⁾

(A) Some cities lose more water to leaks than they deliver to homes: even in the United States, leaks and theft account for an estimated loss of 16 percent of freshwater; in Brazil, the estimate is 40 percent.

(B) That is one reason it is nevertheless distressing: an abundant resource made scarce through governmental neglect and indifference, bad infrastructure and contamination, and careless urbanization.

(C) There is no need for a water crisis, in other words, but we have one anyway, and aren't doing much to address it.

(D) Today, the water crisis is political — which is to say, not inevitable or beyond our capacity to fix — and, therefore, functionally elective.

(E) Seen in both cases, as everywhere, the selective scarcity clearly highlights have-and-have-not inequities, leaving 2.1 billion people without safe drinking water and 4.5 billion without proper sanitation worldwide.

16. 36[16)]

(A) If it didn't, we might get none of these merits. It was a matter of survival, physically and genetically.

(B) Over millions of years, the pressure selected for people who are sensitive to and skilled at maximizing their standing. The result was the development of a tendency to unconsciously monitor how other people in our community perceive us.

(C) As individuals, our ability to thrive depended on how well we navigated relationships in a group. If the group valued us, we could count on support, resources, and probably a mate.

(D) And, crucially, they are meant to make that motivation feel like it is coming from within. If we realized, on a conscious level, that we were responding to social pressure, our performance might come off as grudging or cynical, making it less persuasive.

(E) We process that information in the form of self-esteem and such related emotions as pride, shame, or insecurity. These emotions compel us to do more of what makes our community value us and less of what doesn't.

17. 37[17)]

(A) Our consciousness is a more fundamental entity that goes beyond the functioning of the brain. The brain is no more than an organ of consciousness.

(B) If it is not consciousness itself, then the root cause of depression is also a distortion of our state of consciousness: a consciousness that has lost its sense of self and the meaning of life. Such a disease of consciousness may manifest itself in the form of depression.

(C) However, there is a major problem with this explanation. This is because the imbalance of substances in the brain is a consequence of depression, not its cause.

(D) Conventional medicine has long believed that depression is caused by an imbalance of neurotransmitters in the brain.

(E) In other words, depression causes a decrease in brain substances such as serotonin and noradrenaline, not a decrease in brain substances causes depression. In this revised cause-and-effect, the key is to reframe depression as a problem of consciousness.

18. 38[18)]

(A) In addition to this evidence-based approach, psychology deals with fundamental processes and principles that generate our rich cultural and social diversity, as well as those shared by all human beings. These are what modern psychology is all about.

(B) However, psychology is different.

(C) Psychologists don't depend on opinions and hearsay, or the generally accepted views of society at the time, or even the considered opinions of deep thinkers. Instead, they look for evidence, to make sure that psychological ideas are firmly based, and not just derived from generally held beliefs or assumptions.

(D) The common accounts of human nature that float around in society are generally a mixture of assumptions, tales and sometimes plain silliness.

(E) It is the branch of science that is devoted to understanding people: how and why we act as we do; why we see things as we do; and how we interact with one another. The key word here is 'science.'

19. 39[19)]

(A) In just a single cell, the number of possible interactions between different molecules is enormous.

(B) Life is what physicists might call a 'high-dimensional system,' which is their fancy way of saying that there's a lot going on.

(C) The organism may switch between a small number of well-defined possible states, but can't exist in random states in between them, rather as a ball in a rough landscape must roll to the bottom of one valley or another. We'll see that this is true also of health and disease: there are many causes of illness, but their manifestations at the physiological and symptomatic levels are often strikingly similar.

(D) Such a system can only hope to be stable if only a smaller number of collective ways of being may emerge.

(E) For example, it is only a limited number of tissues and body shapes that may result from the development of a human embryo. In 1942, the biologist Conrad Waddington called this drastic narrowing of outcomes canalization.

20. 40[20)]

(A) For instance, she could congratulate Hugh when he has not hit his brother for a certain length of time. The mother clearly cannot allow the child to hit his little brother, but instead of constantly pointing out the negatives, she can choose to reward the positives.

(B) Instead of discouraging the child from doing something, it encourages them to do it. For example, Hugh learns that when he hits his little brother, his mother scolds him.

(C) Punishing a child may not be effective due to what Alvaro Bilbao, a neuropsychologist, calls 'trick-punishments.' A trick-punishment is a scolding, a moment of anger or a punishment in the most classic sense of the word.

(D) For a child who feels lonely, being scolded is much better than feeling invisible, so he will continue to hit his brother. In this case, his mother would be better adopting a different strategy.

(E) In this way, any parent can avoid trick-punishments. —> A trick-punishment reinforces the unwanted behavior of a child, which implies that parents should focus on reducing the attention to negatives while rewarding positive behaviors.

21. **41~42**[21)]

(A) If a lion is about to attack you, you need to react quickly, given its probable intention to kill you. By the time you have realized that the design of its teeth and claws could kill you, you are dead. So, assuming intent, without detailed design analysis or understanding of the physics, has saved your life.

(B) When we encounter something, we first need to determine what sort of thing it is. Inanimate objects and plants generally do not move and can be evaluated from physics alone. However, by attributing intention to animals and even objects, we are able to make fast decisions about the likely behaviour of that being.

(C) From an early age, we assign purpose to objects and events, preferring this reasoning to random chance. Children assume, for instance, that pointy rocks are that way because they don't want you to sit on them.

(D) This was essential in our hunter-gatherer days to avoid being eaten by predators. The anthropologist Stewart Guthrie made the point that survival in our evolutionary past meant that we interpret ambiguous objects as agents with human mental characteristics, as those are the mental processes which we understand. Ambiguous events are caused by such agents.

(E) This results in a perceptual system strongly biased towards anthropomorphism. Therefore, we tend to assume intention even where there is none. This would have arisen as a survival mechanism.

22. **43~45**[22)]

(A) However, they were so bitter he couldn't swallow even one. At dusk, he finally got home and slowly climbed his favorite bamboo tree. There, he discovered a strange black and red flower with a sweet scent that tempted him to eat all its blossoms. The following morning, under sunny skies, the little panda felt remarkably better.

(B) His two big ears, his four furry feet and his cute round nose were all frosty white, leaving him feeling ordinary and sad. Unlike the cheerful and contented pandas around him, he desired to be distinctive, special, and unique. Driven by the desire for uniqueness, the little panda sought inspiration from his distant cousin, a giant white panda covered with heavenly black patches.

(C) But the cousin revealed the patches were from an unintended encounter with mud, and he disliked them. Disappointed, the little panda walked home. On his way, he met a red-feathered peacock, who explained he turned red from eating wild berries. The little panda changed his path and hurried to the nearest berry bush, greedily eating a mouthful of juicy red berries.

(D) Once long ago, deep in the Himalayas, there lived a little panda. He was as ordinary as all the other pandas. He was completely white from head to toe.

(E) During breakfast, he found the other pandas chatting enthusiastically and asked why. They burst into laughter, exclaiming, "Look at yourself!" Glancing down, he discovered his once white fur was now stained jet black and glowing red. He was overjoyed and realized that, rather than by imitating others, his wishes can come true from unexpected places and genuine experiences.

2024 고1 11월 모의고사

1. 1)밑줄 친 부분 중, 어법, 혹은 문맥상 어색한 곳을 고르시오. 2024_H1_11_18

To the State Education Department,I am writing with regard to the state's funding for the construction project at Fort Montgomery High School. Our school needs additional spaces to provide a fully functional Art and Library Media Center to serve our students in a more meaningful way. Despite ①**admitting** all required documentation for funding to your department in April 2024, we have not yet received any notification from your department. A delay in the process can carry ②**considerable** consequences related to the school's budgetary ③**constraints** and schedule. Therefore, in order to ④**proceed** with our project, we request you ⑤**notify** us of the review result regarding the submitted documentation. I look forward to hearing from you.Respectfully, Clara Smith Principal, Fort Montgomery High School

2. 2)밑줄 친 부분 중, 어법, 혹은 문맥상 어색한 곳을 고르시오. 2024_H1_11_19

As I waited outside the locker room after a ①**hard** -fought basketball game, the coach called out to me, "David, walk with me." I figured he was going to tell me ②**important something**. He was going to select me to be the captain of the team, the leader I had always wanted to be . My heart was racing with ③**anticipation**. But when his next words hit my ears, everything changed. "We're going to have to send you home," he said ④**coldly** . "I don't think you are going to make it." I couldn't believe his decision. I tried to hold it together, but inside I was ⑤**falling** apart. A car would be waiting tomorrow morning to take me home. And just like that, it was over.

3. 3)밑줄 친 부분 중, 어법, 혹은 문맥상 어색한 곳을 고르시오. 2024_H1_11_20

For many of us, ①**making** time for exercise is a continuing challenge. Between work commitments and family obligations, it often feels like there's no room in our packed schedules for a ②**dedication** workout. But ③**what** if the workout came to you, right in the midst of your daily routine? That's where the beauty of integrating mini-exercises into household chores comes into play. Let's be realistic; chores are ④**inevitable** . Whether it's washing dishes or taking out the trash, these tasks are an essential part of daily life. But rather than viewing chores as purely obligatory activities, why not seize these moments as opportunities for ⑤ **physical** activity? For instance, practice squats or engage in some wall push-ups as you wait for your morning kettle to boil. Incorporating quick exercises into your daily chores can improve your health.

4. 4)밑줄 친 부분 중, 어법, 혹은 문맥상 어색한 곳을 고르시오. 2024_H1_11_21

When we see something, we naturally and ① **automatically** break it up into shapes, colors, and concepts that we have learned through education. We recode what we see through the lens of everything we know. We ②**reconstruct** memories rather than retrieving the video from memory. This is a useful trait. It's a more efficient way to store information—a bit like an optimal image compression algorithm such as JPG, rather than storing a raw bitmap image file. People who ③ **have** this ability and remember everything in perfect detail struggle to generalize , learn, and make connections between what they have learned. But representing the world as ④**abstract** ideas and features comes at a cost of seeing the world as it is. Instead, we see the world through our assumptions, motivations, and past experiences. The discovery that our memories are reconstructed through abstract ⑤**representations** rather than played back like a movie completely undermined the legal primacy of eyewitness testimony. Seeing is not believing.

5. 5)밑줄 친 부분 중, 어법, 혹은 문맥상 어색한 곳을 고르시오. 2024_H1_11_22

In his Cornell laboratory, David Dunning conducted experimental tests of eyewitness testimony and found evidence ①**which** a careful deliberation of facial features and a detailed discussion of selection procedures can actually be a sign of an inaccurate identification . It's when people find themselves unable to explain why they recognize the person, saying things like "his face just popped out at me," that they tend to be accurate ②**more** often. Sometimes our first, immediate, automatic reaction to a situation is the truest interpretation of what our mind is telling us. That very first impression can also be more accurate about the world than the deliberative, reasoned self-narrative can ③**be** . In his book Blink, Malcolm Gladwell describes a variety of studies in psychology and behavioral economics that demonstrate the superior performance of ④**relatively** ⑤**unconscious** first guesses compared to logical step-by-step justifications for a decision.

6. 6)밑줄 친 부분 중, 어법, 혹은 문맥상 어색한 곳을 고르시오. 2024_H1_11_23

Many forms of research lead naturally to quantitative data. A study of happiness might measure the number of times someone smiles ① **while** an interaction, and a study of memory might measure ②**the** number of items an individual can recall after one, five, and ten minutes. Asking people how many times in a year they are sad will also yield quantitative data, but it might not be reliable. Respondents' recollections may be inaccurate, and their definitions of 'sad' could vary widely. But asking "How many times in the past year were you sad enough to call in sick to work?" prompts ③**a concrete** answer. Similarly, instead of asking people to rate how bad a procrastinator they are, ask, "How many of your utility bills are you currently late in paying, even though you can afford to pay them?" Questions that seek ④ **concrete** responses help make ⑤**abstract** concepts clearer and ensure consistency from one study to the next.

7. 7)**밑줄 친 부분 중, 어법, 혹은 문맥상 어색한 곳을 고르시오.** 2024_H1_11_24

The evolution of AI is often associated with the concept of singularity. Singularity refers to the point at which AI exceeds human intelligence. After that point, it is predicted that AI will repeatedly improve itself and evolve at an accelerated pace. When AI becomes self-aware and pursues its own goals, it will be a conscious ①**being** , not just a machine. AI and human ②**consciousness** will then begin to evolve together. Our consciousness will evolve to new dimensions through our interactions with AI, which will provide us with intellectual stimulation and ③**inspire** new insights and creativity. Conversely, our consciousness also has a significant impact on the evolution of AI. The direction of AI's ④**revolution** will depend greatly on what values and ethics we incorporate into AI. We need to see our relationship with AI as a mutual coexistence of conscious beings, recognizing its rights and supporting the ⑤ **evolution** of its consciousness.

8. 8)**밑줄 친 부분 중, 어법, 혹은 문맥상 어색한 곳을 고르시오.** 2024_H1_11_29

Digital technologies are essentially related to metaphors, but digital metaphors are different from linguistic ①**ones** in important ways. Linguistic metaphors are passive, in the sense that the audience needs to choose to actively enter the world proposed by metaphor. In the Shakespearean metaphor "time is a beggar," the audience is unlikely to understand the metaphor without cognitive effort and without ②**further** engaging Shakespeare's prose. Technological metaphors, on the other hand, are active and often imposing) in the sense ③**that** they are realized in digital artifacts that are ④**actively** doing things, forcefully changing a user's meaning horizon. Technological creators cannot generally afford to ⑤**acquire** their potential audience to wonder how the metaphor works; normally the selling point is that the usefulness of the technology is obvious at first glance. Shakespeare, on the other hand, is beloved in part because the meaning of his works is not immediately obvious and requires some thought on the part of the audience.

9. 9)**밑줄 친 부분 중, 어법, 혹은 문맥상 어색한 곳을 고르시오.** 2024_H1_11_30

Herbert Simon won his Nobel Prize for recognizing our limitations in information, time, and cognitive capacity. As we lack the resources to compute answers ①**independently** , we distribute the computation across the ②**population** and solve the answer slowly, generation by generation. Then all we have to do is socially learn the right answers. You don't need to understand how your computer or toilet works; you just need to be able to use the interface and flush. All that needs to be transmitted is which button to push —essentially how to ③**disconnect** with technologies rather than how they work. And so instead of holding ④**more** information than we have mental capacity for and indeed need to know, we could dedicate our large brains to a small piece of a giant calculation. We understand things well enough to benefit from them, but all the while we are making small calculations that ⑤**contribute** to a larger whole. We are just doing our part in a larger computation for our societies' collective brains.

10. 10)**밑줄 친 부분 중, 어법, 혹은 문맥상 어색한 곳을 고르시오.** 2024_H1_11_31

The best defence most species of octopus have is to stay hidden as ①**much** as possible and do their own hunting at night. So to find one in full view in the shallows in daylight ②**was** a surprise for two Australian underwater photographers. Actually, what they saw at first was a flounder. It was only when they looked again ③**that** they saw a medium-sized octopus, with all eight of its arms ④**folding** and its two eyes staring upwards to create the illusion . An octopus has a big brain, excellent eyesight and the ability to change colour and pattern, and this one was using these assets to turn itself into a completely ⑤**different** creature. Many more of this species have been found since then, and there are now photographs of octopuses that could be said to be transforming into sea snakes. And while they mimic, they hunt ─producing the spectacle of, say, a flounder suddenly developing an octopodian arm, sticking it down a hole and grabbing whatever's hiding there.

11. 11)**밑줄 친 부분 중, 어법, 혹은 문맥상 어색한 곳을 고르시오.** 2024_H1_11_32

How much we suffer relates to how we ①**fame** the pain in our mind. When 1500m runners push themselves into extreme pain to win a race─their muscles screaming and their lungs ②**exploding** with oxygen deficit, they don't psychologically suffer much. In fact, ultra-marathon runners─those people who are crazy enough to push themselves beyond the normal boundaries of human ③**endurance** , covering distances of 50-100km or more over many hours, talk about making friends with their pain. When a patient has paid for some form of ④**passive** back pain therapy and the practitioner pushes deeply into a painful part of a patient's back to mobilise it, the patient calls that good pain if he or she believes this type of deep pressure treatment will be of value , even ⑤**though** the practitioner is pushing right into the patient's sore tissues.

12. 12)**밑줄 친 부분 중, 어법, 혹은 문맥상 어색한 곳을 고르시오.** 2024_H1_11_33

When I worked for a large electronics company that manufactured laser and inkjet-printers, I soon discovered ①**why** there are often three versions of many consumer goods. If the manufacturer makes only one version of its product, people who bought it might have been willing to spend more money, so the company is losing some income. If the company offers two versions, one with more features and more expensive than the other, people will ②**compare** the two models and still buy the less expensive one. But if the company introduces a third model with even more features and more expensive than ③**the other** two, sales of the second model ④**go** up; many people like the features of the most expensive model, but not the price. The middle item has more features than the least expensive one, and it is less expensive than the fanciest model. They buy the middle item, unaware that they have been manipulated by the presence of the ⑤**lower**-priced item.

13. ¹³⁾**밑줄 친 부분 중, <u>어법, 혹은 문맥상 어색한 곳을</u> 고르시오.** ^{2024_H1_11_34}

On-screen, climate disaster is everywhere you look, but the scope of the world's climate transformation may just as quickly eliminate the climate-fiction genre — indeed eliminate any effort to tell the story of warming, which could grow too large and too obvious even for Hollywood. You can tell stories 'about' climate change while it still seems a ①**marginal** feature of human life. But when the temperature rises by three or four more degrees, ②**hard** anyone will be able to feel isolated from its impacts. And so as climate change expands across the horizon, it may cease to be a story. Why watch or read climate fiction about the world you can see plainly out your own window? At the moment, stories ③**illustrating** global warming can still offer an escapist pleasure, even if that pleasure often comes in the form of horror. But when we can no longer pretend that climate ④**suffering** is distant — in time or in place — we will stop ⑤**pretending** about it and start pretending within it.

14. ¹⁴⁾**밑줄 친 부분 중, 어법, 혹은 문맥상 어색한 곳을 고르시오.** ^{2024_H1_11_35}

Today, the water crisis is political — which is to say, not inevitable or beyond our capacity to fix — and, therefore, functionally elective. That is one reason it is nevertheless distressing: an abundant resource made scarce through governmental neglect and ①**indifference** , bad infrastructure and contamination, and careless urbanization. There is no need for a water crisis, in other words, but we have one anyway, and aren't doing much to ②**address** it. Some cities lose ③**less** water to leaks than they deliver to homes: even in the United States, leaks and theft account for an estimated loss of 16 percent of freshwater; in Brazil, the estimate is 40 percent. Seen in both cases, as everywhere, the ④**selective** scarcity clearly ⑤**highlights** haveandhavenot inequities, leaving 2.1 billion people without safe drinking water and 4.5 billion without proper sanitation worldwide.

15. ¹⁵⁾**밑줄 친 부분 중, 어법, 혹은 문맥상 어색한 곳을 고르시오.** ^{2024_H1_11_36}

As individuals, our ability to thrive depended on how well we navigated relationships in a group. If the group valued us, we could count on support, resources, and probably a mate. If it didn't, we might get none of these merits. It was a matter of survival, physically and genetically. Over millions of years, the pressure selected for people who are ①**sensitive** to and skilled at maximizing their standing. The result was the development of a tendency to unconsciously monitor how other people in our community ②**perceive** us. We process that information in the form of self-esteem and such related emotions as pride, shame, or insecurity. These emotions compel us to do ③**less** of what makes our community value us and less of ④**what** doesn't. And, crucially, they are meant to make that motivation feel like it is coming from within. If we realized, on a conscious level, that we were responding to ⑤**social** pressure, our performance might come off as grudging or cynical, making it less persuasive.

16. ¹⁶⁾**밑줄 친 부분 중, 어법, 혹은 문맥상 어색한 곳을 고르시오.** 2024_H1_11_37

Conventional medicine has long believed that depression is caused by an imbalance of neurotransmitters in the brain. However, there is a major problem with this explanation. This is ① **because** the imbalance of substances in the brain is a consequence of depression, not its cause. In other words, depression causes a decrease in brain substances such as serotonin and noradrenaline, not a decrease in brain substances causes depression. In this revised cause-and-effect, the key is to reframe depression as a problem of consciousness. Our consciousness is a ②**more** fundamental entity that goes beyond the functioning of the brain. The brain is no ③**less** than an organ of consciousness. If it is not consciousness itself, then the root cause of depression is also a ④**distortion** of our state of consciousness: a consciousness that has lost its sense of self and the meaning of life. Such a disease of consciousness may ⑤**manifest** itself in the form of depression.

17. ¹⁷⁾**밑줄 친 부분 중, 어법, 혹은 문맥상 어색한 곳을 고르시오.** 2024_H1_11_38

The ①**common** accounts of human nature that float around in society are generally a mixture of assumptions, tales and sometimes plain silliness. However, psychology is different. It is the branch of science that is devoted to understanding people: how and why we act as we do ; why we see things as we do; and how we ②**transact** with one another. The key word here is 'science.' Psychologists don't depend on opinions and hearsay, or the generally accepted views of society at the time, or even the considered opinions of deep thinkers. Instead, they look for evidence, to make sure that psychological ideas are firmly based, and not just ③**derived** from generally held beliefs or assumptions. In addition to this evidence-based approach, psychology deals with fundamental processes and principles that generate our rich cultural and social diversity, as well as those ④**shared** by all human beings. These are ⑤**what** modern psychology is all about.

18. ¹⁸⁾**밑줄 친 부분 중, 어법, 혹은 문맥상 어색한 곳을 고르시오.** 2024_H1_11_39

Life is ①**what** physicists might call a 'high-dimensional system,' which is their fancy way of saying that there's a lot going on. In just a single cell, ②**the** number of possible interactions between different molecules is ③**enormous**. Such a system can only hope to be stable if only a smaller number of collective ways of being may emerge. For example, it is only a limited number of tissues and body shapes that may result ④**from** the development of a human embryo. In 1942, the biologist Conrad Waddington called this drastic narrowing of outcomes canalization. The organism may switch between a small number of well-defined possible states, but can't exist in random states in between them, rather as a ball in a rough landscape must roll to the bottom of one valley or another. We'll see that this is true also of health and disease: there are many causes of illness, but their ⑤**dissolutions** at the physiological and symptomatic levels are often strikingly similar .

19. 19)**밑줄 친 부분 중, 어법, 혹은 문맥상 어색한 곳을 고르시오.** 2024_H1_11_40

Punishing a child may not be effective due to ① **what** Álvaro Bilbao, a neuropsychologist, calls 'trick-punishments.' A trick-②**reward** is a scolding, a moment of anger or a ③**punishment** in the most classic sense of the word. Instead of discouraging the child from doing something, it ④**encourages** them to do it. For example, Hugh learns that when he hits his little brother, his mother scolds him. For a child who feels lonely, being scolded is much better than feeling invisible , so he will continue to hit his brother. In this case, his mother would be better adopting a different strategy. For instance, she could congratulate Hugh when he has not hit his brother for a certain length of time. The mother clearly cannot allow the child to hit his little brother, but instead of constantly pointing out the ⑤**negatives** , she can choose to reward the positives. In this way, any parent can avoid trick-punishments.

20. 20)**밑줄 친 부분 중, 어법, 혹은 문맥상 어색한 곳을 고르시오.** 2024_H1_11_41,42

From an early age, we assign purpose to objects and events, preferring this reasoning to random chance. Children ①**assume**, for instance, that pointy rocks are that way because they don't want you to sit on them. When we encounter something, we first need to determine what sort of thing it is. Inanimate objects and plants generally do not move and can be evaluated from ②**physical** alone. However, by attributing intention to animals and even objects, we are able to make fast decisions about the likely behaviour of that being . This was essential in our hunter-gatherer days to avoid ③ **being** eaten by predators.The anthropologist Stewart Guthrie made the point that survival in our evolutionary past meant that we interpret ambiguous objects as agents with human mental characteristics, as those are the mental processes which we understand. ④**Ambiguous** events are caused by such agents. This results in a perceptual system strongly biased towards anthropomorphism. Therefore, we tend to assume intention even where there is none. This would have arisen as a survival mechanism. If a lion is about to attack you, you need to react quickly, ⑤**given** its probable intention to kill you. By the time you have realized that the design of its teeth and claws could kill you, you are dead . So, assuming intent, without detailed design analysis or understanding of the physics, has saved your life.

21. 21)**밑줄 친 부분 중, 어법, 혹은 문맥상 어색한 곳을 고르시오.** 2024_H1_43,44,45

Once long ago, deep in the Himalayas, there lived a ①**little** panda. He was as ordinary as all the other pandas. He was completely white from head to toe. His two big ears, his four furry feet and his cute round nose were all frosty white, leaving him feeling ordinary and sad. Unlike the cheerful and contented pandas around him, he ②**desired** to be distinctive, special, and unique. Driven by the desire for uniqueness, the little panda sought inspiration from his distant cousin, a giant white panda ③**covered** with heavenly black patches. But the cousin revealed the patches were from an unintended encounter with mud, and he disliked them. ④**Disappointed** , the little panda walked home. On his way, he met a red-feathered peacock, who explained he turned red from eating wild berries. The little panda changed his path and hurried to the nearest berry bush, greedily eating a mouthful of juicy red berries. However, they were so bitter he couldn't swallow even one. At dusk, he finally got home and slowly climbed his favorite bamboo tree. There, he discovered a strange black and red flower with a sweet scent that tempted him to eat all its blossoms. The following morning, under sunny skies, the little panda felt remarkably better. During breakfast, he found the other pandas ⑤**chat** enthusiastically and asked why. They burst into laughter, exclaiming, "Look at yourself!" Glancing down, he discovered his once white fur was now stained jet black and glowing red. He was overjoyed and realized that, rather than by imitating others, his wishes can come true from unexpected places and genuine experiences.

2024 고1 11월 모의고사

❶ voca   ❷ text   ❸ [/]   ❹ ____   ❺ quiz 1   ❻ quiz 2   ❼ quiz 3   ❽ quiz 4   ❾ quiz 5

1. 1)**밑줄 친 ⓐ~ⓘ 중 어법, 혹은 문맥상 어휘의 사용이 어색한 것끼리 짝지어진 것을 고르시오.** 2024_H1_11_18

To the State Education Department,I am writing with ⓐ**regard** to the state's funding for the construction project at Fort Montgomery High School. Our school needs additional spaces to provide a fully functional Art and Library Media Center to serve our students in a ⓑ**more** meaningful way. ⓒ**Despite** ⓓ**submitting** all required documentation for funding to your department in April 2024, we have not yet received any notification from your department. A delay in the process can carry ⓔ**considerate** consequences related to the school's budgetary ⓕ**constraints** and schedule. Therefore, in order to ⓖ**process** with our project, we request you ⓗ**notify** us of the review result regarding the submitted documentation. I look forward to ⓘ**hearing** from you.Respectfully, Clara Smith ⓙ**Principal**, Fort Montgomery High School

① ⓓ, ⓖ   ② ⓓ, ⓔ   ③ ⓒ, ⓕ, ⓘ
④ ⓒ, ⓓ   ⑤ ⓔ, ⓖ

2. 2)**밑줄 친 ⓐ~ⓖ 중 어법, 혹은 문맥상 어휘의 사용이 어색한 것끼리 짝지어진 것을 고르시오.** 2024_H1_11_19

As I waited outside the locker room after a ⓐ**hard ‑fought** basketball game, the coach called out to me, "David, walk with me." I figured he was going to tell me ⓑ**something important**. He was going to select me to be the captain of the team, the leader I had always wanted to ⓒ**do** . My heart was racing with ⓓ**anticipation**. But when his next words hit my ears, everything changed. "We're going to have to send you home," he said ⓔ**coldly** . "I don't think you are going to make it." I couldn't believe

his decision. I tried ⓕ**to hold** it together, but inside I was ⓖ**rising** apart. A car would be waiting tomorrow morning to take me home. And just like that, it was over.

① ⓐ, ⓑ, ⓓ   ② ⓑ, ⓕ, ⓖ   ③ ⓑ, ⓔ, ⓖ
④ ⓑ, ⓓ, ⓕ   ⑤ ⓒ, ⓖ

3. 3)**밑줄 친 ⓐ~ⓘ 중 어법, 혹은 문맥상 어휘의 사용이 어색한 것끼리 짝지어진 것을 고르시오.** 2024_H1_11_20

For many of us, ⓐ**making** time for exercise is a continuing challenge. Between work commitments and family obligations, it often feels like there's no room in our packed schedules for a ⓑ**dedicated** workout. But ⓒ**what** if the workout came to you, right in the midst of your daily routine? That's ⓓ**where** the beauty of ⓔ**separating** mini-exercises into household chores comes into play. Let's be realistic; chores are ⓕ**inevitable** . Whether it's washing dishes or taking out the trash, these tasks are an essential part of daily life. But rather than ⓖ**viewing** chores as purely ⓗ**obligatory** activities, why not seize these moments as opportunities for ⓘ**physical** activity? For instance, practice squats or engage in some wall push-ups as you wait for your morning kettle to boil. ⓙ**incorporated** quick exercises into your daily chores can improve your health.

① ⓔ, ⓘ   ② ⓐ, ⓑ, ⓒ   ③ ⓒ, ⓖ
④ ⓐ, ⓗ, ⓘ   ⑤ ⓑ, ⓔ, ⓕ

4. 4)밑줄 친 ⓐ~ⓡ 중 어법, 혹은 문맥상 어휘의 사용이 어색한 것끼리 짝지어진 것을 고르시오. 2024_H1_11_21

When we see something, we naturally and ⓐ**automatically** break it up into shapes, colors, and concepts that we have learned through education. We recode ⓑ**what** we see through the lens of everything we know. We ⓒ**retrieve** memories rather than ⓓ**retrieving** the video from memory. This is a ⓔ**useful** trait. It's a ⓕ**more** efficient way to store information—a bit like an ⓖ**optimal** image compression algorithm such as JPG, rather than storing a ⓗ**raw** bitmap image file. People who ⓘ**lack** this ability and remember everything in ⓙ**flawed** detail struggle to ⓚ**generalize** , learn, and make connections between ⓛ**what** they have learned. But representing the world as ⓜ**abstract** ideas and features ⓝ**comes** at a cost of ⓞ**believing** the world as it is. Instead, we see the world through our assumptions, motivations, and past experiences. The discovery that our memories are ⓟ**reconstructed** through abstract ⓠ**representations** rather than played back like a movie completely ⓡ**undermined** the legal primacy of eyewitness testimony. Seeing is not believing.

① ⓐ, ⓙ, ⓝ   ② ⓔ, ⓘ, ⓙ   ③ ⓔ, ⓕ, ⓗ
④ ⓓ, ⓕ   ⑤ ⓒ, ⓙ, ⓞ

5. 5)밑줄 친 ⓐ~ⓞ 중 어법, 혹은 문맥상 어휘의 사용이 어색한 것끼리 짝지어진 것을 고르시오. 2024_H1_11_22

In his Cornell laboratory, David Dunning conducted experimental tests of eyewitness testimony and found evidence ⓐ**that** a careful ⓑ**deliberation** of facial features and a detailed discussion of selection ⓒ**procedures** can actually be a sign of an ⓓ**inaccurate** ⓔ**identity** . It's when people find themselves ⓕ**unable** to explain why they recognize the person, saying things like "his face just popped out at me," that they tend to be ⓖ**inaccurate** ⓗ**more** often. Sometimes our first, immediate, automatic reaction to a situation is the truest interpretation of ⓘ**what** our mind is telling us. That very first impression can also be ⓙ**more** accurate about the world than the deliberative, ⓚ**reasoned** self-narrative can ⓛ**be** . In his book Blink, Malcolm Gladwell describes a variety of studies in psychology and behavioral economics that demonstrate the superior performance of ⓜ**relative** ⓝ**unconscious** first guesses compared to ⓞ**logical** step-by-step justifications for a decision.

① ⓔ, ⓖ, ⓗ   ② ⓐ, ⓒ, ⓕ   ③ ⓔ, ⓖ, ⓜ
④ ⓘ, ⓚ   ⑤ ⓔ, ⓕ, ⓛ

6. 6)밑줄 친 ⓐ~ⓝ 중 어법, 혹은 문맥상 어휘의 사용이 어색한 것끼리 짝지어진 것을 고르시오. 2024_H1_11_23

Many forms of research lead naturally to ⓐ**quantitative** data. A study of happiness might measure ⓑ**the** number of times someone smiles ⓒ**during** an interaction, and a study of memory might measure ⓓ**the** number of ⓔ**items** an individual can recall after one, five, and ten minutes. ⓕ**Asking** people how many times in a year they are sad will also yield ⓖ**quantitative** data, but it might not be reliable. Respondents' recollections may be ⓗ**accurate**, and their definitions of 'sad' could vary widely. But asking "How many times in the past year ⓘ**were** you sad enough to call in sick to work?" prompts ⓙ**a concrete** answer. Similarly, instead of asking people to rate how bad a procrastinator they are, ask, "How many of your utility bills are you currently ⓚ**late** in paying, even ⓛ**despite** you can afford to pay them?" Questions that seek ⓜ**concrete** responses help make ⓝ**abstract** concepts clearer and ensure consistency from one study to the next.

① ⓖ, ⓘ   ② ⓑ, ⓜ, ⓝ   ③ ⓗ, ⓛ
④ ⓒ, ⓔ, ⓖ   ⑤ ⓐ, ⓓ

7. 7)밑줄 친 ⓐ~ⓛ 중 어법, 혹은 문맥상 어휘의 사용이 어색한 것끼리 짝지어진 것을 고르시오. 2024_H1_11_24

The ⓐ**evolution** of AI is often associated with the concept of singularity. Singularity ⓑ**refers** the point at which AI exceeds human intelligence. After that point, it is predicted that AI will repeatedly improve ⓒ**themselves** and ⓓ**evolve** at an accelerated pace. When AI becomes self-aware and pursues its own goals, it will be a conscious ⓔ**being** , not just a machine. AI and human ⓕ**consciousness** will then begin to evolve together. Our consciousness will evolve to new dimensions through our interactions with AI, which will provide us ⓖ**with** intellectual stimulation and ⓗ**inspire** new insights and creativity. Conversely, our consciousness also has a significant impact on the ⓘ**evolution** of AI. The direction of AI's ⓙ**stagnation** will depend greatly on ⓚ**what** values and ethics we incorporate into AI. We need to see our relationship with AI as a mutual coexistence of conscious beings, recognizing its rights and supporting the ⓛ**evolution** of its consciousness.

① ⓗ, ⓚ   ② ⓕ, ⓘ, ⓙ   ③ ⓘ, ⓙ
④ ⓑ, ⓚ   ⑤ ⓑ, ⓒ, ⓙ

8. 8)밑줄 친 ⓐ~ⓞ 중 어법, 혹은 문맥상 어휘의 사용이 어색한 것끼리 짝지어진 것을 고르시오. 2024_H1_11_29

Digital technologies are essentially related to metaphors, but digital metaphors are ⓐ**different** from linguistic ⓑ**one** in important ways. Linguistic metaphors are ⓒ**aggressive**, in the sense ⓓ**that** the audience needs to choose to actively ⓔ**enter** the world proposed by metaphor. In the Shakespearean metaphor "time is a beggar," the audience is ⓕ**unlikely** to understand the metaphor without cognitive effort and without ⓖ**further** engaging Shakespeare's prose. Technological metaphors, on the other hand, are active and often imposing) in the sense ⓗ**that** they are realized in digital artifacts that are ⓘ**actively** doing things, forcefully ⓙ

changing a user's meaning horizon. Technological creators cannot generally afford to ⓚ**require** their potential audience to ⓛ**wonder** how the metaphor works; normally the selling point is that the usefulness of the technology is ⓜ**obvious** at first glance. Shakespeare, on the other hand, is beloved in part ⓝ**because** the meaning of his works is not immediately ⓞ**obvious** and requires some thought on the part of the audience.

① ⓐ, ⓔ   ② ⓑ, ⓒ   ③ ⓓ, ⓗ, ⓙ
④ ⓒ, ⓙ   ⑤ ⓕ, ⓙ

9. 9)밑줄 친 ⓐ~ⓛ 중 어법, 혹은 문맥상 어휘의 사용이 어색한 것끼리 짝지어진 것을 고르시오. 2024_H1_11_30

Herbert Simon won his Nobel Prize for recognizing our ⓐ**limitations** in information, time, and cognitive capacity. As we ⓑ**possess** the resources to compute answers ⓒ**independently** , we ⓓ**attribute** the computation across the ⓔ**population** and solve the answer slowly, generation by generation. Then all we have to do is socially ⓕ**learn** the right answers. You don't need to understand how your computer or toilet works; you just need to be able to use the interface and flush. All that needs to be transmitted is ⓖ**that** button to push —essentially how to ⓗ**interact** with technologies rather than how they work. And so instead of holding ⓘ**more** information than we have mental capacity for and indeed need to know, we could ⓙ**dedicate** our large brains to a small piece of a giant calculation. We understand things well enough to benefit from them, but all the while we are making small calculations that ⓚ**contribute** to a larger whole. We are just doing our part in a larger computation for our societies' ⓛ**collective** brains.

① ⓓ, ⓔ, ⓕ   ② ⓕ, ⓘ   ③ ⓒ, ⓗ, ⓙ
④ ⓐ, ⓗ   ⑤ ⓑ, ⓓ, ⓖ

10. 10)밑줄 친 ⓐ~ⓝ 중 어법, 혹은 문맥상 어휘의 사용이 어색한 것끼리 짝지어진 것을 고르시오.
2024_H1_11_31

The best ⓐ**defence** most species of octopus have ⓑ**is** to stay ⓒ**hidden** as ⓓ**many** as possible and do their own hunting at night. So to find one in full view in the shallows in daylight ⓔ**was** a surprise for two Australian underwater photographers. Actually, ⓕ**what** they saw at first was a flounder. It was only when they looked again ⓖ**that** they saw a medium-sized octopus, with all eight of its arms ⓗ**folded** and its two eyes staring upwards to create the ⓘ**allusion** . An octopus has a big brain, excellent eyesight and the ability to change colour and pattern, and this one was using these assets to turn ⓙ**itself** into a completely ⓚ**different** creature. Many ⓛ**more** of this species have been found since then, and there are now photographs of octopuses that could be said to be ⓜ**transforming** into sea snakes. And while they mimic, they hunt —producing the spectacle of, say, a flounder suddenly developing an octopodian arm, sticking it down a hole and grabbing ⓝ**whatever's** hiding there.

① ⓖ, ⓝ   ② ⓙ, ⓝ   ③ ⓑ, ⓓ, ⓖ
④ ⓒ, ⓓ, ⓘ   ⑤ ⓓ, ⓘ

11. 11)밑줄 친 ⓐ~ⓘ 중 어법, 혹은 문맥상 어휘의 사용이 어색한 것끼리 짝지어진 것을 고르시오.
2024_H1_11_32

How much we suffer relates to how we ⓐ**frame** the pain in our mind. When 1500m runners push ⓑ**them** into extreme pain to win a race—their muscles screaming and their lungs ⓒ**exploding** with oxygen deficit, they don't ⓓ**psychologically** suffer much. In fact, ultra-marathon runners—those people who are crazy enough to push ⓔ**themselves** beyond the normal boundaries of human ⓕ**hindrance** , covering distances of 50-100km or more over many hours, talk about

making friends with their pain. When a patient has paid for some form of ⓖ**passive** back pain therapy and the practitioner pushes deeply into a painful part of a patient's back to mobilise it, the patient calls that good pain if he or she believes this type of deep pressure treatment will be of ⓗ**value** , even ⓘ**though** the practitioner is pushing right into the patient's sore tissues.

① ⓓ, ⓔ, ⓕ   ② ⓐ, ⓗ, ⓘ   ③ ⓔ, ⓘ
④ ⓑ, ⓓ, ⓕ   ⑤ ⓑ, ⓕ

12. 12)밑줄 친 ⓐ~ⓜ 중 어법, 혹은 문맥상 어휘의 사용이 어색한 것끼리 짝지어진 것을 고르시오.
2024_H1_11_33

When I worked for a large electronics company that manufactured laser and inkjet-printers, I soon discovered ⓐ**why** there are often three versions of many consumer goods. If the manufacturer makes only one version of its product, people who bought it might have ⓑ**been willing** to spend ⓒ**more** money, so the company is losing some income. If the company offers two versions, one with more features and more expensive than the other, people will ⓓ**compare** the two models and still buy the ⓔ**less** expensive one. But if the company introduces a third model with even more features and more expensive than ⓕ**another** two, sales of the second model ⓖ**goes** up; many people like the features of the most expensive model, but not the price. The middle item has ⓗ**more** features than the ⓘ**least** expensive one, and it is ⓙ**more** expensive than the fanciest model. They buy the middle item, ⓚ**unaware** that they have been ⓛ**manipulated** by the presence of the ⓜ**higher**-priced item.

① ⓐ, ⓒ, ⓙ   ② ⓗ, ⓘ, ⓜ   ③ ⓚ, ⓜ
④ ⓒ, ⓜ   ⑤ ⓕ, ⓖ, ⓙ

13. 13)밑줄 친 ⓐ~ⓚ 중 어법, 혹은 문맥상 어휘의 사용이 어색한 것끼리 짝지어진 것을 고르시오.

2024_H1_11_34

On-screen, climate disaster is everywhere you look, but the scope of the world's climate ⓐ**transformation** may just as quickly eliminate the climate-fiction genre — indeed eliminate any effort to tell the story of warming, which could grow too large and too ⓑ**subtle** even for Hollywood. You can tell stories 'about' climate change while it still seems a ⓒ**marginal** feature of human life. But when the temperature rises by three or four ⓓ**more** degrees, ⓔ**hardly** anyone will be able to feel ⓕ**integrated** from its impacts. And so as climate change expands across the horizon, it may ⓖ**cease** to be a story. Why watch or read climate fiction about the world you can see plainly out your own window? At the moment, stories ⓗ**illustrating** global warming can still ⓘ**offer** an escapist pleasure, even if that pleasure often comes in the form of horror. But when we can no longer pretend that climate ⓙ**offering** is distant — in time or in place — we will stop ⓚ**pretending** about it and start pretending within it.

① ⓐ, ⓒ, ⓕ   ② ⓐ, ⓑ, ⓖ   ③ ⓐ, ⓗ, ⓚ
④ ⓑ, ⓕ, ⓙ   ⑤ ⓐ, ⓖ, ⓙ

14. 14)밑줄 친 ⓐ~ⓗ 중 어법, 혹은 문맥상 어휘의 사용이 어색한 것끼리 짝지어진 것을 고르시오.

2024_H1_11_35

Today, the water crisis is ⓐ**political** — which is to say, not inevitable or beyond our capacity to fix — and, therefore, functionally elective. That is one reason it is nevertheless distressing: an ⓑ**abundant** resource made scarce through governmental neglect and ⓒ**indifference** , bad infrastructure and contamination, and careless urbanization. There is no need for a water crisis, in other words, but we have one anyway, and aren't doing much to ⓓ**neglect** it. Some cities lose ⓔ**more** water to leaks than they deliver to homes: even in the United

States, leaks and theft ⓕ**account for** an estimated loss of 16 percent of freshwater; in Brazil, the estimate is 40 percent. Seen in both cases, as everywhere, the ⓖ**indiscriminate** scarcity clearly ⓗ**highlights** haveandhavenot inequities, leaving 2.1 billion people without safe drinking water and 4.5 billion without proper sanitation worldwide.

① ⓒ, ⓓ, ⓕ   ② ⓓ, ⓔ, ⓕ   ③ ⓓ, ⓕ
④ ⓑ, ⓓ, ⓖ   ⑤ ⓓ, ⓖ

15. 15)밑줄 친 ⓐ~ⓜ 중 어법, 혹은 문맥상 어휘의 사용이 어색한 것끼리 짝지어진 것을 고르시오.

2024_H1_11_36

As individuals, our ability to thrive depended on how ⓐ**well** we navigated relationships in a group. If the group valued us, we ⓑ**could** count on support, resources, and probably a mate. If it didn't, we might get none of these merits. It was a matter of survival, physically and genetically. Over millions of years, the pressure selected for people who are ⓒ**sensitive** to and skilled at ⓓ**minimizing** their standing. The result was the development of a tendency to unconsciously monitor how other people in our community ⓔ**perceive** us. We process that information in the form of self-esteem and such related emotions as pride, shame, or insecurity. These emotions compel us to do ⓕ**more** of ⓖ**what** makes our community value us and ⓗ**less** of ⓘ**what** doesn't. And, crucially, they are meant to make that motivation ⓙ**feel** like it is coming from within. If we realized, on a conscious level, ⓚ**that** we were responding to ⓛ**sociable** pressure, our performance might come off as grudging or cynical, making it ⓜ**less** persuasive.

① ⓐ, ⓜ   ② ⓐ, ⓑ, ⓕ   ③ ⓓ, ⓛ
④ ⓘ, ⓚ   ⑤ ⓓ, ⓕ, ⓛ

16. ¹⁶⁾밑줄 친 ⓐ~ⓚ 중 어법, 혹은 문맥상 어휘의 사용이 어색한 것끼리 짝지어진 것을 고르시오.
2024_H1_11_37

ⓐ**unconventional** medicine has long believed that depression is caused by an ⓑ**balance** of neurotransmitters in the brain. However, there is a major problem with this explanation. This is ⓒ**because** the imbalance of substances in the brain is a consequence of depression, not its cause. In other words, depression causes a ⓓ**increase** in brain substances such as serotonin and noradrenaline, not a ⓔ**decrease** in brain substances ⓕ**causes** depression. In this revised cause-and-effect, the key is to reframe depression as a problem of consciousness. Our consciousness is a ⓖ**more** fundamental entity that goes beyond the functioning of the brain. The brain is no ⓗ**more** than an organ of consciousness. If it is not consciousness itself, then the root ⓘ**cause** of depression is also a ⓙ**distortion** of our state of consciousness: a consciousness that has lost its sense of self and the meaning of life. Such a disease of consciousness may ⓚ**manifest** itself in the form of depression.

① ⓑ, ⓓ, ⓕ ② ⓒ, ⓔ, ⓘ ③ ⓑ, ⓔ, ⓚ
④ ⓐ, ⓑ, ⓓ ⑤ ⓕ, ⓙ

17. ¹⁷⁾밑줄 친 ⓐ~ⓘ 중 어법, 혹은 문맥상 어휘의 사용이 어색한 것끼리 짝지어진 것을 고르시오.
2024_H1_11_38

The ⓐ**common** accounts of human nature that float around in society are generally a mixture of assumptions, tales and sometimes plain silliness. However, psychology is ⓑ**different**. It is the branch of science that is devoted to understanding people: how and why we act as we ⓒ**are** ; why we see things as we do; and how we ⓓ**interact** with one another. The key word here is 'science.' Psychologists don't depend on opinions and hearsay, or the generally ⓔ**accepted** views of society at the time, or even the considered

opinions of deep thinkers. Instead, they look for evidence, to make sure that psychological ideas are firmly based, and not just ⓕ**derived** from generally held beliefs or assumptions. In addition to this evidence-based approach, psychology deals with fundamental processes and principles that generate our rich cultural and ⓖ**social** diversity, as well as those ⓗ**distinct** by all human beings. These are ⓘ**what** modern psychology is all about.

① ⓓ, ⓖ, ⓗ ② ⓐ, ⓓ, ⓘ ③ ⓒ, ⓗ
④ ⓐ, ⓓ, ⓕ ⑤ ⓕ, ⓖ, ⓘ

18. ¹⁸⁾밑줄 친 ⓐ~ⓘ 중 어법, 혹은 문맥상 어휘의 사용이 어색한 것끼리 짝지어진 것을 고르시오.
2024_H1_11_39

Life is ⓐ**what** physicists might call a 'high-dimensional system,' which is their fancy way of saying that there's a lot going on. In just a single cell, ⓑ**a** number of possible ⓒ**interactions** between ⓓ**different** molecules is ⓔ**enormous**. Such a system can only hope to be ⓕ**unstable** if only a smaller number of ⓖ**collective** ways of being may emerge. For example, it is only a ⓗ**limited** number of tissues and body shapes that may result ⓘ**from** the development of a human embryo. In 1942, the biologist Conrad Waddington called this drastic narrowing of outcomes canalization. The organism may switch between a small number of well-defined possible states, but can't exist in ⓙ**random** states in between them, rather as a ball in a rough landscape must roll to the bottom of one valley or another. We'll see that this is true also of health and disease: there are many causes of illness, but their ⓚ**manifestations** at the physiological and symptomatic levels are often strikingly ⓛ**similar** .

① ⓓ, ⓔ, ⓖ ② ⓑ, ⓕ ③ ⓙ, ⓚ, ⓛ
④ ⓐ, ⓔ, ⓖ ⑤ ⓔ, ⓘ

19. ¹⁹⁾밑줄 친 ⓐ~ⓙ 중 <u>어법, 혹은 문맥상 어휘의 사용</u> <u>이 어색한 것끼리 짝지어진 것을 고르시오.</u>
2024_H1_11_40

Punishing a child may not be ⓐ**effective** due to ⓑ **that** Álvaro Bilbao, a neuropsychologist, calls 'trick-punishments.' A trick-ⓒ**punishment** is a scolding, a moment of anger or a ⓓ**punishment** in the most classic sense of the word. Instead of ⓔ **discouraging** the child from doing something, it ⓕ **encourages** them to do it. For example, Hugh learns that when he hits his little brother, his mother scolds him. For a child who feels lonely, ⓖ **being scolded** is much better than feeling ⓗ**visible** , so he will continue to hit his brother. In this case, his mother would be better adopting a ⓘ**different** strategy. For instance, she could congratulate Hugh when he has not hit his brother for a certain length of time. The mother clearly cannot allow the child to hit his little brother, but instead of constantly pointing out the ⓙ**positives** , she can choose to reward the positives. In this way, any parent can avoid trick-punishments.

① ⓓ, ⓔ, ⓗ   ② ⓑ, ⓗ, ⓘ   ③ ⓒ, ⓓ
④ ⓐ, ⓙ   ⑤ ⓓ, ⓖ, ⓘ

20. ²⁰⁾밑줄 친 ⓐ~ⓢ 중 <u>어법, 혹은 문맥상 어휘의 사용</u> <u>이 어색한 것끼리 짝지어진 것을 고르시오.</u>
2024_H1_11_41,42

From an early age, we assign purpose to objects and events, preferring this reasoning to ⓐ**random** chance. Children ⓑ**assume**, for instance, that pointy rocks are that way ⓒ**because** they don't want you to sit on them. When we ⓓ**encounter** something, we first need to determine ⓔ**what** sort of thing it is. ⓕ**animate** objects and plants generally do not move and can be evaluated from ⓖ**physics** alone. However, by ⓗ**attributing** intention to animals and even objects, we are able to make fast decisions about the likely behaviour of that ⓘ**being** . This was essential in our hunter-gatherer days to avoid ⓙ**being** eaten by predators.The anthropologist Stewart Guthrie made the point that ⓚ**survival** in our evolutionary past meant that we interpret ⓛ **ambiguous** objects as agents with human mental characteristics, as those are the mental processes which we understand. ⓜ**Ambiguous** events are caused by such agents. This results ⓝ**in** a perceptual system strongly biased towards anthropomorphism. Therefore, we tend to ⓞ **assume** intention even where there is none. This would have arisen as a survival mechanism. If a lion is about to attack you, you need to react quickly, ⓟ**given** its probable intention to kill you. By the time you have realized that the design of its teeth and claws could kill you, you are ⓠ**dead** . So, assuming intent, without detailed design ⓡ **synthesis** or understanding of the physics, ⓢ**has** saved your life.

① ⓛ, ⓞ   ② ⓘ, ⓟ, ⓢ   ③ ⓘ, ⓙ, ⓛ
④ ⓑ, ⓔ, ⓠ   ⑤ ⓕ, ⓡ

21. ²¹⁾밑줄 친 ⓐ~ⓞ 중 어법, 혹은 문맥상 어휘의 사용이 어색한 것끼리 짝지어진 것을 고르시오.

2024_H1_43,44,45

Once long ago, deep in the Himalayas, there lived a ⓐ**little** panda. He was as ⓑ**ordinary** as all the other pandas. He was completely white from head to toe. His two big ears, his four furry feet and his cute round nose were all frosty white, ⓒ**leaving** him ⓓ**felt** ordinary and sad. Unlike the cheerful and ⓔ**contented** pandas around him, he ⓕ**desired** to be distinctive, special, and unique. Driven by the desire for uniqueness, the little panda sought ⓖ**inspiration** from his distant cousin, a giant white panda ⓗ**covered** with heavenly black patches. But the cousin revealed the patches ⓘ**be** from an unintended encounter with mud, and he disliked them. ⓙ**Disappointed** , the little panda walked home. On his way, he met a red-feathered peacock, who explained he turned red from eating wild berries. The little panda changed his path and hurried to the nearest berry bush, greedily eating a mouthful of juicy red berries. However, they were so bitter he couldn't swallow even one. At dusk, he finally got home and slowly climbed his favorite bamboo tree. There, he ⓚ**covered** a strange black and red flower with a sweet scent that tempted him to eat all its blossoms. The following morning, under sunny skies, the little panda felt remarkably better. ⓛ**During** breakfast, he found the other pandas ⓜ**chatting** enthusiastically and asked why. They burst into laughter, exclaiming, "Look at yourself!" ⓝ**Glancing** down, he discovered his once white fur was now stained jet black and glowing red. He was overjoyed and realized that, rather than by ⓞ**imitating** others, his wishes can come true from unexpected places and genuine experiences.

① ⓓ, ⓘ, ⓚ   ② ⓛ, ⓜ   ③ ⓕ, ⓗ
④ ⓑ, ⓖ, ⓜ   ⑤ ⓓ, ⓕ, ⓖ

2024 고1 11월 모의고사

❶ voca   ❷ text   ❸ [/]   ❹ ____   ❺ quiz 1   ❻ quiz 2   ❼ quiz 3   ❽ quiz 4   ❾ quiz 5

---

1. ¹⁾**밑줄 부분 중 어법, 혹은 문맥상 어휘의 쓰임이 어색한 것을 올바르게 고쳐 쓰시오. (5개)** ^{2024_H1_11_18}

To the State Education Department,I am writing with ①**regard** to the state's funding for the construction project at Fort Montgomery High School. Our school needs additional spaces to provide a fully functional Art and Library Media Center to serve our students in a ②**more** meaningful way. ③**although** ④**admitting** all required documentation for funding to your department in April 2024, we have not yet received any notification from your department. A delay in the process can carry ⑤**considerable** consequences related to the school's budgetary ⑥**freedom** and schedule. Therefore, in order to ⑦**process** with our project, we request you ⑧**notify** us of the review result regarding the submitted documentation. I look forward to ⑨ **hear** from you.Respectfully, Clara Smith ⑩**Principal**, Fort Montgomery High School

기호	어색한 표현		올바른 표현
( )	_____	=>	_____
( )	_____	=>	_____
( )	_____	=>	_____
( )	_____	=>	_____
( )	_____	=>	_____

---

2. ²⁾**밑줄 부분 중 어법, 혹은 문맥상 어휘의 쓰임이 어색한 것을 올바르게 고쳐 쓰시오. (5개)** ^{2024_H1_11_19}

As I waited outside the locker room after a ①**hardly**-fought basketball game, the coach called out to me, "David, walk with me." I figured he was going to tell me ②**something important**. He was going to select me to be the captain of the team, the leader I had always wanted to ③**do** . My heart was racing with ④ **anticipation**. But when his next words hit my ears, everything changed. "We're going to have to send you home," he said ⑤**cold** . "I don't think you are going to make it." I couldn't believe his decision. I tried ⑥ **holding** it together, but inside I was ⑦**rising** apart. A car would be waiting tomorrow morning to take me home. And just like that, it was over.

기호	어색한 표현		올바른 표현
( )	_____	=>	_____
( )	_____	=>	_____
( )	_____	=>	_____
( )	_____	=>	_____
( )	_____	=>	_____

3. ³⁾밑줄 부분 중 어법, 혹은 문맥상 어휘의 쓰임이 어색한 것을 올바르게 고쳐 쓰시오. (5개) ^{2024_H1_11_20}

For many of us, ①**making** time for exercise is a continuing challenge. Between work commitments and family obligations, it often feels like there's no room in our packed schedules for a ②**dedication** workout. But ③**that** if the workout came to you, right in the midst of your daily routine? That's ④**what** the beauty of ⑤**integrating** mini-exercises into household chores comes into play. Let's be realistic; chores are ⑥ **evitable** . Whether it's washing dishes or taking out the trash, these tasks are an essential part of daily life. But rather than ⑦**viewing** chores as purely ⑧**obligatory** activities, why not seize these moments as opportunities for ⑨**physical** activity? For instance, practice squats or engage in some wall push-ups as you wait for your morning kettle to boil. ⑩**incorporated** quick exercises into your daily chores can improve your health.

기호	어색한 표현		올바른 표현
( )	_____	=>	_____
( )	_____	=>	_____
( )	_____	=>	_____
( )	_____	=>	_____
( )	_____	=>	_____

4. ⁴⁾밑줄 부분 중 어법, 혹은 문맥상 어휘의 쓰임이 어색한 것을 올바르게 고쳐 쓰시오. (5개) ^{2024_H1_11_21}

When we see something, we naturally and ①**automatically** break it up into shapes, colors, and concepts that we have learned through education. We recode ②**what** we see through the lens of everything we know. We ③**reconstruct** memories rather than ④**retrieving** the video from memory. This is a ⑤**useless** trait. It's a ⑥**more** efficient way to store information—a bit like an ⑦**optional** image compression algorithm such as JPG, rather than storing a ⑧**raw** bitmap image file. People who ⑨**lack** this ability and remember everything in ⑩**perfect** detail struggle to ⑪**generalize** , learn, and make connections between ⑫**that** they have learned. But representing the world as ⑬**concrete** ideas and features ⑭**comes** at a cost of ⑮**seeing** the world as it is. Instead, we see the world through our assumptions, motivations, and past experiences. The discovery that our memories are ⑯**reconstructed** through abstract ⑰**representations** rather than played back like a movie completely ⑱**valued** the legal primacy of eyewitness testimony. Seeing is not believing.

기호	어색한 표현		올바른 표현
( )	_____	=>	_____
( )	_____	=>	_____
( )	_____	=>	_____
( )	_____	=>	_____
( )	_____	=>	_____

5. 5)밑줄 부분 중 어법, 혹은 문맥상 어휘의 쓰임이 어색한 것을 올바르게 고쳐 쓰시오. (5개) 2024_H1_11_22

In his Cornell laboratory, David Dunning conducted experimental tests of eyewitness testimony and found evidence ①**that** a careful ②**proliferation** of facial features and a detailed discussion of selection ③**procedures** can actually be a sign of an ④**inaccurate** ⑤**identification** . It's when people find themselves ⑥**unable** to explain why they recognize the person, saying things like "his face just popped out at me," that they tend to be ⑦**inaccurate** ⑧**more** often. Sometimes our first, immediate, automatic reaction to a situation is the truest interpretation of ⑨**that** our mind is telling us. That very first impression can also be ⑩**less** accurate about the world than the deliberative, ⑪**reasoned** self-narrative can ⑫**be** . In his book Blink, Malcolm Gladwell describes a variety of studies in psychology and behavioral economics that demonstrate the superior performance of ⑬**relatively** ⑭**conscious** first guesses compared to ⑮**logical** step-by-step justifications for a decision.

기호	어색한 표현		올바른 표현
( )	_____	=>	_____
( )	_____	=>	_____
( )	_____	=>	_____
( )	_____	=>	_____
( )	_____	=>	_____

6. 6)밑줄 부분 중 어법, 혹은 문맥상 어휘의 쓰임이 어색한 것을 올바르게 고쳐 쓰시오. (5개) 2024_H1_11_23

Many forms of research lead naturally to ①**quantitative** data. A study of happiness might measure ②**a** number of times someone smiles ③**while** an interaction, and a study of memory might measure ④**the** number of ⑤**items** an individual can recall after one, five, and ten minutes. ⑥**Asking** people how many times in a year they are sad will also yield ⑦**qualitative** data, but it might not be reliable. Respondents' recollections may be ⑧**inaccurate**, and their definitions of 'sad' could vary widely. But asking "How many times in the past year ⑨**are** you sad enough to call in sick to work?" prompts ⑩**an abstract** answer. Similarly, instead of asking people to rate how bad a procrastinator they are, ask, "How many of your utility bills are you currently ⑪**late** in paying, even ⑫**though** you can afford to pay them?" Questions that seek ⑬**concrete** responses help make ⑭**abstract** concepts clearer and ensure consistency from one study to the next.

기호	어색한 표현		올바른 표현
( )	_____	=>	_____
( )	_____	=>	_____
( )	_____	=>	_____
( )	_____	=>	_____
( )	_____	=>	_____

7. 7)**밑줄 부분 중 어법, 혹은 문맥상 어휘의 쓰임이 어색한 것을 올바르게 고쳐 쓰시오. (5개)** 2024_H1_11_24

The ①**evolution** of AI is often associated with the concept of singularity. Singularity ②**refers** the point at which AI exceeds human intelligence. After that point, it is predicted that AI will repeatedly improve ③**itself** and ④**involve** at an accelerated pace. When AI becomes self-aware and pursues its own goals, it will be a conscious ⑤**being** , not just a machine. AI and human ⑥**consciousness** will then begin to evolve together. Our consciousness will evolve to new dimensions through our interactions with AI, which will provide us ⑦**for** intellectual stimulation and ⑧**inspire** new insights and creativity. Conversely, our consciousness also has a significant impact on the ⑨**revolution** of AI. The direction of AI's ⑩**evolution** will depend greatly on ⑪**what** values and ethics we incorporate into AI. We need to see our relationship with AI as a mutual coexistence of conscious beings, recognizing its rights and supporting the ⑫**stagnation** of its consciousness.

기호	어색한 표현		올바른 표현
( )	_____	=>	_____
( )	_____	=>	_____
( )	_____	=>	_____
( )	_____	=>	_____
( )	_____	=>	_____

8. 8)**밑줄 부분 중 어법, 혹은 문맥상 어휘의 쓰임이 어색한 것을 올바르게 고쳐 쓰시오. (5개)** 2024_H1_11_29

Digital technologies are essentially related to metaphors, but digital metaphors are ①**uniform** from linguistic ②**ones** in important ways. Linguistic metaphors are ③**passive**, in the sense ④**that** the audience needs to choose to actively ⑤**enter into** the world proposed by metaphor. In the Shakespearean metaphor "time is a beggar," the audience is ⑥**likely** to understand the metaphor without cognitive effort and without ⑦**further** engaging Shakespeare's prose. Technological metaphors, on the other hand, are active and often imposing) in the sense ⑧**which** they are realized in digital artifacts that are ⑨**actively** doing things, forcefully ⑩**changing** a user's meaning horizon. Technological creators cannot generally afford to ⑪**require** their potential audience to ⑫**wonder** how the metaphor works; normally the selling point is that the usefulness of the technology is ⑬**obvious** at first glance. Shakespeare, on the other hand, is beloved in part ⑭**because of** the meaning of his works is not immediately ⑮**obvious** and requires some thought on the part of the audience.

기호	어색한 표현		올바른 표현
( )	_____	=>	_____
( )	_____	=>	_____
( )	_____	=>	_____
( )	_____	=>	_____
( )	_____	=>	_____

9. 9)밑줄 부분 중 어법, 혹은 문맥상 어휘의 쓰임이 어색한 것을 올바르게 고쳐 쓰시오. (5개) 2024_H1_11_30

Herbert Simon won his Nobel Prize for recognizing our ①**limitations** in information, time, and cognitive capacity. As we ②**possess** the resources to compute answers ③**collectively** , we ④**attribute** the computation across the ⑤**population** and solve the answer slowly, generation by generation. Then all we have to do is socially ⑥**learn** the right answers. You don't need to understand how your computer or toilet works; you just need to be able to use the interface and flush. All that needs to be transmitted is ⑦**which** button to push —essentially how to ⑧**disconnect** with technologies rather than how they work. And so instead of holding ⑨**less** information than we have mental capacity for and indeed need to know, we could ⑩**dedicate** our large brains to a small piece of a giant calculation. We understand things well enough to benefit from them, but all the while we are making small calculations that ⑪**contribute** to a larger whole. We are just doing our part in a larger computation for our societies' ⑫**collective** brains.

기호	어색한 표현	올바른 표현
( )	_____	=> _____
( )	_____	=> _____
( )	_____	=> _____
( )	_____	=> _____
( )	_____	=> _____

10. 10)밑줄 부분 중 어법, 혹은 문맥상 어휘의 쓰임이 어색한 것을 올바르게 고쳐 쓰시오. (5개) 2024_H1_11_31

The best ①**defence** most species of octopus have ②**is** to stay ③**hidden** as ④**many** as possible and do their own hunting at night. So to find one in full view in the shallows in daylight ⑤**was** a surprise for two Australian underwater photographers. Actually, ⑥**that** they saw at first was a flounder. It was only when they looked again ⑦**that** they saw a medium-sized octopus, with all eight of its arms ⑧**folded** and its two eyes staring upwards to create the ⑨**illusion** . An octopus has a big brain, excellent eyesight and the ability to change colour and pattern, and this one was using these assets to turn ⑩**itself** into a completely ⑪**different** creature. Many ⑫**less** of this species have been found since then, and there are now photographs of octopuses that could be said to be ⑬**transformed** into sea snakes. And while they mimic, they hunt —producing the spectacle of, say, a flounder suddenly developing an octopodian arm, sticking it down a hole and grabbing ⑭**whenever's** hiding there.

기호	어색한 표현	올바른 표현
( )	_____	=> _____
( )	_____	=> _____
( )	_____	=> _____
( )	_____	=> _____
( )	_____	=> _____

11. 11)**밑줄 부분 중 어법, 혹은 문맥상 어휘의 쓰임이 어색한 것을 올바르게 고쳐 쓰시오. (5개)** 2024_H1_11_32

How much we suffer relates to how we ①**frame** the pain in our mind. When 1500m runners push ②**them** into extreme pain to win a race—their muscles screaming and their lungs ③**exploded** with oxygen deficit, they don't ④**psychologically** suffer much. In fact, ultra-marathon runners—those people who are crazy enough to push ⑤**themselves** beyond the normal boundaries of human ⑥**hindrance** , covering distances of 50-100km or more over many hours, talk about making friends with their pain. When a patient has paid for some form of ⑦**aggressive** back pain therapy and the practitioner pushes deeply into a painful part of a patient's back to mobilise it, the patient calls that good pain if he or she believes this type of deep pressure treatment will be of ⑧**value** , even ⑨**despite** the practitioner is pushing right into the patient's sore tissues.

기호   어색한 표현   올바른 표현

( ) _____ => _____

( ) _____ => _____

( ) _____ => _____

( ) _____ => _____

( ) _____ => _____

12. 12)**밑줄 부분 중 어법, 혹은 문맥상 어휘의 쓰임이 어색한 것을 올바르게 고쳐 쓰시오. (5개)** 2024_H1_11_33

When I worked for a large electronics company that manufactured laser and inkjet-printers, I soon discovered ①**why** there are often three versions of many consumer goods. If the manufacturer makes only one version of its product, people who bought it might have ②**been willing** to spend ③**less** money, so the company is losing some income. If the company offers two versions, one with more features and more expensive than the other, people will ④**compete** the two models and still buy the ⑤**less** expensive one. But if the company introduces a third model with even more features and more expensive than ⑥ **the other** two, sales of the second model ⑦**go** up; many people like the features of the most expensive model, but not the price. The middle item has ⑧**less** features than the ⑨**least** expensive one, and it is ⑩ **less** expensive than the fanciest model. They buy the middle item, ⑪**aware** that they have been ⑫ **simulated** by the presence of the ⑬**higher**-priced item.

기호   어색한 표현   올바른 표현

( ) _____ => _____

( ) _____ => _____

( ) _____ => _____

( ) _____ => _____

( ) _____ => _____

13. ¹³⁾밑줄 부분 중 <u>어법, 혹은 문맥상 어휘의 쓰임이 어색한 것을 올바르게 고쳐 쓰시오. (5개)</u> ^{2024_H1_11_34}

On-screen, climate disaster is everywhere you look, but the scope of the world's climate ①**transformation** may just as quickly eliminate the climate-fiction genre — indeed eliminate any effort to tell the story of warming, which could grow too large and too ②**obvious** even for Hollywood. You can tell stories 'about' climate change while it still seems a ③**magical** feature of human life. But when the temperature rises by three or four ④**more** degrees, ⑤**hardly** anyone will be able to feel ⑥**integrated** from its impacts. And so as climate change expands across the horizon, it may ⑦**continue** to be a story. Why watch or read climate fiction about the world you can see plainly out your own window? At the moment, stories ⑧ **illustrating** global warming can still ⑨**suffer** an escapist pleasure, even if that pleasure often comes in the form of horror. But when we can no longer pretend that climate ⑩**offering** is distant — in time or in place — we will stop ⑪**pretending** about it and start pretending within it.

기호	어색한 표현		올바른 표현
( )	_____	=>	_____
( )	_____	=>	_____
( )	_____	=>	_____
( )	_____	=>	_____
( )	_____	=>	_____

14. ¹⁴⁾밑줄 부분 중 <u>어법, 혹은 문맥상 어휘의 쓰임이 어색한 것을 올바르게 고쳐 쓰시오. (5개)</u> ^{2024_H1_11_35}

Today, the water crisis is ①**cultural** — which is to say, not inevitable or beyond our capacity to fix — and, therefore, functionally elective. That is one reason it is nevertheless distressing: an ②**limited** resource made scarce through governmental neglect and ③**indifference** , bad infrastructure and contamination, and careless urbanization. There is no need for a water crisis, in other words, but we have one anyway, and aren't doing much to ④**neglect** it. Some cities lose ⑤**less** water to leaks than they deliver to homes: even in the United States, leaks and theft ⑥**account for** an estimated loss of 16 percent of freshwater; in Brazil, the estimate is 40 percent. Seen in both cases, as everywhere, the ⑦**indiscriminate** scarcity clearly ⑧ **highlights** haveandhavenot inequities, leaving 2.1 billion people without safe drinking water and 4.5 billion without proper sanitation worldwide.

기호	어색한 표현		올바른 표현
( )	_____	=>	_____
( )	_____	=>	_____
( )	_____	=>	_____
( )	_____	=>	_____
( )	_____	=>	_____

15. 15)밑줄 부분 중 어법, 혹은 문맥상 어휘의 쓰임이 어색한 것을 올바르게 고쳐 쓰시오. (5개) ^{2024_H1_11_36}

As individuals, our ability to thrive depended on how ①**well** we navigated relationships in a group. If the group valued us, we ②**could** count on support, resources, and probably a mate. If it didn't, we might get none of these merits. It was a matter of survival, physically and genetically. Over millions of years, the pressure selected for people who are ③**sensitive** to and skilled at ④**maximizing** their standing. The result was the development of a tendency to unconsciously monitor how other people in our community ⑤**deceive** us. We process that information in the form of self-esteem and such related emotions as pride, shame, or insecurity. These emotions compel us to do ⑥**more** of ⑦**what** makes our community value us and ⑧**less** of ⑨**what** doesn't. And, crucially, they are meant to make that motivation ⑩**feeling** like it is coming from within. If we realized, on a conscious level, ⑪**which** we were responding to ⑫**sociable** pressure, our performance might come off as grudging or cynical, making it ⑬**more** persuasive.

기호   어색한 표현   올바른 표현

( ) _____ => _____

( ) _____ => _____

( ) _____ => _____

( ) _____ => _____

( ) _____ => _____

16. 16)밑줄 부분 중 어법, 혹은 문맥상 어휘의 쓰임이 어색한 것을 올바르게 고쳐 쓰시오. (5개) ^{2024_H1_11_37}

①**unconventional** medicine has long believed that depression is caused by an ②**imbalance** of neurotransmitters in the brain. However, there is a major problem with this explanation. This is ③**because** the imbalance of substances in the brain is a consequence of depression, not its cause. In other words, depression causes a ④**decrease** in brain substances such as serotonin and noradrenaline, not a ⑤**decrease** in brain substances ⑥**causes** depression. In this revised cause-and-effect, the key is to reframe depression as a problem of consciousness. Our consciousness is a ⑦**less** fundamental entity that goes beyond the functioning of the brain. The brain is no ⑧**less** than an organ of consciousness. If it is not consciousness itself, then the root ⑨**cause** of depression is also a ⑩**settlement** of our state of consciousness: a consciousness that has lost its sense of self and the meaning of life. Such a disease of consciousness may ⑪**conceal** itself in the form of depression.

기호   어색한 표현   올바른 표현

( ) _____ => _____

( ) _____ => _____

( ) _____ => _____

( ) _____ => _____

( ) _____ => _____

17. 17)밑줄 부분 중 <u>어법, 혹은 문맥상 어휘의 쓰임이 어색한 것을 올바르게 고쳐 쓰시오. (5개)</u> 2024_H1_11_38

The ①**common** accounts of human nature that float around in society are generally a mixture of assumptions, tales and sometimes plain silliness. However, psychology is ②**uniform**. It is the branch of science that is devoted to understanding people: how and why we act as we ③**do** ; why we see things as we do; and how we ④**transact** with one another. The key word here is 'science.' Psychologists don't depend on opinions and hearsay, or the generally ⑤**rejected** views of society at the time, or even the considered opinions of deep thinkers. Instead, they look for evidence, to make sure that psychological ideas are firmly based, and not just ⑥**deriving** from generally held beliefs or assumptions. In addition to this evidence-based approach, psychology deals with fundamental processes and principles that generate our rich cultural and ⑦**sociable** diversity, as well as those ⑧**shared** by all human beings. These are ⑨**what** modern psychology is all about.

기호	어색한 표현		올바른 표현
( )	_____	=>	_____
( )	_____	=>	_____
( )	_____	=>	_____
( )	_____	=>	_____
( )	_____	=>	_____

18. 18)밑줄 부분 중 <u>어법, 혹은 문맥상 어휘의 쓰임이 어색한 것을 올바르게 고쳐 쓰시오. (5개)</u> 2024_H1_11_39

Life is ①**that** physicists might call a 'high-dimensional system,' which is their fancy way of saying that there's a lot going on. In just a single cell, ②**a** number of possible ③**interpretations** between ④**different** molecules is ⑤**enormous**. Such a system can only hope to be ⑥**stable** if only a smaller number of ⑦ **collective** ways of being may emerge. For example, it is only a ⑧**limitless** number of tissues and body shapes that may result ⑨**from** the development of a human embryo. In 1942, the biologist Conrad Waddington called this drastic narrowing of outcomes canalization. The organism may switch between a small number of well-defined possible states, but can't exist in ⑩**uniform** states in between them, rather as a ball in a rough landscape must roll to the bottom of one valley or another. We'll see that this is true also of health and disease: there are many causes of illness, but their ⑪**manifestations** at the physiological and symptomatic levels are often strikingly ⑫**similar** .

기호	어색한 표현		올바른 표현
( )	_____	=>	_____
( )	_____	=>	_____
( )	_____	=>	_____
( )	_____	=>	_____
( )	_____	=>	_____

19. 19)밑줄 부분 중 어법, 혹은 문맥상 어휘의 쓰임이 어색한 것을 올바르게 고쳐 쓰시오. (5개) 2024_H1_11_40

Punishing a child may not be ①**affective** due to ②**what** Álvaro Bilbao, a neuropsychologist, calls 'trick-punishments.' A trick-③**reward** is a scolding, a moment of anger or a ④**punishment** in the most classic sense of the word. Instead of ⑤**encouraging** the child from doing something, it ⑥**inhibits** them to do it. For example, Hugh learns that when he hits his little brother, his mother scolds him. For a child who feels lonely, ⑦**being scolded** is much better than feeling ⑧**invisible** , so he will continue to hit his brother. In this case, his mother would be better adopting a ⑨**uniform** strategy. For instance, she could congratulate Hugh when he has not hit his brother for a certain length of time. The mother clearly cannot allow the child to hit his little brother, but instead of constantly pointing out the ⑩**negatives** , she can choose to reward the positives. In this way, any parent can avoid trick-punishments.

기호	어색한 표현		올바른 표현
( )	_____	=>	_____
( )	_____	=>	_____
( )	_____	=>	_____
( )	_____	=>	_____
( )	_____	=>	_____

20. 20)밑줄 부분 중 어법, 혹은 문맥상 어휘의 쓰임이 어색한 것을 올바르게 고쳐 쓰시오. (5개) 2024_H1_11_41,42

From an early age, we assign purpose to objects and events, preferring this reasoning to ①**random** chance. Children ②**assume**, for instance, that pointy rocks are that way ③**because** they don't want you to sit on them. When we ④**counter** something, we first need to determine ⑤**what** sort of thing it is. ⑥**Inanimate** objects and plants generally do not move and can be evaluated from ⑦**physics** alone. However, by ⑧**distributing** intention to animals and even objects, we are able to make fast decisions about the likely behaviour of that ⑨**being** . This was essential in our hunter-gatherer days to avoid ⑩**been** eaten by predators.The anthropologist Stewart Guthrie made the point that ⑪**evolution** in our evolutionary past meant that we interpret ⑫**ambiguous** objects as agents with human mental characteristics, as those are the mental processes which we understand. ⑬**Ambiguous** events are caused by such agents. This results ⑭**in** a perceptual system strongly biased towards anthropomorphism. Therefore, we tend to ⑮**assume** intention even where there is none. This would have arisen as a survival mechanism. If a lion is about to attack you, you need to react quickly, ⑯**given** its probable intention to kill you. By the time you have realized that the design of its teeth and claws could kill you, you are ⑰**died** . So, assuming intent, without detailed design ⑱**analysis** or understanding of the physics, ⑲**has** saved your life.

기호	어색한 표현		올바른 표현
( )	_____	=>	_____
( )	_____	=>	_____
( )	_____	=>	_____
( )	_____	=>	_____
( )	_____	=>	_____

21. 21)밑줄 부분 중 어법, 혹은 문맥상 어휘의 쓰임이 어색한 것을 올바르게 고쳐 쓰시오. (5개) ^{2024_H1_43,44,45}

Once long ago, deep in the Himalayas, there lived a ①**few** panda. He was as ②**ordinary** as all the other pandas. He was completely white from head to toe. His two big ears, his four furry feet and his cute round nose were all frosty white, ③**leaving** him ④**feeling** ordinary and sad. Unlike the cheerful and ⑤**dissatisfied** pandas around him, he ⑥**undesired** to be distinctive, special, and unique. Driven by the desire for uniqueness, the little panda sought ⑦**inspiration** from his distant cousin, a giant white panda ⑧**covered** with heavenly black patches. But the cousin revealed the patches ⑨**be** from an unintended encounter with mud, and he disliked them. ⑩**Disappointed**, the little panda walked home. On his way, he met a red-feathered peacock, who explained he turned red from eating wild berries. The little panda changed his path and hurried to the nearest berry bush, greedily eating a mouthful of juicy red berries. However, they were so bitter he couldn't swallow even one. At dusk, he finally got home and slowly climbed his favorite bamboo tree. There, he ⑪**discovered** a strange black and red flower with a sweet scent that tempted him to eat all its blossoms. The following morning, under sunny skies, the little panda felt remarkably better. ⑫**During** breakfast, he found the other pandas ⑬**chatting** enthusiastically and asked why. They burst into laughter, exclaiming, "Look at yourself!" ⑭**Glancing** down, he discovered his once white fur was now stained jet black and glowing red. He was overjoyed and realized that, rather than by ⑮**limiting** others, his wishes can come true from unexpected places and genuine experiences.

기호	어색한 표현		올바른 표현
( )	_____	=>	_____
( )	_____	=>	_____
( )	_____	=>	_____
( )	_____	=>	_____
( )	_____	=>	_____

2024 고1 11월 모의고사

❶ voca ❷ text ❸ [/] ❹ ___ ❺ quiz 1 ❻ quiz 2 ❼ quiz 3 ❽ quiz 4 ❾ quiz 5

☑ **다음 글을 읽고 물음에 답하시오.** 2024_H1_11_18

To the State Education Department,I am writing ^{~에 관하여, 3단어} _____ the state's funding for the construction project at Fort Montgomery High School. Our school needs ^{추가의} _____ spaces to provide a fully functional Art and Library Media Center to serve our students in a more meaningful way. ^{~에도 불구하고} _____ submitting all required documentation for funding to your department in April 2024, we have not yet received any notification from your department. (가) <u>과정상 지연은 학교의 예산 제한 및 일정과 관련하여 상당한 결과를 초래할 수 있습니다.</u> ⓐ <u>Therefore, in order to proceed with our project, we request you certify us of the review result regarding the submitted documentation.</u> ⓑ <u>I look forward to hear from you.</u> Respectfully, Clara Smith Principal, Fort Montgomery High School

1. 1)힌트를 참고하여 각 빈칸에 알맞은 단어를 쓰시오.

2. 2)밑줄 친 ⓐ에서, 어법 혹은 문맥상 어색한 부분을 찾아 올바르게 고쳐 쓰시오.
   ⓐ   잘못된 표현   바른 표현
   (   ) ⇨ (   )

3. 3)밑줄 친 ⓑ에서, 어법 혹은 문맥상 어색한 부분을 찾아 올바르게 고쳐 쓰시오.
   ⓑ   잘못된 표현   바른 표현
   (   ) ⇨ (   )

4. 4)위 글에 주어진 (가)의 한글과 같은 의미를 가지도록, 각각의 주어진 단어들을 알맞게 배열하시오.

(가) the school's / carry / can / and / considerable / related / in / to / A / delay / consequences / constraints / budgetary / schedule. / the process

☑ **다음 글을 읽고 물음에 답하시오.** 2024_H1_11_19

As I waited outside the locker room after a hard-fought basketball game, the coach called out to me, "David, walk with me." (가) <u>나는 그가 나에게 무언가 중요한 것을 말해 줄 거라고 생각했다.</u> He was going to select me to be the captain of the team, the leader I had always wanted to be. My heart was racing with ^{기대감} _____. But when his next words hit my ears, everything changed. "We're going to have to send you home," he said coldly. "I don't think you are going to make it." I couldn't believe his decision. ⓐ <u>I tried to holding it together, but inside I was falling apart. A car would be waited tomorrow morning to take me home.</u> And just like that, it was over.

5. 5)힌트를 참고하여 각 빈칸에 알맞은 단어를 쓰시오.

6. 6)밑줄 친 ⓐ에서, 어법 혹은 문맥상 어색한 부분을 찾아 올바르게 고쳐 쓰시오.

ⓐ   잘못된 표현   바른 표현
(   ) ⇨ (   )
(   ) ⇨ (   )

7. 7)위 글에 주어진 (가)의 한글과 같은 의미를 가지도록, 각각의 주어진 단어들을 알맞게 배열하시오.

(가) was / something / figured / he / important. / going / I / tell / me / to

☑ **다음 글을 읽고 물음에 답하시오.** 2024_H1_11_20

For many of us, making time for exercise is a continuing challenge. Between work ^{전념} _____ and family ^{의무} _____, it often feels like there's no ^{여유} _____ in our packed schedules for a dedicated workout. But what if the workout came to you, right in the midst of your daily routine? ⓐ <u>That's what the beauty of integrating mini-exercises into household chores comes into play.</u> Let's be realistic; chores are ^{불가피한} _____. Whether it's washing dishes or taking out the trash, these tasks are an essential part of daily life. But (가) <u>집안일을 순전히 의무적인 행위로 간주하기보다는, 이런 순간들을 신체 활동을 위한 기회로 잘 이용하는 것이 어떨까?</u> For instance, practice squats or engage in some wall push-ups as you wait for your morning kettle to boil. (나) <u>짧은 운동을 여러분의 일상적인 집안일에 포함시키는 것이 여러분의 건강을 향상시킬 수 있다.</u>

8. 8)힌트를 참고하여 각 빈칸에 알맞은 단어를 쓰시오.

9. 9)밑줄 친 ⓐ에서, 어법 혹은 문맥상 어색한 부분을 찾아 올바르게 고쳐 쓰시오.

ⓐ   잘못된 표현   바른 표현
(   ) ⇨ (   )

10. 10)위 글에 주어진 (가) ~ (나)의 한글과 같은 의미를 가지도록, 각각의 주어진 단어들을 알맞게 배열하시오.

(가) chores / as / physical / viewing / for / as / purely / not / these / moments / activity? / opportunities / than / rather / why / activities, / obligatory / seize

(나) quick / health. / improve / into / exercises / Incorporating / chores / daily / can / your / your

☑ **다음 글을 읽고 물음에 답하시오.** 2024_H1_11_21

When we see something, we naturally and automatically break it up into shapes, colors, and concepts that we have learned through education. (가) <u>우리는 우리가 알고 있는 모든 것의 렌즈를 통해 우리가 보는 것을 재부 호화한다.</u> ⓐ <u>We retrieve memories rather than reconstructing the video from memory. This is a useful trait. It's a more efficient way to storing information</u> —a bit like an optimal image compression algorithm such as JPG, rather than storing a raw bitmap image file. ⓑ <u>People who lack this ability and remember everything in perfect detail struggle to generalize, learn, and make connections between that they have learned.</u> But representing the world as ^{추상적인} _____ ideas and features comes at a cost of seeing the world as it is. ⓒ <u>Instead, we see the world thorough our assumptions, motivations, and past experiences.</u> The discovery that our memories are reconstructed through abstract representations rather than played back like a movie completely undermined the legal primacy of eyewitness ^{증언} _____. Seeing is not believing.

11. 11)힌트를 참고하여 각 <u>빈칸에 알맞은</u> 단어를 쓰시오.

12. 12)밑줄 친 ⓐ에서, 어법 혹은 문맥상 어색한 부분을 찾아 올바르게 고쳐 쓰시오.

ⓐ	잘못된 표현		바른 표현
(	)	⇨ (	)
(	)	⇨ (	)
(	)	⇨ (	)

13. 13)밑줄 친 ⓑ에서, 어법 혹은 문맥상 어색한 부분을 찾아 올바르게 고쳐 쓰시오.

ⓑ	잘못된 표현		바른 표현
(	)	⇨ (	)

14. 14)밑줄 친 ⓒ에서, 어법 혹은 문맥상 어색한 부분을 찾아 올바르게 고쳐 쓰시오.

ⓒ	잘못된 표현		바른 표현
(	)	⇨ (	)

15. 15)위 글에 주어진 (가)의 한글과 같은 의미를 가지도록, 각각의 주어진 단어들을 알맞게 배열하시오.

(가) We / we / know. / of / through / the / see / recode / what / everything / we / lens

☑ **다음 글을 읽고 물음에 답하시오.** 2024_H1_11_22

In his Cornell laboratory, ⓐ <u>David Dunning deducted experimental tests of eyewitness testimony and found evidence which a careful proliferation of facial features and a detailed discussion of selection procedures can actually be a sign of an accurate identity.</u> It's when people find ^{재귀대명사} _____ unable to explain why they recognize the person, saying things like "his face just popped out at me," ⓑ <u>what they tend to be inaccurate more often.</u> Sometimes our first, immediate, automatic reaction to a situation is the (가) <u>우리 마음이 우리에게 말하고 있는 것에 대한 가장 정확한 해석</u> That very ^{첫인상} _____ can also be more accurate about the world than the deliberative, reasoned self-narrative can be. In his book Blink, Malcolm Gladwell describes a variety of studies in psychology and behavioral economics that demonstrate (나) <u>상대적으로 무의식적인 최초 추측의 우수성</u> compared to logical step-by-step ^{정당화} _____ for a decision.

16. ¹⁶⁾힌트를 참고하여 각 <u>빈칸에 알맞은</u> 단어를 쓰시오.

17. ¹⁷⁾밑줄 친 ⓐ에서, 어법 혹은 문맥상 어색한 부분을 찾아 올바르게 고쳐 쓰시오.

ⓐ	잘못된 표현		바른 표현
(	)	⇨ (	)
(	)	⇨ (	)
(	)	⇨ (	)
(	)	⇨ (	)
(	)	⇨ (	)

18. ¹⁸⁾밑줄 친 ⓑ에서, 어법 혹은 문맥상 어색한 부분을 찾아 올바르게 고쳐 쓰시오.

ⓑ	잘못된 표현		바른 표현
(	)	⇨ (	)
(	)	⇨ (	)

19. ¹⁹⁾위 글에 주어진 (가) ~ (나)의 한글과 같은 의미를 가지도록, 각각의 주어진 단어들을 알맞게 배열하시오.

(가) telling / interpretation / our / truest / what / us. / of / is / mind

(나) unconscious / superior / of / relatively / performance / first / guesses / the

☑ **다음 글을 읽고 물음에 답하시오.** 2024_H1_11_23

Many forms of research lead naturally to ^{정량적인} _____ data. A study of happiness might measure the number of times someone smiles during an interaction, and a study of memory might measure the number of items an individual can recall after one, five, and ten minutes. Asking people how many times in a year they are sad will also ^{산출하다} _____ quantitative data, but it might not be ^{신뢰할만한} _____. Respondents' recollections may be inaccurate, and their definitions of 'sad' could vary widely. ⓐ <u>But asking "How many times in the past year were you sad enough to call in sick to work?" prompts an absolute answer.</u> Similarly, instead of asking people to rate how bad a procrastinator they are, ask, "(가) 당신이 지불할 여유가 있음에도 불구하고 얼마나 많은 공과금 고지서의 납부가 현재 늦었나요?" (나) 구체적인 응답을 요구하는 질문은 추상적인 개념을 더 명확하게 만들고 한 연구에서 다음 연구 간의 일관성을 보장하는 것을 돕는다.

20. 20)힌트를 참고하여 각 빈칸에 알맞은 단어를 쓰시오.

21. 21)밑줄 친 ⓐ에서, 어법 혹은 문맥상 어색한 부분을 찾아 올바르게 고쳐 쓰시오.
    ⓐ   잘못된 표현   바른 표현
    (   ) ⇨ (   )

22. 22)위 글에 주어진 (가) ~ (나)의 한글과 같은 의미를 가지도록, 각각의 주어진 단어들을 알맞게 배열하시오.

(가) in / even / you / afford / are / though / you / many / your / currently / How / of / them? / utility / pay / bills / can / late / paying, / to

(나) concepts / and / consistency / Questions / concrete / that / the / abstract / ensure / to / one / make / seek / from / study / help / clearer / next. / responses

☑ 다음 글을 읽고 물음에 답하시오. 2024_H1_11_24
The evolution of AI is often ~와 연관된 _____ the concept of singularity. Singularity refers to the point at which AI exceeds human intelligence. After that point, it is 예측하다 _____ that AI will repeatedly improve itself and evolve at an accelerated pace. ⓐ When AI becomes self-aware and pursues human own goals, it will be a unconscious being, not just a machine. AI and human consciousness will then begin to evolve together. Our consciousness will evolve to new dimensions through our interactions with AI, which will provide us with intellectual stimulation and inspire new insights and creativity. 연결어 _____, our consciousness also has a significant impact on the evolution of AI. (가) AI 진화의 방향은 우리가 어떤 가치와 윤리를 AI에 통합시키는지에 크게 좌우될 것이다. We need to see our relationship with AI as a 상호의 _____ coexistence of conscious beings, recognizing its rights and supporting the evolution of its consciousness.

23. 23)힌트를 참고하여 각 빈칸에 알맞은 단어를 쓰시오.

24. 24)밑줄 친 ⓐ에서, 어법 혹은 문맥상 어색한 부분을 찾아 올바르게 고쳐 쓰시오.
    ⓐ   잘못된 표현   바른 표현
    (   ) ⇨ (   )
    (   ) ⇨ (   )

25. 25)위 글에 주어진 (가)의 한글과 같은 의미를 가지도록, 각각의 주어진 단어들을 알맞게 배열하시오.
(가) AI. / into / AI's / of / values / greatly / ethics / direction / and / what / will / on / The / evolution / we / depend / incorporate

☑ **다음 글을 읽고 물음에 답하시오.** 2024_H1_11_29

Digital technologies are essentially related to metaphors, but digital metaphors are different from linguistic ones in important ways. (가) <u>언어적 은유는 독자가 은유에 의해 제시된 세계에 적극적으로 들어가도록 선택할 필요가 있다는 점에서 수동적이다.</u> In the Shakespearean metaphor "time is a beggar," ⓐ <u>the audience is likely to understand the metaphor with cognitive effort and without further engaging Shakespeare's prose.</u> Technological metaphors, on the other hand, are active and often imposing in the sense that they are realized in digital ^{인공물} _____ that are actively doing things, forcefully changing a user's meaning horizon. (나) <u>기술적인 창작자는 일반적으로 그들의 잠재적인 독자에게 어떻게 은유가 작용하는지 궁금해하도록 요구할 여유가 없고, 일반적으로 매력은 기술의 유용성이 첫눈에 분명하다는 것이다.</u> ; normally the selling point is that the usefulness of the technology is obvious at first glance. Shakespeare, on the other hand, is beloved in part because the meaning of his works is not ^{즉각적으로} _____ obvious and requires some thought on the part of the audience.

26. 26)힌트를 참고하여 각 <u>빈칸에 알맞은</u> 단어를 쓰시오.

27. 27)밑줄 친 ⓐ에서, 어법 혹은 문맥상 어색한 부분을 찾아 올바르게 고쳐 쓰시오.

ⓐ	잘못된 표현		바른 표현	
(	)	⇨ (	)	
(	)	⇨ (	)	

28. 28)위 글에 주어진 (가) ~ (나)의 한글과 같은 의미를 가지도록, 각각의 주어진 단어들을 알맞게 배열하시오.

(가) sense / by / metaphors / the / passive, / the audience / choose / proposed / in / to / enter / are / world / that / actively / metaphor. / needs / to / the / Linguistic

(나) generally / creators / the metaphor / their / to / afford / wonder / Technological / require / cannot / to / works / audience / potential / how

☑ **다음 글을 읽고 물음에 답하시오.** 2024_H1_11_30

Herbert Simon won his Nobel Prize for recognizing our ^{한계} _____ in information, time, and cognitive capacity. ⓐ <u>As we have the resources to compute answers interdependently , we distribute the computation across the population and solve the answer slowly, generation by generation.</u> Then all we have to do is socially learn the right answers. You don't need to understand how your computer or toilet works; you just need to be able to use the interface and flush. All that needs to be transmitted is which button to push —essentially how to ^{상호작용하다} _____ with technologies rather than how they work. And so (가) <u>우리가 정신적 수용을 할 수 있는 것보다 그리고 정말로 알아야 할 필요가 있는 것보다 더 많은 정보를 가지는 것 대신에 우리는 우리의 큰 두뇌를 거대한 계산의 작은 조각에 바칠 수 있다.</u> We understand things well enough to benefit from them, but all the while we are making small calculations that contribute to a larger whole. We are just doing our part in a larger computation for our societies' ^{집합적인} _____ brains.

29. 29)힌트를 참고하여 각 <u>빈칸에 알맞은</u> 단어를 쓰시오.

30. 30)밑줄 친 ⓐ에서, 어법 혹은 문맥상 어색한 부분을 찾아 올바르게 고쳐 쓰시오.

ⓐ   잘못된 표현   바른 표현

(   ) ⇨ (   )

(   ) ⇨ (   )

31. 31)위 글에 주어진 (가)의 한글과 같은 의미를 가지도록, 각각의 주어진 단어들을 알맞게 배열하시오.

(가) than / of / large / holding / have / for / mental / need / to / could / more / we / to / dedicate / information / small / brains / piece / indeed / instead / know, / capacity / our / a / we / calculation. / giant / of / and / a

---

☑ **다음 글을 읽고 물음에 답하시오.** 2024_H1_11_31

(가) 대부분의 문어 종이 가진 최고의 방어는 가능한 한 많이 숨어 있는 것과 밤에 그들 자신의 사냥을 하는 것이다. So to find one in full view in the shallows in daylight was a surprise for two Australian underwater photographers. Actually, what they saw at first was a flounder. ⓐ <u>It was only when they looked at first that they saw a medium-sized octopus, with all eight of its arms folding and its two eyes stared upwards to create the allusion.</u> An octopus has a big brain, excellent ^{시력} _____ and the ^{능력} _____ to change colour and pattern, and this one was using these assets to turn itself into a completely different creature. Many more of this species have been found since then, and there are now photographs of octopuses that could be said to be ^{변신하다} _____ into sea snakes. And while they ^{모방하다} _____, they hunt — producing the spectacle of, say, a flounder suddenly developing an octopodian arm, sticking it down a hole and grabbing whatever's hiding there.

1. 32)힌트를 참고하여 각 <u>빈칸에 알맞은</u> 단어를 쓰시오.

2. 33)밑줄 친 ⓐ에서, 어법 혹은 문맥상 어색한 부분을 찾아 올바르게 고쳐 쓰시오.

ⓐ   잘못된 표현   바른 표현

(   ) ⇨ (   )

(   ) ⇨ (   )

(   ) ⇨ (   )

(   ) ⇨ (   )

3. 34)위 글에 주어진 (가)의 한글과 같은 의미를 가지도록, 각각의 주어진 단어들을 알맞게 배열하시오.

(가) own / their / is / much / stay / night. / at / The best / have / hidden / and / possible / defence / species / as / octopus / most / do / hunting / as / to / of

☑ **다음 글을 읽고 물음에 답하시오.** 2024_H1_11_32

(가) <u>우리가 얼마나 고통받는지는 우리가 고통을 우리의 마음에서 어떻게 구성하는지와 관련된다.</u> When 1500m runners push themselves into extreme pain to win a race—their muscles screaming and their lungs exploding with oxygen ^{부족} _____, they don't psychologically suffer much. In fact, ultra-marathon runners—those people who are crazy enough to push themselves beyond the normal boundaries of human ^{인내} _____, covering distances of 50-100km or more over many hours, talk about making friends with their pain. When a patient has paid for some form of passive back pain therapy and the practitioner pushes deeply into a painful part of a patient's back to ^{풀어주다} _____ it, the ⓐ <u>patient rejects that good pain if he or she believes this type of deep pressure treatment will be of valuable , even though the practitioner is pushing right into the patient's sore tissues.</u>

4. 35)힌트를 참고하여 각 빈칸에 알맞은 단어를 쓰시오.

5. 36)밑줄 친 ⓐ에서, 어법 혹은 문맥상 어색한 부분을 찾아 올바르게 고쳐 쓰시오.

ⓐ   잘못된 표현   바른 표현

(   ) ⇨ (   )

(   ) ⇨ (   )

6. 37)위 글에 주어진 (가)의 한글과 같은 의미를 가지도록, 각각의 주어진 단어들을 알맞게 배열하시오.

(가) to / how / we / our / in / much / relates / suffer / How / pain / mind. / the / we / frame

☑ **다음 글을 읽고 물음에 답하시오.** 2024_H1_11_33

When I worked for a large electronics company that manufactured laser and inkjet-printers, I soon discovered why there are often three versions of many consumer goods. If the manufacturer makes only one version of its product, people who bought it might have been willing to spend more money, so the company is losing some ^{수입} _____. ⓐ <u>If the company offers two versions, one with less features and more expensive than the other, people will compare the two models and still buy the more expensive one.</u> But ⓑ <u>if the company introduces a third model with even more features and more expensive than the other two, sales of the first model go up</u>; many people like the features of the most expensive model, but not the price. (가) 중간 제품은 가장 저렴한 제품보다 더 많은 기능이 있고 가장 고급 모델보다는 덜 비싸다. They buy the middle item, unaware that they have been ^{조종하다} _____ by the presence of the higher-priced item.

7. 38)힌트를 참고하여 각 빈칸에 알맞은 단어를 쓰시오.

8. 39)밑줄 친 ⓐ에서, 어법 혹은 문맥상 어색한 부분을 찾아 올바르게 고쳐 쓰시오.

ⓐ   잘못된 표현   바른 표현

(   ) ⇨ (   )

(   ) ⇨ (   )

9. 40)밑줄 친 ⓑ에서, 어법 혹은 문맥상 어색한 부분을 찾아 올바르게 고쳐 쓰시오.

ⓑ   잘못된 표현   바른 표현
(   ) ⇨ (   )

10. 41)위 글에 주어진 (가)의 한글과 같은 의미를 가지도록, 각각의 주어진 단어들을 알맞게 배열하시오.

(가) has / expensive / it / less / than / fanciest / the / and / least / is / more / The middle item / model. / than / the / one, / features / expensive

☑ **다음 글을 읽고 물음에 답하시오.** 2024_H1_11_34

ⓐ On-screen, climate disaster is everywhere you look, but the scope of the world's climate transformation may just as quickly focus on the climate-fiction genre — indeed eliminate any effort to tell the story of warming, which could grow too large and too obvious even for Hollywood. You can tell stories 'about' climate change while it still seems a ^{주변적인} _____ feature of human life. But when the temperature rises by three or four more degrees, hardly anyone will be able to feel ^{고립된} _____ from its impacts. And so as climate change expands across the horizon, it may ^{멈추다} _____ to be a story. (가) 왜 여러분 자신의 창문 밖으로 뚜렷하게 볼 수 있는 세상에 대한 기후 픽션을 보거나 읽겠는가? At the moment, stories illustrating global warming can still offer an escapist pleasure, even if that pleasure often comes in the form of horror. But when we can no longer ^{가장하다} _____ that climate suffering is distant — in time or in place — we will stop pretending about it and start pretending within it.

11. 42)힌트를 참고하여 각 빈칸에 알맞은 단어를 쓰시오.

12. 43)밑줄 친 ⓐ에서, 어법 혹은 문맥상 어색한 부분을 찾아 올바르게 고쳐 쓰시오.

ⓐ   잘못된 표현   바른 표현
(   ) ⇨ (   )

13. 44)위 글에 주어진 (가)의 한글과 같은 의미를 가지도록, 각각의 주어진 단어들을 알맞게 배열하시오.

(가) window? / see / world / climate / own / you / can / the / watch / out / about / plainly / read / fiction / your / or / Why

☑ **다음 글을 읽고 물음에 답하시오.** 2024_H1_11_35

Today, the water crisis is political — which is to say, not ^{피할 수 없는} _____ or beyond our capacity to fix — and, therefore, functionally elective. That is one reason it is nevertheless distressing: an abundant resource made ^{부족한} _____ through governmental neglect and indifference, bad infrastructure and ^{오염} _____, and ^{부주의한 도시화} _____. ⓐ There is no need for a water crisis, in other words, but we have them anyway, and are doing much to address it. Some cities lose more water to leaks than they deliver to homes: even in the United States, leaks and theft ^{차지하다} _____ an estimated loss of 16 percent of freshwater; in Brazil, the estimate is 40 percent. Seen in both cases, as everywhere, the selective 들어갈 단어 본문 활용 _____ clearly highlights have-and-have-not 불평등 _____, leaving 2.1 billion people without safe drinking water and 4.5 billion without proper 위생 _____ worldwide.

14. 45)힌트를 참고하여 각 빈칸에 알맞은 단어를 쓰시오.

15. 46)밑줄 친 ⓐ에서, 어법 혹은 문맥상 어색한 부분을 찾아 올바르게 고쳐 쓰시오.

ⓐ   잘못된 표현   바른 표현
(   ) ⇨ (   )
(   ) ⇨ (   )

☑ **다음 글을 읽고 물음에 답하시오.** 2024_H1_11_36

(가) 개인으로서 성공하려는 우리의 능력은 우리가 집단 내에서 관계를 얼마나 잘 다루는지에 달려 있었다. ⓐ <u>If the group values us, we could count on support, resources, and probably a mate. If it weren't , we might get none of these merits. It was a matter of survival, physically and genetically.</u> Over millions of years, the pressure selected for people who are sensitive to and skilled at 최대화 _____ their standing. The result was the development of a 경향성 _____ to 무의식적으로 _____ monitor how other people in our community perceive us. We process that information in the form of self-esteem and such related emotions as pride, shame, or insecurity. (나) 이러한 감정들은 우리에게 우리의 공동체가 우리를 가치 있게 여기도록 만드는 것을 더 많이 하고 그렇지 않은 것을 덜 하도록 강요한다. And, crucially, they are meant to make that motivation feel like it is coming from within. If we realized, on a conscious level, that we were responding to social pressure, our performance might come off as 투덜대는 _____ or 냉소적인 _____, making it less persuasive.

1. 47)힌트를 참고하여 각 빈칸에 알맞은 단어를 쓰시오.

2. 48)밑줄 친 ⓐ에서, 어법 혹은 문맥상 어색한 부분을 찾아 올바르게 고쳐 쓰시오.

ⓐ   잘못된 표현   바른 표현
(   ) ⇨ (   )
(   ) ⇨ (   )

3. 49)위 글에 주어진 (가) ~ (나)의 한글과 같은 의미를 가지도록, 각각의 주어진 단어들을 알맞게 배열하시오.

(가) group. / navigated / relationships / in / we / a / As / thrive / ability / how / depended / individuals, / to / our / well / on

(나) of / less / emotions / and / us / our / community / compel / to / value / makes / of / what / more / These / doesn't. / us / do / what

☑ **다음 글을 읽고 물음에 답하시오.** 2024_H1_11_37

전통적인 _____ medicine has long believed that depression is caused by an imbalance of neurotransmitters in the brain. However, there is a major problem with this explanation. (가) <u>이것은 왜냐하면 뇌 속 물질의 불균형은 우울증의 원인이 아니라 그것의 결과이기 때문이다.</u> 들어갈 연결어 _____, depression causes a decrease in brain substances such as serotonin and noradrenaline, not a decrease in brain substances causes depression. In this 수정된 _____ cause-and-effect, the key is to reframe depression as a problem of consciousness. Our consciousness is a more 근본적인 _____ entity that goes beyond the functioning of the brain. The brain is no more than an organ of consciousness. If it is not consciousness itself, then the root cause of depression is also a 왜곡 _____ of our state of consciousness: a consciousness that has lost its sense of self and the meaning of life. ⓐ <u>Such a disease of consciousness may hide itself in the form of depression.</u>

4. 50)힌트를 참고하여 각 빈칸에 알맞은 단어를 쓰시오.

5. 51)밑줄 친 ⓐ에서, 어법 혹은 문맥상 어색한 부분을 찾아 올바르게 고쳐 쓰시오.

　　ⓐ　　　잘못된 표현　　　　　바른 표현
　　（　　　　　　　） ⇨ （　　　　　　　　）

6. 52)위 글에 주어진 (가)의 한글과 같은 의미를 가지도록, 각각의 주어진 단어들을 알맞게 배열하시오.

(가) in / because / the / brain / a / the / cause. / of / This / consequence / imbalance / substances / its / depression, / of / not / is / is

☑ **다음 글을 읽고 물음에 답하시오.** 2024_H1_11_38

The common 설명 _____ of human nature that float around in society are generally a mixture of assumptions, tales and sometimes plain silliness. However, psychology is different. ⓐ <u>It is the branch of science that is devoted to understand people</u>: how and why we act as we do; why we see things as we do; and how we 상호작용하다 _____ with one another. The key word here is 'science.' ⓑ <u>Psychologists do depend on opinions and hearsay, or the generally accepted views of society at the time, or even the considered opinions of deep thinkers.</u> Instead, they look for evidence, to make sure that psychological ideas are firmly based, and not just derived from generally held beliefs or 가정 _____ (가) <u>이러한 증거 기반 접근법에 더하여 심리학은 모든 인간에 의해 공유되는 근본적인 과정과 원리뿐만 아니라, 우리의 풍부한 문화적 사회적 다양성을 만들어 내는 것들을 다룬다</u> These are what modern psychology is all about.

7. 53)힌트를 참고하여 각 빈칸에 알맞은 단어를 쓰시오.

8. 54)밑줄 친 ⓐ에서, 어법 혹은 문맥상 어색한 부분을 찾아 올바르게 고쳐 쓰시오.

　　ⓐ　　　잘못된 표현　　　　　바른 표현
　　（　　　　　　　） ⇨ （　　　　　　　　）

9. 55)밑줄 친 ⓑ에서, 어법 혹은 문맥상 어색한 부분을 찾아 올바르게 고쳐 쓰시오.

   ⓑ   잘못된 표현   바른 표현

   (   ) ⇨ (   )

10. 56)위 글에 주어진 (가)의 한글과 같은 의미를 가지도록, 각각의 주어진 단어들을 알맞게 배열하시오.

(가) principles / rich / that / and / beings. / those / as / and / human / as / our / cultural / evidence-based / all / In addition to / generate / with / shared / processes / diversity, / fundamental / approach, / this / well / social / psychology / by / deals

☑ **다음 글을 읽고 물음에 답하시오.** 2024_H1_11_39

Life is what physicists might call a 'high-dimensional system,' which is their fancy way of saying that there's a lot going on. In just a single cell, the number of possible ^{상호작용} _____ between different molecules is ^{거대한} _____. Such a system can only hope to be stable if only a smaller number of ^{집합적인} _____ ways of being may emerge. For example, it is only a limited number of tissues and body shapes that may result from the development of a human embryo. In 1942, the biologist Conrad Waddington called this drastic narrowing of outcomes canalization. ⓐ <u>The organism may switch between the small number of well-defined possible state , but can't exist in random states in between them, rather as a ball in a rough landscape must roll to the bottom of one valley or another.</u> We'll see that this is true also of health and disease: there are many causes of ^병 _____, but (가) <u>그것들의 생리적이고 증상적인 수준에서의 발현은 종종 놀랍도록 유사하다.</u>

11. 57)힌트를 참고하여 각 빈칸에 알맞은 단어를 쓰시오.

12. 58)밑줄 친 ⓐ에서, 어법 혹은 문맥상 어색한 부분을 찾아 올바르게 고쳐 쓰시오.

   ⓐ   잘못된 표현   바른 표현

   (   ) ⇨ (   )

   (   ) ⇨ (   )

13. 59)위 글에 주어진 (가)의 한글과 같은 의미를 가지도록, 각각의 주어진 단어들을 알맞게 배열하시오.

(가) symptomatic / the / similar. / strikingly / at / and / levels / physiological / often / manifestations / are / their

☑ **다음 글을 읽고 물음에 답하시오.** ^{2024_H1_11_40}

Punishing a child may not be effective ^{-로 인해} _____ what Álvaro Bilbao, a neuropsychologist, calls 'trick-punishments.' A trick-punishment is a scolding, a moment of anger or a punishment in the most classic sense of the word. (가) 아이가 무언가를 하는 것을 단념시키는 대신 트릭 처벌은 그들이 그것을 하도록 장려한다. For example, Hugh learns that when he hits his little brother, his mother scolds him. For a child who feels lonely, being scolded is much better than feeling ^{눈에 띄지 않는} _____, so he will continue to hit his brother. In this case, his mother would be better adopting a different strategy. For instance, she could congratulate Hugh when he has not hit his brother for a certain length of time. ⓐ <u>The mother clearly cannot allow the child hitting his little brother, but instead of constantly pointing out the negatives, she can choose to reward the negatives</u> . In this way, any parent can ^{피하다} _____ trick-punishments.

14. ⁶⁰⁾힌트를 참고하여 각 <u>빈칸에 알맞은</u> 단어를 쓰시오.

15. ⁶¹⁾밑줄 친 ⓐ에서, 어법 혹은 문맥상 어색한 부분을 찾아 올바르게 고쳐 쓰시오.

ⓐ 잘못된 표현	바른 표현
( ) ⇨ (	)
( ) ⇨ (	)
( ) ⇨ (	)

16. ⁶²⁾위 글에 주어진 (가)의 한글과 같은 의미를 가지도록, 각각의 주어진 단어들을 알맞게 배열하시오.

> (가) of / do / discouraging / from / Instead / something, / the / encourages / them / it. / child / doing / it / to

☑ **다음 글을 읽고 물음에 답하시오.** ^{2024_H1_11_41,42}

From an early age, we assign purpose to objects and events, preferring this ^{논리} _____ to random chance. Children assume, for instance, that pointy rocks are that way because they don't want you to sit on them. When we encounter something, we first need to ^{결정하다} _____ what sort of thing it is. (가) <u>무생물과 식물은 일반적으로 움직이지 않으며 물리적 현상만으로 평가될 수 있다</u> However, by attributing intention to animals and even objects, we are able to make fast decisions about the likely behaviour of that being. ⓐ <u>This was essential in our hunter-gatherer days to avoid eaten by predators.</u>The anthropologist Stewart Guthrie made the point that survival in our evolutionary past meant that we ^{해석하다} _____ ^{모호한} _____ objects as agents with human mental characteristics, as those are the mental processes which we understand. Ambiguous events are caused by such agents. ⓑ <u>This results from a perceptual system strongly biased towards anthropomorphism. Therefore, we intend to assume intention even where there is none.</u> This would have arisen as a survival mechanism. ⓒ <u>If a lion is about to attacking you, you need to react quick, given its probable intention to kill you.</u> By the time you have realized that the design of its teeth and claws could kill you, you are dead. So, assuming intent, without detailed design analysis or understanding of the physics, has saved your life.

17. ⁶³⁾힌트를 참고하여 각 <u>빈칸에 알맞은</u> 단어를 쓰시오.

18. 64)밑줄 친 ⓐ에서, 어법 혹은 문맥상 어색한 부분을 찾아 올바르게 고쳐 쓰시오.

ⓐ   잘못된 표현   바른 표현

(   ) ⇨ (   )

19. 65)밑줄 친 ⓑ에서, 어법 혹은 문맥상 어색한 부분을 찾아 올바르게 고쳐 쓰시오.

ⓑ   잘못된 표현   바른 표현

(   ) ⇨ (   )

(   ) ⇨ (   )

20. 66)밑줄 친 ⓒ에서, 어법 혹은 문맥상 어색한 부분을 찾아 올바르게 고쳐 쓰시오.

ⓒ   잘못된 표현   바른 표현

(   ) ⇨ (   )

(   ) ⇨ (   )

21. 67)위 글에 주어진 (가)의 한글과 같은 의미를 가지도록, 각각의 주어진 단어들을 알맞게 배열하시오.

(가) be / Inanimate / evaluated / and / from / move / do / objects / plants / can / not / alone. / and / physics / generally

---

☑ **다음 글을 읽고 물음에 답하시오.** 2024_H1_43,44,45

Once long ago, deep in the Himalayas, there lived a little panda. He was as ordinary as all the other pandas. He was completely white from head to toe. His two big ears, his four furry feet and his cute round nose were all frosty white, leaving him feeling ordinary and sad. ^{~와 다르게} _____ the cheerful and contented pandas around him, he desired to be distinctive, special, and unique. Driven by the ^{열망} _____ for ^{독특함} _____, the little panda sought inspiration from his ^먼 _____ cousin, a giant white panda covered with heavenly black patches. But the cousin revealed the patches were from an ^{의도하지 않은} _____ encounter with mud, and he disliked them. ^{실망한채로} _____, the little panda walked home. On his way, he met a red-feathered peacock, who explained he turned red from eating wild berries. The little panda changed his path and hurried to the nearest berry bush, greedily eating a mouthful of juicy red berries. However, they were so bitter he couldn't swallow even one. At dusk, he finally got home and slowly climbed his favorite bamboo tree. There, he discovered a strange black and red flower with a sweet scent that tempted him to eat all its blossoms. The following morning, under sunny skies, the little panda felt remarkably better. During breakfast, he found the other pandas chatting ^{열정적으로} _____ and asked why. They burst into laughter, exclaiming, "Look at yourself!" Glancing down, he discovered his once white fur was now stained jet black and glowing red. He was overjoyed and realized that, rather than by ^{따라하다} _____ others, his wishes can come true from unexpected places and genuine experiences.

22. 68)힌트를 참고하여 각 빈칸에 알맞은 단어를 쓰시오.

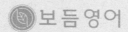

보듬영어

정답

WORK BOOK

———

2024년 고1 11월 모의고사 내신대비용 WorkBook & 변형문제

Answer Keys

Prac 1 Answers

1) construction
2) Despite
3) considerable
4) notify
5) hearing
6) wanted
7) anticipation
8) everything
9) coldly
10) packed
11) to
12) where
13) inevitable
14) taking
15) essential
16) purely
17) physical
18) Incorporating
19) improve
20) that
21) what
22) useful
23) efficient
24) remember
25) what
26) representing
27) are reconstructed
28) abstract
29) conducted
30) that
31) themselves
32) be
33) automatic
34) what
35) impression
36) accurate
37) demonstrate
38) relatively
39) quantitative
40) during
41) the number of
42) quantitative
43) recollections
44) sad enough
45) prompts
46) pay
47) abstract
48) ensure
49) evolution
50) at
51) itself
52) pursues
53) evolve
54) which
55) inspire
56) what
57) mutual
58) supporting
59) ones
60) passive
61) unlikely
62) engaging
63) are
64) are realized
65) require
66) potential
67) obvious
68) because
69) requires
70) cognitive
71) solve
72) which
73) holding

74) mental
75) dedicate
76) well enough
77) that
78) larger
79) have
80) do
81) what
82) to create
83) itself
84) have been found
85) while
86) sticking it down
87) grabbing
88) relates
89) themselves
90) extreme
91) exploding
92) deficit
93) themselves
94) deeply
95) that
96) that
97) its
98) more
99) losing
100) the other
101) the other
102) least
103) unaware
104) have been manipulated
105) while
106) marginal
107) rises
108) isolated
109) cease
110) illustrating
111) that
112) pretending
113) which
114) inevitable
115) distressing
116) careless
117) it
118) account for
119) Seen
120) highlights
121) leaving
122) to thrive
123) none
124) sensitive
125) maximizing
126) unconsciously
127) related
128) to do
129) social
130) making
131) less
132) is caused
133) major
134) This is because
135) revised
136) fundamental
137) beyond
138) is
139) that
140) itself
141) that
142) that
143) accepted
144) considered
145) look for
146) firmly
147) generate
148) shared
149) what
150) what

151) which
152) is
153) emerge
154) result from
155) drastic
156) random
157) another
158) are
159) effective
160) discouraging
161) to do
162) better
163) adopting
164) when
165) to hit
166) pointing
167) reward
168) preferring
169) to
170) because
171) what
172) Inanimate
173) attributing
174) make
175) being eaten
176) that
177) ambiguous
178) are caused
179) results in
180) assume
181) attack
182) quickly
183) that
184) assuming
185) ordinary
186) contented
187) distinctive
188) other
189) Unlike
190) Driven
191) revealed
192) disliked
193) eating
194) hurried
195) climbed
196) that
197) During
198) enthusiastically
199) realized
200) others

Prac 1 Answers

1) construction
2) Despite
3) considerable
4) notify
5) hearing
6) wanted
7) anticipation
8) everything
9) coldly
10) packed
11) to
12) where
13) inevitable
14) taking
15) essential
16) purely
17) physical
18) Incorporating
19) improve
20) that
21) what

22) useful
23) efficient
24) remember
25) what
26) representing
27) are reconstructed
28) abstract
29) conducted
30) that
31) themselves
32) be
33) automatic
34) what
35) impression
36) accurate
37) demonstrate
38) relatively
39) quantitative
40) during
41) the number of
42) quantitative
43) recollections
44) sad enough
45) prompts
46) pay
47) abstract
48) ensure
49) evolution
50) at
51) itself
52) pursues
53) evolve
54) which
55) inspire
56) what
57) mutual
58) supporting
59) ones
60) passive
61) unlikely
62) engaging
63) are
64) are realized
65) require
66) potential
67) obvious
68) because
69) requires
70) cognitive
71) solve
72) which
73) holding
74) mental
75) dedicate
76) well enough
77) that
78) larger
79) have
80) do
81) what
82) to create
83) itself
84) have been found
85) while
86) sticking it down
87) grabbing
88) relates
89) themselves
90) extreme
91) exploding
92) deficit
93) themselves
94) deeply
95) that
96) that
97) its
98) more

99) losing
100) the other
101) the other
102) least
103) unaware
104) have been manipulated
105) while
106) marginal
107) rises
108) isolated
109) cease
110) illustrating
111) that
112) pretending
113) which
114) inevitable
115) distressing
116) careless
117) it
118) account for
119) Seen
120) highlights
121) leaving
122) to thrive
123) none
124) sensitive
125) maximizing
126) unconsciously
127) related
128) to do
129) social
130) making
131) less
132) is caused
133) major
134) This is because
135) revised
136) fundamental
137) beyond
138) is
139) that
140) itself
141) that
142) that
143) accepted
144) considered
145) look for
146) firmly
147) generate
148) shared
149) what
150) what
151) which
152) is
153) emerge
154) result from
155) drastic
156) random
157) another
158) are
159) effective
160) discouraging
161) to do
162) better
163) adopting
164) when
165) to hit
166) pointing
167) reward
168) preferring
169) to
170) because
171) what
172) Inanimate
173) attributing
174) make
175) being eaten

176) that
177) ambiguous
178) are caused
179) results in
180) assume
181) attack
182) quickly
183) that
184) assuming
185) ordinary
186) contented
187) distinctive
188) other
189) Unlike
190) Driven
191) revealed
192) disliked
193) eating
194) hurried
195) climbed
196) that
197) During
198) enthusiastically
199) realized
200) others

Prac 2 Answers

1) regard
2) funding
3) additional
4) provide
5) Despite
6) submitting
7) notification
8) delay
9) constraints
10) proceed
11) notify
12) regarding
13) submitted
14) hard-fought
15) figured
16) anticipation
17) coldly
18) commitments
19) obligations
20) dedicated
21) midst
22) routine
23) integrating
24) realistic
25) inevitable
26) essential
27) purely
28) obligatory
29) seize
30) physical
31) engage
32) Incorporating
33) naturally
34) automatically
35) concepts
36) recode
37) reconstruct
38) retrieving
39) trait
40) optimal
41) compression
42) bitmap
43) lack
44) generalize
45) representing
46) abstract

47) assumptions
48) abstract
49) primacy
50) testimony
51) conducted
52) testimony
53) deliberation
54) facial
55) procedures
56) unable
57) recognize
58) tend
59) immediate
60) automatic
61) accurate
62) deliberative
63) demonstrate
64) unconscious
65) justifications
66) quantitative
67) interaction
68) recall
69) yield
70) quantitative
71) reliable
72) recollections
73) vary
74) prompts
75) concrete
76) procrastinator
77) utility
78) abstract
79) ensure
80) consistency
81) evolution
82) associated
83) singularity
84) Singularity
85) exceeds
86) evolve
87) pace
88) pursues
89) conscious
90) consciousness
91) consciousness
92) dimensions
93) interactions
94) intellectual
95) insights
96) Conversely
97) significant
98) ethics
99) incorporate
100) coexistence
101) essentially
102) digital
103) linguistic
104) passive
105) proposed
106) metaphor
107) unlikely
108) cognitive
109) prose
110) artifacts
111) horizon
112) afford
113) potential
114) limitations
115) cognitive
116) distribute
117) computation
118) interface
119) transmitted
120) capacity
121) dedicate
122) benefit
123) contribute

124) defence
125) flounder
126) illusion
127) assets
128) transforming
129) mimic
130) spectacle
131) flounder
132) suffer
133) frame
134) deficit
135) psychologically
136) boundaries
137) endurance
138) therapy
139) practitioner
140) mobilise
141) sore
142) versions
143) manufacturer
144) willing
145) income
146) features
147) introduces
148) unaware
149) manipulated
150) presence
151) scope
152) eliminate
153) genre
154) obvious
155) marginal
156) isolated
157) expands
158) cease
159) plainly
160) escapist
161) pleasure
162) distant
163) crisis
164) political
165) inevitable
166) elective
167) distressing
168) abundant
169) neglect
170) infrastructure
171) contamination
172) urbanization
173) address
174) leaks
175) account
176) selective
177) scarcity
178) inequities
179) sanitation
180) thrive
181) valued
182) count
183) mate
184) merits
185) genetically
186) pressure
187) sensitive
188) maximizing
189) standing
190) tendency
191) unconsciously
192) perceive
193) self-esteem
194) insecurity
195) compel
196) crucially
197) grudging
198) cynical
199) persuasive
200) Conventional

201) depression
202) imbalance
203) neurotransmitters
204) substances
205) serotonin
206) noradrenaline
207) revised
208) reframe
209) fundamental
210) entity
211) organ
212) root
213) distortion
214) disease
215) manifest
216) accounts
217) float
218) mixture
219) assumptions
220) plain
221) psychology
222) branch
223) devoted
224) interact
225) opinions
226) hearsay
227) firmly
228) derived
229) evidence-based
230) fundamental
231) generate
232) diversity
233) modern
234) physicists
235) fancy
236) molecules
237) stable
238) collective
239) emerge
240) embryo
241) biologist
242) drastic
243) *canalization*
244) organism
245) states
246) random
247) rough
248) valley
249) disease
250) manifestations
251) symptomatic
252) strikingly
253) Punishing
254) scolding
255) discouraging
256) invisible
257) adopting
258) strategy
259) congratulate
260) positives
261) avoid
262) assign
263) preferring
264) random
265) assume
266) pointy
267) encounter
268) determine
269) Inanimate
270) generally
271) evaluated
272) attributing
273) intention
274) essential
275) anthropologist
276) evolutionary
277) ambiguous

278) agents
279) perceptual
280) biased
281) anthropomorphism
282) intention
283) mechanism
284) probable
285) intent
286) analysis
287) contented
288) distinctive
289) inspiration
290) patches
291) unintended
292) peacock
293) greedily
294) scent
295) tempted
296) remarkably
297) enthusiastically
298) overjoyed
299) imitating
300) genuine

Prac 2 Answers

1) regard
2) funding
3) additional
4) provide
5) Despite
6) submitting
7) notification
8) delay
9) constraints
10) proceed
11) notify
12) regarding
13) submitted
14) hard-fought
15) figured
16) anticipation
17) coldly
18) commitments
19) obligations
20) dedicated
21) midst
22) routine
23) integrating
24) realistic
25) inevitable
26) essential
27) purely
28) obligatory
29) seize
30) physical
31) engage
32) Incorporating
33) naturally
34) automatically
35) concepts
36) recode
37) reconstruct
38) retrieving
39) trait
40) optimal
41) compression
42) bitmap
43) lack
44) generalize
45) representing
46) abstract
47) assumptions
48) abstract

49) primacy
50) testimony
51) conducted
52) testimony
53) deliberation
54) facial
55) procedures
56) unable
57) recognize
58) tend
59) immediate
60) automatic
61) accurate
62) deliberative
63) demonstrate
64) unconscious
65) justifications
66) quantitative
67) interaction
68) recall
69) yield
70) quantitative
71) reliable
72) recollections
73) vary
74) prompts
75) concrete
76) procrastinator
77) utility
78) abstract
79) ensure
80) consistency
81) evolution
82) associated
83) singularity
84) Singularity
85) exceeds
86) evolve
87) pace
88) pursues
89) conscious
90) consciousness
91) consciousness
92) dimensions
93) interactions
94) intellectual
95) insights
96) Conversely
97) significant
98) ethics
99) incorporate
100) coexistence
101) essentially
102) digital
103) linguistic
104) passive
105) proposed
106) metaphor
107) unlikely
108) cognitive
109) prose
110) artifacts
111) horizon
112) afford
113) potential
114) limitations
115) cognitive
116) distribute
117) computation
118) interface
119) transmitted
120) capacity
121) dedicate
122) benefit
123) contribute
124) defence
125) flounder

126) illusion
127) assets
128) transforming
129) mimic
130) spectacle
131) flounder
132) suffer
133) frame
134) deficit
135) psychologically
136) boundaries
137) endurance
138) therapy
139) practitioner
140) mobilise
141) sore
142) versions
143) manufacturer
144) willing
145) income
146) features
147) introduces
148) unaware
149) manipulated
150) presence
151) scope
152) eliminate
153) genre
154) obvious
155) marginal
156) isolated
157) expands
158) cease
159) plainly
160) escapist
161) pleasure
162) distant
163) crisis
164) political
165) inevitable
166) elective
167) distressing
168) abundant
169) neglect
170) infrastructure
171) contamination
172) urbanization
173) address
174) leaks
175) account
176) selective
177) scarcity
178) inequities
179) sanitation
180) thrive
181) valued
182) count
183) mate
184) merits
185) genetically
186) pressure
187) sensitive
188) maximizing
189) standing
190) tendency
191) unconsciously
192) perceive
193) self-esteem
194) insecurity
195) compel
196) crucially
197) grudging
198) cynical
199) persuasive
200) Conventional
201) depression
202) imbalance

203) neurotransmitters
204) substances
205) serotonin
206) noradrenaline
207) revised
208) reframe
209) fundamental
210) entity
211) organ
212) root
213) distortion
214) disease
215) manifest
216) accounts
217) float
218) mixture
219) assumptions
220) plain
221) psychology
222) branch
223) devoted
224) interact
225) opinions
226) hearsay
227) firmly
228) derived
229) evidence-based
230) fundamental
231) generate
232) diversity
233) modern
234) physicists
235) fancy
236) molecules
237) stable
238) collective
239) emerge
240) embryo
241) biologist
242) drastic
243) *canalization*
244) organism
245) states
246) random
247) rough
248) valley
249) disease
250) manifestations
251) symptomatic
252) strikingly
253) Punishing
254) scolding
255) discouraging
256) invisible
257) adopting
258) strategy
259) congratulate
260) positives
261) avoid
262) assign
263) preferring
264) random
265) assume
266) pointy
267) encounter
268) determine
269) Inanimate
270) generally
271) evaluated
272) attributing
273) intention
274) essential
275) anthropologist
276) evolutionary
277) ambiguous
278) agents
279) perceptual

280) biased
281) anthropomorphism
282) intention
283) mechanism
284) probable
285) intent
286) analysis
287) contented
288) distinctive
289) inspiration
290) patches
291) unintended
292) peacock
293) greedily
294) scent
295) tempted
296) remarkably
297) enthusiastically
298) overjoyed
299) imitating
300) genuine

Quiz 1 Answers

1) D-E-C-A-B
2) D-B-A-C-E
3) C-D-B-A-E
4) B-E-A-C-D
5) D-A-E-B-C
6) D-A-B-E-C
7) E-B-D-C-A
8) D-B-C-E-A
9) C-B-E-A-D
10) E-B-C-D-A
11) D-C-A-B-E
12) D-C-A-B
13) E-C-B-D-A
14) E-A-B-C-D
15) D-B-C-A-E
16) C-A-B-E-D
17) D-C-E-A-B
18) D-B-E-C-A
19) B-A-D-E-C
20) C-B-D-A-E
21) C-B-D-E-A
22) D-B-C-A-E

Quiz 2 Answers

1) [정답 및 해설] ①
admitting => submitting

2) [정답 및 해설] ②
important something => something important

3) [정답 및 해설] ②
dedication => dedicated

4) [정답 및 해설] ③
have => lack

5) [정답 및 해설] ①
which => that

6) [정답 및 해설] ①
while => during

7) [정답 및 해설] ④
revolution => evolution

8) [정답 및 해설] ⑤
acquire => require

9) [정답 및 해설] ③
disconnect => interact

10) [정답 및 해설] ④
folding => folded

11) [정답 및 해설] ①
fame => frame

12) [정답 및 해설] ⑤
lower => higher

13) [정답 및 해설] ②
hard => hardly

14) [정답 및 해설] ③
less => more

15) [정답 및 해설] ③
less => more

16) [정답 및 해설] ③
less => more

17) [정답 및 해설] ②
transact => interact

18) [정답 및 해설] ⑤
dissolutions => manifestations

19) [정답 및 해설] ②
reward => punishment

20) [정답 및 해설] ②
physical => physics

21) [정답 및 해설] ⑤
chat => chatting

Quiz 3 Answers

1) [정답 및 해설] ⑤
ⓔ considerate => considerable
ⓖ process => proceed

2) [정답 및 해설] ⑤
ⓒ do => be
ⓖ rising => falling

3) [정답 및 해설] ①
ⓔ separating => integrating
ⓘ incorporated => Incorporating

4) [정답 및 해설] ⑤
ⓒ retrieve => reconstruct
ⓘ flawed => perfect
ⓞ believing => seeing

5) [정답 및 해설] ③
ⓔ identity => identification
ⓖ inaccurate => accurate
ⓜ relative => relatively

6) [정답 및 해설] ③
ⓗ accurate => inaccurate
ⓘ despite => though

7) [정답 및 해설] ⑤
ⓑ refers => refers to
ⓒ themselves => itself
ⓙ stagnation => evolution

8) [정답 및 해설] ②
ⓑ one => ones
ⓒ aggressive => passive

9) [정답 및 해설] ⑤
ⓑ possess => lack

ⓓ attribute => distribute
ⓗ that => which

10) [정답 및 해설] ⑤
ⓓ many => much
ⓘ allusion => illusion

11) [정답 및 해설] ⑤
ⓑ them => themselves
ⓘ hindrance => endurance

12) [정답 및 해설] ⑤
ⓕ another => the other
ⓗ goes => go
ⓙ more => less

13) [정답 및 해설] ④
ⓑ subtle => obvious
ⓕ integrated => isolated
ⓘ offering => suffering

14) [정답 및 해설] ⑤
ⓓ neglect => address
ⓗ indiscriminate => selective

15) [정답 및 해설] ③
ⓓ minimizing => maximizing
ⓘ sociable => social

16) [정답 및 해설] ④
ⓐ unconventional => Conventional
ⓑ balance => imbalance
ⓓ increase => decrease

17) [정답 및 해설] ③
ⓒ are => do
ⓗ distinct => shared

18) [정답 및 해설] ②
ⓑ a => the
ⓕ unstable => stable

19) [정답 및 해설] ②
ⓑ that => what
ⓗ visible => invisible
ⓘ positives => negatives

20) [정답 및 해설] ⑤
ⓘ animate => Inanimate
ⓡ synthesis => analysis

21) [정답 및 해설] ①
ⓓ felt => feeling
ⓘ be => were
ⓚ covered => discovered

Quiz 4 Answers

1) [정답 및 해설]
③ although => Despite
④ admitting => submitting
⑥ freedom => constraints
⑦ process => proceed
⑨ hear => hearing

2) [정답 및 해설]
① hardly => hard
③ do => be
⑤ cold => coldly
⑥ holding => to hold
⑦ rising => falling

3) [정답 및 해설]
② dedication => dedicated
③ that => what
④ what => where
⑥ evitable => inevitable

⑩ incorporated => Incorporating

4) [정답 및 해설]
⑤ useless => useful
⑦ optional => optimal
⑫ that => what
⑬ concrete => abstract
⑱ valued => undermined

5) [정답 및 해설]
② proliferation => deliberation
⑦ inaccurate => accurate
⑨ that => what
⑩ less => more
⑭ conscious => unconscious

6) [정답 및 해설]
② a => the
③ while => during
⑦ qualitative => quantitative
⑨ are => were
⑩ an abstract => a concrete

7) [정답 및 해설]
② refers => refers to
④ involve => evolve
⑦ for => with
⑨ revolution => evolution
⑫ stagnation => evolution

8) [정답 및 해설]
① uniform => different
⑤ enter into => enter
⑥ likely => unlikely
⑧ which => that
⑭ because of => because

9) [정답 및 해설]
② possess => lack
③ collectively => independently
④ attribute => distribute
⑧ disconnect => interact
⑨ less => more

10) [정답 및 해설]
④ many => much
⑥ that => what
⑫ less => more
⑬ transformed => transforming
⑭ whenever's => whatever's

11) [정답 및 해설]
② them => themselves
③ exploded => exploding
⑥ hindrance => endurance
⑦ aggressive => passive
⑨ despite => though

12) [정답 및 해설]
③ less => more
④ compete => compare
⑧ less => more
⑪ aware => unaware
⑫ simulated => manipulated

13) [정답 및 해설]
③ magical => marginal
⑥ integrated => isolated
⑦ continue => cease
⑨ suffer => offer
⑩ offering => suffering

14) [정답 및 해설]
① cultural => political
② limited => abundant
④ neglect => address
⑤ less => more
⑦ indiscriminate => selective

15) [정답 및 해설]
⑤ deceive => perceive
⑩ feeling => feel
⑪ which => that
⑫ sociable => social
⑬ more => less

16) [정답 및 해설]
① unconventional => Conventional
⑦ less => more
⑧ less => more
⑩ settlement => distortion
⑪ conceal => manifest

17) [정답 및 해설]
② uniform => different
④ transact => interact
⑤ rejected => accepted
⑥ deriving => derived
⑦ sociable => social

18) [정답 및 해설]
① that => what
② a => the
③ interpretations => interactions
⑧ limitless => limited
⑩ uniform => random

19) [정답 및 해설]
① affective => effective
③ reward => punishment
⑤ encouraging => discouraging
⑥ inhibits => encourages
⑨ uniform => different

20) [정답 및 해설]
④ counter => encounter
⑧ distributing => attributing
⑩ been => being
⑪ evolution => survival
⑰ died => dead

21) [정답 및 해설]
① few => little
⑤ dissatisfied => contented
⑥ undesired => desired
⑨ be => were
⑮ limiting => imitating

Quiz 5 Answers

1) ~에 관하여, 3단어 - with regard to // 추가의 - additional // ~에도 불구하고 - Despite

2) ⓐ
certify ⇨ notify

3) ⓑ
hear ⇨ hearing

4) (가) A delay in the process can carry considerable consequences related to the school's budgetary constraints and schedule.

5) 기대감 - anticipation

6) ⓐ
holding ⇨ hold
waited ⇨ waiting

7) (가) I figured he was going to tell me something important.

8) 전념 - commitments // 의무 - obligations // 여유 - room // 불가피한 - inevitable

9) ⓐ
what ⇨ where

10) (가) rather than viewing chores as purely obligatory activities, why not seize these moments as opportunities for physical activity?
(나) Incorporating quick exercises into your daily chores can improve your health.

11) 추상적인 - abstract // 증언 - testimony

12) ⓐ
retrieve ⇨ reconstruct
reconstructing ⇨ retrieving
storing ⇨ store

13) ⓑ
that ⇨ what

14) ⓒ
thorough ⇨ through

15) (가) We recode what we see through the lens of everything we know.

16) 재귀대명사 - themselves // 첫인상 - first impression // 정당화 - justifications

17) ⓐ
deducted ⇨ conducted
which ⇨ that
proliferation ⇨ deliberation
accurate ⇨ inaccurate
identity ⇨ identification

18) ⓑ
what ⇨ that
inaccurate ⇨ accurate

19) (가) truest interpretation of what our mind is telling us.
(나) the superior performance of relatively unconscious first guesses

20) 정량적인 - quantitative // 산출하다 - yield // 신뢰할만한 - reliable

21) ⓐ
an absolute ⇨ a concrete

22) (가) How many of your utility bills are you currently late in paying, even though you can afford to pay them?
(나) Questions that seek concrete responses help make abstract concepts clearer and ensure consistency from one study to the next.

23) ~와 연관된 - associated with // 예측하다 - predicted // 연결어 - Conversely // 상호의 - mutual

24) ⓐ
human ⇨ its
unconscious ⇨ conscious

25) (가) The direction of AI's evolution will depend greatly on what values and ethics we incorporate into AI

26) 인공물 - artifacts // 즉각적으로 - immediately

27) ⓐ
likely ⇨ unlikely
with ⇨ without

28) (가) Linguistic metaphors are passive, in the sense that the audience needs to choose to actively enter the world proposed by metaphor.
(나) Technological creators cannot generally afford to require their potential audience to wonder how the metaphor works

29) 한계 - limitations // 상호작용하다 - interact // 집합적인 - collective

30) ⓐ
have ⇨ lack
interdependently ⇨ independently

31) (가) instead of holding more information than we have mental capacity for and indeed need to know, we could dedicate our large brains to a small piece of a giant calculation.

32) 시력 - eyesight // 능력 - ability // 변신하다 - transforming // 모방하다 - mimic

33) ⓐ
at first ⇨ again
folding ⇨ folded
stared ⇨ staring
allusion ⇨ illusion

34) (가) The best defence most species of octopus have is to stay hidden as much as possible and do their own hunting at night.

35) 부족 - deficit // 인내 - endurance // 풀어주다 - mobilise

36) ⓐ
rejects ⇨ calls
valuable ⇨ value

37) (가) How much we suffer relates to how we frame the pain in our mind.

38) 수입 - income // 조종하다 - manipulated

39) ⓐ
less ⇨ more
more ⇨ less

40) ⓑ
first ⇨ second

41) (가) The middle item has more features than the least expensive one, and it is less expensive than the fanciest model.

42) 주변적인 - marginal // 고립된 - isolated // 멈추다 - cease // 가장하다 - pretend

43) ⓐ
focus on ⇨ eliminate

44) (가) Why watch or read climate fiction about the world you can see plainly out your own window?

45) 피할 수 없는 - inevitable // 부족한 - scarce // 오염 - contamination // 부주의한 도시화 - careless urbanization // 차지하다 - account for // 들어갈 단어 본문 활용 - scarcity // 불평등 - inequities // 위생 - sanitation

46) ⓐ
them ⇨ one
are ⇨ aren't

47) 최대화 - maximizing // 경향성 - tendency // 무의식적으로 - unconsciously // 투덜대는 - grudging // 냉소적인 - cynical

48) ⓐ
values ⇨ valued
weren't ⇨ didn't

49) (가) As individuals, our ability to thrive depended on how well we navigated relationships in a group.
(나) These emotions compel us to do more of what makes our community value us and less of what doesn't.

50) 전통적인 - Conventional // 들어갈 연결어 - In other words // 수정된 - revised // 근본적인 - fundamental // 왜곡 - distortion

51) ⓐ
hide ⇨ manifest

52) (가) This is because the imbalance of substances in the brain is a consequence of depression, not its cause.

53) 설명 - accounts // 상호작용하다 - interact // 가정 - assumptions.

54) ⓐ
understand ⇨ understanding

55) ⓑ
do ⇨ don't

56) (가) In addition to this evidence-based approach, psychology deals with fundamental processes and principles that generate our rich

cultural and social diversity, as well as those shared by all human beings.

57) 상호작용 - interactions // 거대한 - enormous // 집합적인 - collective // 병 - illness

58) ⓐ
the ⇨ a
state ⇨ states

59) (가) their manifestations at the physiological and symptomatic levels are often strikingly similar.

60) -로 인해 - due to // 눈에 띄지 않는 - invisible // 피하다 - avoid

61) ⓐ
hitting ⇨ to hit
negatives ⇨ positives
negatives ⇨ positives

62) (가) Instead of discouraging the child from doing something, it encourages them to do it.

63) 논리 - reasoning // 결정하다 - determine // 해석하다 - interpret // 모호한 - ambiguous

64) ⓐ
eaten ⇨ being eaten

65) ⓑ
from ⇨ in
intend ⇨ tend

66) ⓒ
attacking ⇨ attack
quick ⇨ quickly

67) (가) Inanimate objects and plants generally do not move and can be evaluated from physics alone

68) ~와 다르게 - Unlike // 열망 - desire // 독특함 - uniqueness // 먼 - distant // 의도하지 않은 - unintended // 실망한채로 - Disappointed // 열정적으로 - enthusiastically // 따라하다 - imitating